2.50

*DEMOCRACY
AND EXCELLENCE
IN AMERICAN
SECONDARY
EDUCATION*

DEMOCRACY
AND EXCELLENCE
IN AMERICAN
SECONDARY
EDUCATION

A STUDY IN CURRICULUM THEORY

HARRY S. BROUDY

B. OTHANEL SMITH

JOE R. BURNETT

University of Illinois

RAND McNALLY & COMPANY • CHICAGO

RAND McNALLY EDUCATION SERIES

B. Othanel Smith, *Advisory Editor*

Broudy, Smith, and Burnett, *Democracy and Excellence in American Secondary Education*

Farwell and Peters, eds., *Guidance Readings for Counselors*

Foshay, ed., *Rand McNally Handbook of Education*

Haines, *Guiding the Student Teaching Process in Elementary Education*

Johnson and Jackson, *Modern Statistical Methods: Descriptive and Inductive*

Lewenstein, *Teaching Social Studies in Junior and Senior High Schools*

Norris, Zeran, and Hatch, *The Information Service in Guidance: Occupational, Educational, Social*

Peters and Farwell, *Guidance: A Developmental Approach*

Smith and Ennis, eds., *Language and Concepts in Education*

Trump and Baynham, *Focus on Change: Guide to Better Schools*

Zeran and Riccio, *Organization and Administration of Guidance Services*

PREFACE

The development of new curricula in mathematics and science, the discussion of cognition in learning theory, professional and lay dissatisfaction with prevailing curricula modes, and a host of related phenomena have developed to a point where everyone knows that something important and pervasive is happening in American education. It is not so obvious that there is any coherent or comprehensive view of what the developments signify—especially with regard to democracy, excellence, and educative ideals. The outstanding problem of our time is precisely that of providing excellence in the educational context of popular or mass democracy. There are those who say that there is no solution for this problem. Nevertheless, this volume affirms that it can be solved. We need not indicate the prospects for many of our society's historic ideals if we are incorrect.

This volume is in part the outgrowth of a year of meetings with several of our colleagues who, like us, were concerned over the lack of order in the curriculum procedures of modern education. To those colleagues—Professors Archibald W. Anderson, Foster McMurray, and William O. Stanley—we are indebted more than could ever be specifically acknowledged. Influential as they were, however, the views are the authors' own, and the authors alone must be held responsible for them.

We wish to acknowledge with gratitude the help we received from individuals who read and made critical comments on the manuscript. Particularly we are indebted to Professor Arno Bellack, Miss Margaret Gill, Professor Harold Hand, Professor L. J. Hetenyi, Professor Lloyd E. McCleary, Professor Van Cleve Morris, and Professor Celia B. Stendler. Again, however, it must be noted that the authors alone are responsible for the views expressed herein.

Finally, we wish to express our appreciation for the assistance which Mrs. Barbara Bergan rendered in helping prepare the manuscript.

H.S.B.
B.O.S.
J.R.B.

Urbana, Illinois
November 31, 1963

TABLE OF CONTENTS

PART THREE: A CURRICULUM RESPONSE TO THE NEW DEMANDS

PART ONE

SOCIAL DEMANDS ON
THE SECONDARY SCHOOL

CHAPTER I

EDUCATIONAL IDEALS AND
THE SECONDARY CURRICULUM

As education goes, so go the life and future of a nation. The more this truism is recognized, and the more evident that pressing, specific problems of a nation's life and future become, the more educational institutions are likely to be challenged to perfect themselves.

The saying itself is perhaps trite. Certainly there is a sense in which the idea it expresses has always been accepted in American society. But today it has a new significance, and it is being seen in a new light because we are face to face with problems of great moment, the solutions to which can be arrived at only through bold but soberly considered educational measures.

INDIVIDUAL AND SOCIAL CLAIMS ON THE SCHOOL

In an older conception, education was regarded as a process whereby the individual became a "true person" whose innate capacities for a life of virtue, justice, and wisdom were expressed and refined. Not only this, but salvation, too, was seen as contingent upon schooling. The use of schooling for specifically institutional and social ends was often emphasized—as it was in the nineteenth century for the crises of wars and the necessity of building a national spirit or character—but the overriding purpose of school was the liberation of the individual's creative abilities. At the verbal level, at least, education was seen as being preeminently a moral endeavor, and it was often described in terms that equated its function with that of religion. Thus, one finds the literature of education filled with such statements as "education is the training of the human soul," "the teacher affects eternity," and so on.

But things were happening in the Western world, and particularly in America, which resulted in education's being explicitly seen as both more secular a process and one more directly instrumental to the ends of society's dominant institutions. In America, there was the need for massive development of universal education in order to weld a polyglot population into a unified nation. There were burgeoning industrialization, technology, and urbanization, all of which increasingly demanded new and greater sophistication. Rapid mobility in thought and transportation sped these processes along. More recently, there has been the dramatic increase in the scope of government and its needs for trained intelligence; and currently we see the growth of a military complex which rivals, if not exceeds, the rest of national government in its requirement for intellectual resources.

American public education had little or no historical precedent to guide it in its early, formative years, except that it should be kept within the political-economic tradition of local control. But the power center was shifting away from the local community, and the local community itself was becoming highly fluid in character, secular in outlook, and certainly less individualistic than before. Power gathered and intensified in centralized, corporate structures whose essential features are generally connoted by the term "bureaucracies." We need note only a few of those features: the aims of bureaucracies were to be highly specialized, they were often to be narrow aims, and they demanded trained people to accomplish them. What keeps a bureaucracy in power in a democratic society? Laugh though we may at the jokes about bureaucracies having inherent powers of self-perpetuation and growth, the fact is that they must accomplish their aims and they must justify them. And bureaucracies in America have shown an amazing ability to do both of those things—partly because they have had a great ability to swing educational endeavors this way and that as their aims required new and different resources.

The almost purely instrumental function of education has become increasingly obvious not only in America but throughout the world. Perhaps no American has seen it and stated it in such monolithic and cold terms as did a Russian, Joseph Stalin: "Education is a weapon, the effect of which depends . . . on who controls this weapon, and at whom, it is intended, it should strike."[1] But there are disturbing signs that curricula are more and more criticized and determined by groups primarily concerned with the schools as agencies for attaining the often narrow aims of those groups. Their motives are generally good, and their demands are to some extent legitimate. Understandably, the political, military, industrial, and business interests demand large numbers of scientists and technicians; they demand a search for and an exploitation of scholastic talent. Understandably, the authorities of educational institutions, themselves under financial and social pressure, reward in rank and pay the educators who are identified with the projects which satisfy the demands of those interest groups. Understandably, special interest groups can forget the education of the whole man. But can the professional educator ever forget it? Can he forget self-cultivation, citizenship that is more than ethnocentric chest-thumping, vocational competence that is more than a temporary chit for a low-level job with no future? If research project money is not flowing into these areas of concern, if the citizenry is not aroused to demand excellence there, are we supposed to conclude that these aims serve no useful purpose in our national policy?

The massive movement which seems to threaten a reduction of education to the status of being merely an instrument of momentary military, economic, and political policy is clearly no answer to the curriculum problem when looked at in the light of our tra-

[1] Quoted by Maurice J. Shore in *Soviet Education* (New York: Philosophical Library, 1947), p. 220.

ditional democratic ideals. Those who would argue to the contrary might well reflect on the fact that totalitarian governments have been able to produce educational plants which turned out impressive amounts of scientific and technological manpower, which somehow kept employment high, and which found something for every child to do. This type of schooling aim is no more distinctive of democracy than of Nazi Germany or Communist Russia.

It seems clear that, before this decade is over, events may shape the future of the United States in a decisive way. What the role of this country is to be and how well the United States can play it depends in extraordinary measure on the educational strategy which we adopt now. The pivot of this educational strategy is the secondary-school curriculum, because it is the high school that mediates between the potentialities of childhood and the actualities of adulthood.

The actualities of adulthood in a modern mass society threaten us with a hard choice between material abundance and spiritual scarcity, between mass power and individual insignificance.

Such a choice the American ethos rejects. The American ethos affirms that the technological resources of modern society can and should be exploited to enhance the excellence and significance of all, rather than an elite, and that education can significantly help to bring this about.

It seems perfectly clear that it must be professional educators who take the lead if the secondary curriculum is to meet the individual and social ideals of democracy in the years ahead. The natural and legally appointed guardians of those ideals in public education are the educators; but it manifestly remains to be seen if they can justify the adequacy of their programs for attaining the ideals.

It also seems perfectly clear that educators will lose what control they now have if their reactions amount to no more than patching up old curriculum devices and shifting around the physical and administrative furniture of schooling.

There is going to be tremendous power vested in education in the future, power made overt and explicit instead of the covert and implicit power of the past. One prominent forecaster of business and general social trends has said:

I submit . . . that there are already definite signs that the new power groups, the ones for the next ten or fifteen years, are three entirely different ones. The first group is the *public administrators*, especially those in state and regional areas. This is where the challenge of policy is today. The second group is the *educators* on all levels; and the third, *the armed forces*. I submit that these are our emerging real power structures. Forget about business and labor, they represent the spent forces of yesterday.[2]

There is no question that the power will be used, either *by* professional educators or *through* educators by laymen who are concerned to use the schools for interests which are narrow and perhaps selfish (as has happened notably in recent China and Russia). The disjunction need not be made so sharply, nor the alternatives be so few; but there is always the danger that it might be a sharp disjunction, and even the danger that only the second of the two alternatives remains open to us.

Too, the writers see no harm in giving the prospects for professional educators in America in their bleakest aspect. Counting themselves among them, they nevertheless must note that no other group has so consistently (and against such a mass of evidence) claimed that American public education was the source of everything good, true, and beautiful. It is not that the professional educators are going to be asked to "put up or shut up." More likely they are going to "put up" or be left muttering in the wilderness of the past. There are other groups which have quite specific purposes for education, for the specificity of their own aims makes it easy to accommodate the educational process to them.

It may be argued that what we need, instead of the current

[2] Peter F. Drucker, a remark made in Howard J. Ehrlich (Ed.), "Discussing the Issues," in William V. D'Antonio and Howard J. Ehrlich (Eds.), *Power and Democracy in America* (South Bend: University of Notre Dame Press, 1961), pp. 122-23.

and heated debate, are decisions—*forced* decisions, if necessary. Indeed, this seems to be exactly what many of the combatants on the curriculum scene of battle are struggling to achieve; but, so long as we are a democratic nation, and so long as the forces arrayed on the field are so well entrenched, any battle which is won will at best secure an uneasy and brief peace. Forced decisions in such matters as the ones under discussion end only in creating minor discords which eventually grow and overpower whatever good has been done. And when those discords swell to a full crescendo, their creators elicit opposition which in turn produces the same kinds of disruptive discords.

The point underlying the metaphor is obvious to anyone who is familiar with the literature of education and with the popular press in which criticisms of education are discussed; there simply is an impasse in so-called curriculum debate, and it is not going to be overcome with profit to anyone by a continuation of selective reporting, name-calling, assignments of guilt by association (whether with Dewey or Rickover), or even appeals to force.

The answer appropriate for professional educators would seem to be to create a curriculum view which is defensible in regard to the school's obligation to a *democratic* mass society and excellence of individual life in that society.

Given such an ideal, and given the fact that the dominant institutions are still amenable to some leadership from educational institutions, could they help but respond with support? Given such an ideal, could one feel at all false in saying that it would help in unifying the major components of our society and would help work the narrow interests into a schema which would profit all?

THE CHARACTER OF THIS STUDY

Considerations such as these have served in part, but only in part, to prompt the present study. To say that it represents *the* answer by professional education would be presumptuous; but the writers do think it an answer in the right direction. And they believe there are other considerations which today make it increasingly possible to move in the right direction. Some of these are discussed in detail in the following chapters. Here, one can briefly note such developments as the recent work being done in the study of the logical structure of content areas, in the relation of various domains of content, in the logic and psychology of teaching, in the use of new physical and administrative devices, in enrichment programs. This work has already produced valuable clues for general curriculum design.

In essence, this is a study in curriculum theory. It represents a speculative but reasoned interpretation and organization of facts in order to project an ideal for use in the development of the secondary curriculum. The emphasis is upon the ideal and upon the concepts which are necessary to clarify and justify the ideal. In this the study is similar to many others, but there are some significant differences with respect to which the reader should be alerted.

First, even though the emphasis is upon the speculative and ideal, the work concludes with a description of a program of studies which should illustrate the feasibility of the ideal. Thus, the reader is not left with a purely theoretical account which must be interpreted in all details.

Second, the focus of the work is upon the content of instruction. Many curriculum theories deal with the school as a place to live as well as a place in which formal learning occurs. Some of them end by being almost indistinguishable from theories of the general socialization of youth. There is no denying the importance of socialization factors in schooling, and certainly the school should be a good place to live, just as a home, hotel, or hospital should be. But the distinctive feature of a school is that it is a place for formal learning as well as living. And what is to be learned, the content of instruction, thus requires dominant attention. General socialization processes, such as those usually found in extracurricular programs, are necessary. The more a *curriculum* theory makes them central in import, however, the less attention there is to the distinctive function of the school. Thus the emphasis upon the content of instruction.

Third, discussion of the standard curriculum theories—"core," "activity," "broad subjects," "subject matter"—has deliberately been avoided in the presentation, largely because this is a study *in* curriculum theory and not an account *of* curriculum theories. Also, as intimated above, it appears inadvisable to present a curriculum theory in the language of the various existing theories. The theories and their terminology have become emotional rallying points in the current debate; indeed, one sometimes thinks that it is more important to some of the debaters to be identified with the labels of their curriculum position than to be right!

Fourth, the theory described here is radically different in over-all character and intent from those usually encountered, even though it has some major parts in common with them. To note only two contentions which set the theory apart:

1. American secondary education can and should be common education, in the sense that it is basically the same for all in regard to what is taught. Variability for different ability levels can be obtained by adjusting the sophistication and detail of what is taught. This is in contrast to the notion that the requirement of "common education" is met when we provide numerous, different programs in order that everyone can get at least some kind of education. Following Orwell, one might remark that this latter notion amounts to saying that education is common, but for some it is more common than for others.

2. American secondary education can and should be general education, meaning by "general" that what is taught should consist of those central skills, ideas, and evaluations which can be most significantly and widely used in order to deal with life in our times. This notion is in contrast to that which holds general education to be a survey of generally everything.

SHORTCOMINGS OF CURRENT CURRICULA

The positive statement of the theory is the subject of the total work. The remainder of this chapter considers some shortcomings in the current curricula, shortcomings which the theory should help remedy.

It is true that many of the elements of current curriculum thought and practice are highly defensible, but it is also obvious that the total curriculum scene evidences serious shortcomings. In some instances these shortcomings were at one time fairly appropriate responses to the educational problems of previous decades. Most of those mentioned below are of this type; once they were fairly appropriate responses to the needs of universal education in a culture with the features cited earlier—a polyglot population base; burgeoning industrialization, technology, urbanization; and so on.

The shortcomings are ones which sometimes are said to characterize American education. Perhaps it is necessary to indicate the belief that they neither singly nor collectively give an accurate picture of American education. But they are present and talked about. To avoid discussing them would be to neglect one way of making the writers' position clear with regard to what it variously accepts and rejects.

The current debate concerns the scope or extent of the shortcomings in American education. Aside from what has already been said, this study is not intended to be a polemic within that debate.

Diversity and Fragmentation

The first and perhaps most obvious shortcoming is found in the great diversity and fragmentation of a curriculum which purports to meet the need for general education of all American youth. This particular shortcoming is often regarded as a virtue by those who want to laud the flexibility of the American high-school curriculum. They claim that the curriculum is tailored in such a fashion as to allow each individual to find courses which peculiarly suit his needs. The term "tailored" is partly correct, but it also is partly a euphemism to cover the fact that diversity and fragmentation in the curriculum, like Topsy, mainly "just growed."

¶ The source of the growth lay in a great number of historical factors. To mention only one, as secondary education became possible and even legally required for large groups of children who previously would not have sought it, there was an effort to adjust the school programs in order to make them relevant to the diversity of the new school population. Given the fact that the population was an extremely heterogeneous one, largely unable to meet the standards (financial, social, academic) of the grammar school or academy models of the day, the effort was necessary and even noble. But sometimes the schools merely adjusted themselves to individual interests and needs, introducing a curriculum narrowly tailored to individual conditions and expectations. These curricula were not based on a realistic conception of the changing conditions of work, leisure, or life generally in the emerging culture, nor, certainly, did they provide well for a general and common education. Educational opportunity was extended in one sense, but held back in another.

As mentioned above, there is a belief in common education at the secondary level, but many who hold this belief mean by "common" merely that everyone should have a common opportunity for schooling of one kind or another. In this view, the college-preparatory curriculum, the vocational curriculum, the commercial curriculum, and perhaps vocational and commercial curricula designed especially for the potential school dropout, together serve almost the totality of diverse needs.

The arguments used to justify a variety of curricula are often appealing. Diversity of needs, talents, interests, and opportunity are most frequently cited; but the basic assumption is that there is no commonality of need at all, or that it is too small to be significant. Where the arguments are best, on the matter of diversity in talent, one can reply that there is no reason whatever why a program cannot be common in its inputs or content and differentiated in the levels at which it is taught. This is both the reply and the argument of the following chapters.

One cannot deal with this particular shortcoming as briefly as with those yet to be mentioned. This is because one of the strongest arguments in support of multiple curricula for secondary education has been elicited by the problem of the school dropout or potential dropout, for here our society has a pressing human, political, and economic problem which brings to the fore all of the questions of relevancy of need, interest, talent, and opportunity. Since the case is strongest at this point, it should be dealt with rather fully (albeit briefly still), if the perspective and program to be described later are to have a fair hearing amid the legislative and political hue and cry which seem to regard multiple curricula as a panacea for the problem of the dropout.

The dropouts, of whom slum youth and especially Negro slum youth constitute a significant number, are said to need vocational education in the public schools which will fit them for immediate employment. The employment that is referred to is almost always employment in unskilled or semiskilled jobs. It is also said that a general education, and especially a sophisticated, intellectual program of studies, is ludicrously irrelevant to their capacities, concerns, and circumstances.

This is a poor educational argument. The type of program that can insure immediate employment for the dropout is bound to be the most temporary of stopgaps in the rapidly changing labor market. The dropout who gets a job immediately is going to be a social problem by the time he is in his late twenties or thirties, because he will not have the base in knowledge and skills needed for the job mobility and quick retraining in a labor market which is demanding greater and greater intellectual acuteness. Training for immediate employment, usually for a job which makes few intellectual demands, is certainly one way for the school to get rid of its problem; but it can be argued that it merely transfers the problem to the social welfare agencies and labor and industrial organizations a few years later. These might be the places to tackle the problem in the first place.

The argument for such a program is unsound economically, although it generally is grounded in the economic necessity of "putting people back to work" or "finding work for people." When the economy is not in "high gear," when a high rate of unemployment is a fact of economic life (as of this writing), no amount of specialized training is going to get everyone a job, although it may help to determine who will get the available jobs. Even this may not help the slum youth, and especially the Negro slum youth. For example, how many Negroes occupy jobs commensurate with the training they do have? How many whites would settle for the curricula thought necessary for insuring educational and vocational mobility for most Negro youth?[3]

Nor has a variety of curricula demonstrably prevented dropouts. When our society is in a period of high economic growth,

[3] In *Slums and Suburbs* (New York: McGraw-Hill, 1961), James B. Conant wrote as follows about the Dunbar Vocational High School in Chicago:

> Located in a bad slum area now undergoing redevelopment, this school and its program are especially tailored to the vocational aims of its students. Hardly a window has been broken since Dunbar first was opened (and vandalism in schools is a major problem in many slum areas). I discovered in the course of a visit there that almost all the pupils were Negroes. They were learning trades as diverse as shoe repairing, bricklaying, carpentry, cabinet making, auto mechanics, and airplane mechanics. The physical facilities at Dunbar are impressive, but more impressive is the attitude of the pupils. Motivation is good and the students take obvious pride in their work. The academic side of the program is conducted on a high level—high enough so that if a graduate decides he wishes to attend college he may do so. Every year, a few Dunbar graduates do go on to a liberal arts college, but this is not the primary purpose of the school. Most graduates go directly into industry. The Dunbar School, to my mind, approaches the ideal in vocational education (pp. 47–48).

Dunbar would seem to be not only an ideal vocational high school, but an ideal high school for fashionable suburbs as well as for slums, because "if a graduate wishes to attend college he may do so." Why not model all our high schools on the Dunbar pattern? Why is this pattern not recommended for such other Illinois schools as Evanston and New Trier, or for the Westport high schools in Connecticut, or the Westchester schools in New York?

The answer, of course, is that Dunbar is primarily a response to the fact that some American youngsters belong to one socio-economic class rather than to another. This fact, as pointed out, is no more valid a basis for a theory of the curriculum than it is for a theory of democracy.

almost any dropout can get some kind of job with or without training. That is, when economic conditions are good, the low-skilled workers have no great employment problem. To anticipate that our economy will always be so depressed as it is now, or so greatly depressed as it has been in several times past, is hardly a valid basis for curriculum construction.

It is a tautology to say that when there is a high unemployment rate many people will be out of jobs. But the tautology has (or should have) significance in that it suggests the futility of gearing education to a kind of "bad-times" mentality, when the particular problem at the time cannot be solved by education anyway. Better to be educating children for the times when opportunities come, when the country cries out for all of the trained intelligence it can muster. In such times, one fears, the low-level, practicalistic training advocated for dropouts will produce citizens who serve mainly as dead weight. They will find jobs easily in such times, probably, but it is highly doubtful that they will find the jobs which make the most of their and the country's opportunity.

The argument for the special and practicalistic curriculum for slum youth is poor in regard to educational and economic considerations. The argument is also a travesty when the ideals of self-cultivation and citizenship, as well as the vocational competence, are seriously considered. Do the practicalistic programs augur well for the attainment of these ideals which we hold to be possible and desirable for American citizens? Is it not true, rather, that the programs betray these very ideals?

What is envisioned for the potential dropout? A program of common, general education as described above. Not for a moment is it intended to be a watered-down program in regard to content. This means that certain political, economic, and social problems must be looked at in new ways as they bear on the education and life of the dropout or potential dropout. The present course of immediate political, economic, and social expediency is in conflict with our democratic ideals of the quality of life which should be afforded our citizens. The temporary expedient is doomed to be ineffective in the long run; for, as mentioned above, the school "solves" the problem only to have it appear as a problem for other social institutions a few years later.

Gross, Immediate Experience

A second shortcoming is a dangerous emphasis in some programs upon gross, immediate experience as a major pedagogical device. The emphasis is most marked in those programs which make of the immediate community either a model for the school or a "laboratory" in which school learnings are to be tested and reinforced. But the emphasis can also be found in laboratory experiments, classroom demonstrations, and individual assignments in which an inordinate amount of time is given to concrete and crude illustrations of concepts rather than to the concepts themselves. That a child studying, say, the French language should be required to build an accurate model of a French cathedral or town in the course of his work, and should be graded on this as an important aspect of the work, would be a case in point, even if a case infrequently encountered.

As a corollary, where theoretical ideas and systems of thought are dealt with, they tend not to be dealt with thoroughly. Instead, primary attention is given to specific replications of the ideas or systems of thought and not to the intellectual significance and wide-ranging power which can be gained for interpretation of one's experience.

The emphasis is also found in the vocational and commercial curricula, with the undue weight often given to manipulation of the physical objects currently reckoned as basic to "doing business." Such programs, even though they train the students to operate some of the most sophisticated electronic hardware on the present-day market, may well be preparing a wave of school graduates for technological unemployment ten or fifteen years after graduation, because the emphasis is upon merely the gross elements which are mainly of momentary significance. The foundational elements which are basic to understanding, anticipating, and preparing for scientific and technological change are woefully neglected with such an emphasis.

Gross, Overt, Behavioral Roles

Guidance programs today do help youngsters anticipate more wisely than before the job opportunities which are available to them. But it remains true that schooling too often is conceived in a petty fashion with respect to these opportunities. The third major shortcoming, one which other educators will recognize as such, is found in the tendency of the schools to place emphasis upon the youngster's adopting rather mechanically constructed roles for himself, as opposed to his developing a personal *Weltanschauung*, a world view or total ideology, for the conduct of his life.

The criticism is that the current conception of the vocational role at a given time is taken to define the life role. To a considerable extent, this long has been an obvious feature of the commercial and vocational programs in high school, for in these programs what was to be taught has been determined by seeing just what people in contemporary and ordinary occupations needed in order to perform their tasks adequately. This job analysis technique has ended all too often by being the role expectation itself, divorced from normative and aesthetic considerations concerning the character of the individual's total life. The expectation, the role, was in some cases reduced to a recipe statement of precisely what one must minimally do in order to get and keep such-and-such a job under prevailing circumstances. Perhaps it was here that the old ideals of a craft, a calling, and the related sense of individual artistry at work began to be neglected in the schools' training of workers and citizens.

This emphasis upon overt, behavioral roles has extended to the college-preparatory curricula. The pressure of college entrance examinations has produced a spate of recipes for how-to-get-in and how-to-stay-in techniques for youngsters who are crowding the college gates. Where many parents of a given school's children are both anxious and insistent that their children be accepted by colleges of their choice, teachers often are under pressure to teach for just that outcome and only that outcome. For a teacher to have all of his students pass entrance examinations at colleges to which they apply is to allow him to keep his students' parents "off his back" and is likely to assure him of upward mobility in pay and status with his administrators and his school board.

The concern for preparing youth to meet narrow and specific role expectations probably cannot be avoided in the modern era, but it need not be the dominant emphasis in curriculum planning. As long as the ideals of citizenship and self-cultivation are valid for American public education, any curriculum which limits students' role conceptions merely to the character of job or educational openings at a given time is a fraud with respect to those ideals. The situation is that simple.

Neglect in Dealing with Values

A related shortcoming is the neglect of just those evaluative, appreciative, and interpretive models which could do much to furnish the base for the world and life view whose absence was noted above. Even in the college-preparatory curriculum, one finds only literature and perhaps music receiving any attention in the high school, and the latter certainly is not counted as a "solid" subject for college admission. When a portion of the high-school work is set aside for dealing with such models in literature, music, art, and drama, there is a type of learning which too often is either superficial or drily formal. On the one hand there is a surface acquaintance with a host of names of art works and artists, an inferior type of dilettantism, and, on the other hand, there is a dry-as-dust (if thorough) concern for petty details—the type of concern which undoubtedly caused one recent thinker of note to remark, "To this day I cannot read *King Lear*, having had the advantage of studying it accurately at school."

Needless to say, the emphasis upon fashioning school learnings after the prevailing style of community life, which more often than not fails to appreciate excellence in music, art, literature, and drama, does not bode well for even sincere attempts to give proper weight to studies designed for improving the qualitative dimensions of a person's character and career.

Replicative and Applicative Uses of Schooling

The failure properly to emphasize value models in schooling, and the failure properly to cater to the important interpretive use which schooling can provide, is basically an error of omission. But it is one of commission also, resulting from the fact that there is such a massive effort to habituate the student to replicate responses and to apply learnings in the solution of practical problems. These are very important uses of schooling, so no objection can be made on the grounds that schooling devotes itself to developing such uses. It is rather to the way and the extent to which schooling devotes itself to them that objection can be made.

Obviously, there can be no quarrel with the great stress which the schools lay on the replicative uses of the three R's— the symbolics of information. That children should be encouraged habitually to read, write, and calculate well represents one of the constant demands upon American schools. Every theory of education, no matter what its other appeals, has had to argue that it could meet this demand before it has received a serious hearing by American schoolmen and the American public. Beyond the basic symbolics of information, however, are all of the factual details of the sciences, the arts, the humanities, the technologies, the crafts, and the social milieu which are candidates for replicative learning, that is, for learning which allows almost exact duplication of specific things as they were learned in school. Some of the factual details are enormously important for both interpretive and applicative uses, but these often are not the factual details which seem to receive the greatest attention in the curriculum. Instead, one finds widespread emphasis upon the student's learning to cite persons, places, and things of minor import—too often the sorts of things which newspapers use to fill blank spaces when there is no vital copy available. The newspaper filler which informs us, at the end of a major news story, that cotton, rice, peanuts, and karite are the principal money-producing crops of the Republic of Upper Volta may be in some sense interesting. But it is hardly more or less interesting than the report of a student when he informs us of all the members in the United States Cabinet at the time of the Louisiana Purchase.

The context in which facts are used makes a great deal of difference, of course, as to what facts are relevant. Information about the Republic of Upper Volta may be of great significance to one person and of none to another. But the simple and indisputable truth is that some facts are obviously more important than others, if we speak about the contexts which one ordinarily encounters or in general is likely to encounter—the contexts with which a common, general educational program is supposed to prepare the students to deal adequately. Thus, it probably is more important to know how state and national senators and representatives are chosen than to know the names of each of them; probably more important to know the meaning of the Magna Carta than to know the persons, places, and dates associated with its signing; probably more important to know rules of logical inference than to know types of propaganda technique.

There will be occasion to comment on other reasons why this is the case. Here, what has been said about the irrelevance of many of the things taught for replicative use can also be said about many of the things which are taught for applicative use— taught in order to allow a student to use his schooling in the same way as a specialist in a given field. The notion that learning the principles of physics and chemistry should help the student to understand and repair household appliances, autos, and other familiar items with which he might have a problem is a prime example of the error. The error is in part that already described as a mistaken emphasis upon the gross and immediate; it is in part an error in that it represents a failure to stress the interpretive or nonspecialist uses of physics and chemistry; but it is particularly an error in that it overlooks the realities of life in our society.

It is the last aspect of the error which bears particular comment. Technological changes are so diverse, so rapid, and so widespread that this conception of the main use of schooling is hopelessly unrealistic. The notion that specialist competence to deal with the sophisticated and changing machinery around us is a defensible aim of general education is contradicted by almost every aspect of our everyday lives. This point is commented on later. Suffice it to say here that it seems perfectly obvious that the specialized repairman is here to stay. Although it is true that youths with time on their hands do find it possible to learn a great deal about their autos and some household appliances, one finds in later years the same youths at the mercy of further technological changes and hopelessly dependent on the repairmen specially trained to deal with the new malfunctions associated with these changes.

De-Emphasis of the Role of Verbal Behavior

Another significant shortcoming began to appear in the curriculum as the educational program was adjusted to the social and psychological demands of the first half of the current century. There was a revolt against the previously overemphasized verbal behavior which had characterized the educational program of the preceding decades and even centuries. The revolt can be seen as a product of two developments, the rise of pragmatic philosophy and the emergence of experimental psychology. Pragmatic philosophy combined knowing and doing in its reaction against such traditional dualisms as mind-body, leisure-work, theory-practice, and the glorified-mundane. It stressed the thesis that the individual learns best by doing. Pedagogically, the "doing" came to be viewed as mere overt behavior. That the pragmatists had not intended this conclusion to be drawn goes without saying. Nonetheless, the conclusion often was drawn when practical application of the pragmatic tenet was made.

At the same time that pragmatism was coming to the fore, experimental psychology was developing laws of learning based upon studies of the behavior of lower animal forms. These laws of behavior—nonverbal behavior, of course—stressed the activity of the learner in problem situations. The learning curve was plotted with respect to the number of trials that the learner took to acquire a particular way of behaving.

Both of these developments have led in the long run to neglect and distrust of language as an instrument of learning and teaching. This has been true even though teachers continued to teach primarily by talking, and children continued to indicate by talking that they had learned. The deficiency found today lies in the fact that language as an instrument of thought and overt behavior has been sorely devaluated—somehow linguistic behavior does not rank as behavior at all! So far as theory is concerned, the child who reads and verbally gives an accounting of his study, correct though it may be, is thought not to have learned in any genuine sense. So far as practice is concerned, the consequences of the emphasis upon overt "doing" seem to have been several. There has been a lack of concern with language as an instrument of thought and learning. There has been a lack of concern for the logical character of language in communication. Attention to the improvement of the ability of the student to handle ideas has been limited primarily to those problem-solving abilities which can be dealt with in the *psychological* descriptions of problem-solving; and, as a result, the strictly logical character of thinking and discourse largely has been eliminated from consideration in the educative process. Finally, instruction in language has tended to become adjusted to what is basically necessary for ordinary communication as carried on by average students at a given level.

The Shortcomings in Perspective

Some of the major shortcomings which need to be remedied in the secondary curriculum if American education is to meet the challenges of the decades immediately ahead have been discussed briefly. But they and many others of our problems are both causes and effects of a deeper problem, which concerns the traditional ideals of a common, general education and our ineffectiveness in approximating those ideals. Stated briefly, the problem is that of the cultural and personal maladjustments attendant upon America's shifting from essentially a society based upon multiple communal relationships to one which can be characterized as essentially a "mass" society. The cultural shift is discussed briefly in the next chapter, which should indicate how the shortcomings mentioned above can be both explained and understood in the light of one fairly coherent perspective.

CHAPTER II

CURRICULUM DEMANDS OF
A MODERN MASS SOCIETY

The previous chapter briefly called attention to ideals and short-comings of the curriculum of American high schools, and indicated that it is possible to gain a fairly coherent perspective on the problems with which American education is beset by noting the demands which have been placed upon it by a major shift in social modes of organization. This shift can be characterized as one which has led us away from a society predominantly "communal" in nature to one which is predominantly a "mass" society.

"COMMUNAL" AND "MASS" SOCIETIES

By a "communal" society is meant one in which tradition is the main source of values and beliefs, and one in which the tradition is maintained within a relatively small, closely knit group, for example, the neighborhood, the extended family. The communal groups in America at the turn of the century were characterized by certain clusters of values and beliefs: belief in the great importance of practical intelligence and joint effort in the solution of common problems, resistance to innovation from outside individuals or groups, and interdependence and mutual support in times of both joy and crisis. The groups were multifunctional and largely autonomous, taking care of virtually all of their economic, health, recreational, educational, and religious needs themselves.

The educational aspects of the communal groups could be found in the sheltering of the child from outside influences; an insistence on the rites of passage of the particular group; the overseeing of each child by adults who were personally acquainted with him, so that rewards and punishments were on a personal basis; and an education for work and leisure such that the child moved smoothly and fairly easily to a place as an elder in the social group.

Technically, the hallmarks of a communal society are two, both of which highlight the role of tradition. First, by dint of his training, the youth who diligently fulfills the expectations of his elders in turn enforces those expectations on the generations to which he acts as an elder. Second, the youth of oncoming generations have before them an obvious set of expectations which are to be met if they are to attain leadership status, and the youth tend to resist any change which obscures the precise nature of those expectations. In short, it is a situation in which the elders are apt to resist any significant deviation from tradition on the part of neophytes, and the neophytes are apt to resist any significant deviation from tradition on the part of the elders. Aside from changes introduced by charismatic individuals and powerful outside forces, it is a system of almost perfect self-perpetuation.

By contrast, a "mass" society has as one of its features an openness to change. American mass society can be further characterized as one in which change occurs rapidly, largely as a result of scientific and technological developments, and is channeled through vast, highly centralized institutions. The vastness and centralization of the institutions account for another phenomenon of American mass society: the impersonal, formal procedures necessary to accomplish institutional and general social objectives. Whether one considers education, health, religion, recreation, or production, he is struck by the manner in which they have become institutionalized into huge, centralized bureaucracies which are heavily dependent upon specialization of tasks. One is also struck by the impersonality of the bureaucracies in both their internal operations and their relations with the general public. For those old enough to remember the communal neighborhood and tightly-knit extended family, the contrast is tremendous. The self-sufficient, multifunctional communal groups have virtually disappeared as significant modes of American life, and in their place we find today's small family which fulfills mainly the functions of emotional support and procreation. The loss of the functions of education, health, religion, recreation, and production has been accompanied by a loss of traditional modes of controlling the impact which those processes had upon one's life and the lives of those dear to him.

One feels the need to ask, when noting these contrasts, "Has the change been for the better?" Many answer in the negative, citing the growth of anxiety, alienation, and conformity in individual life, in economic life, and in political life. Others answer in the affirmative, noting that specialization and centralization, however impersonal, have brought enormous advances in education, health, religion, recreation, and production. Even if we do not approve of the changes, the chances are slim indeed that the old modes of life can or will return.

The problem thus becomes how to fashion a way of life such that security, identity, and individuality can be retained within the matrix of our mass society. Some argue that there is no solution, for a mass society moves toward an ever increasing autocracy in which fewer and fewer people control the affairs of society with an iron hand. The institutions basic to society become more and more centralized, concentrating more and more power in the hands of the leaders. Some social commentators have argued that there already is an informally organized coterie of such leaders, which acts independently of the general public in forming policies directing major social actions.

Such a possibility, if it is not now an actual fact, is greatly to be feared by a public democratic in its ideals. It is probably just this fear which has made books and articles citing autocratic tendencies so eagerly read in recent times. Nonetheless, there is reason to believe that the loss of popular control is simply a loss of control in its traditional form, and that our mass society does provide the conditions—if they were but wisely used—which could give the people control, and the security and individuality which it confers, in a new form. One can note, for instance, that public opinion has great influence on the actions of institutions and leaders when that opinion is organized to utilize the ground rules for institutional action. One of the basic ground rules is that public opinion, when it makes no impact on an institution, should either seek to rally other institutions to its support, or create an institution specially designed to carry its message. When a few disgruntled soldiers are able to bring the pressure of the mass media and the legislative branch of government to bear on the military, we have an example of the first rule's being employed. When no other major institution will support the opinion, as was the case for years in Negro fights for civil liberties, the answer is to create an institution (for example, the NAACP, Urban League, CORE) which itself can attain social power and thus control.

This is one of the most overlooked phenomena of a mass society. Attention generally is focused on the fact that leaders in our mass society can readily mobilize the public for actions not traditionally sanctioned. Thus the public's fear of autocratic trends on the part of its leaders. But it is also true of our American society that leaders are very sensitive to demands from citizens for actions not traditionally sanctioned. They are sensitive, that is to say, when the citizens know how to clothe their views in the armor of collective power.

The question becomes one of how to prepare citizens who will have the knowledge, skills, and outlooks necessary to attain such effective control. To illustrate the importance of answering this question correctly, let us cite some problems which our mass society has created for a curriculum which is traditional and communally oriented. The illustrations deal with the way in which the conventional curriculum attempts to achieve the school

27

and life outcomes of citizenship, vocational competence, and self-cultivation.

Citizenship

In the conventional curricula, for instance, practical citizenship receives attention through encouraging the students to work together in studying, planning, and taking action on matters which significantly affect them. In strict, formalistic schools, this participation may be reserved for social affairs and recreational activities, dances, outings, safety patrols, student councils, and the like. In some instances, and especially in the schools having a curriculum based on the Deweyian-Kilpatrickian model, the participation of the student in decision-making extends to his studies as well. This "town-meeting" type of participation in arriving at decisions is encouraged by the family and the mass media as well. The child is early taught that this is the way decisions should be made, and stress is placed on the importance of both individual responsibility and group welfare in the town-meeting type of decision-making.

But, except at the family and local community levels, and not always at these, this is not the way decisions affecting social matters are made in our mass society. And there are many instances in which the term "community" refers only to a geographical unit in which group action is organized with respect, not to a core of shared interests, but rather to divergent interests.

Is it any wonder, then, that the child who later finds himself employed by a large organization, public or private, becomes disillusioned? Indeed, the better he has learned the lesson that town-meeting democracy is the ideal against which to judge all forms of social activity, the greater the likelihood that he will be disillusioned.

Consider the factors of loyalty and responsibility in citizenship. The child is taught that these are based on the mutual obligations of persons concretely engaged in advancing the welfare of the group, particularly the family and certain other small groups (scouts, ball teams, clubs, and so on). What happens when he becomes a member of a group formally organized and so large that he never sees either those who give him orders or those who are affected by his actions in the group? When it is not easy for him to discern what his duties are and to whom they extend? Here again, there seems to be a basis either for apathy or the development of interests which run counter to that of the organization's and general society's good. There are indications that many aspects of both blue-collar and white-collar crime can be traced in part to the feeling that the organization is not in any sense "personal," and that the individual may very properly take personal revenge on it for having failed to operate in the ideal democratic manner. Certainly, many people who have been in the armed services have encountered expressions of this feeling and are aware of instances of dereliction of duty resulting from it.

Or consider charity and kindliness. Here again, the child is taught that the ideals begin at home, and the highest form of satisfaction is that to be derived from his concrete expression of the ideals in acts of charity and kindliness to those about him. He is also taught to express his personal appreciation of charity and kindliness on the part of others so that a system of social reinforcement builds up. Social approval complements the individual's own pleasure at doing good, and in some cases probably is the sole cause of his doing good.

Less obviously, but no less powerfully, do song, drama, and story at the popular level of the mass media reinforce these behaviors and expectations. But, again, many of the most important and effective ways of being charitable and kind in a mass society require action in impersonal ways through large organizations. For in the modern world citizenship and perhaps even survival call for more than face-to-face charity and kindliness. We can no longer plead ignorance of the plight of starving Armenians, Indians, and African tribesmen. The groups established to find cures for diseases, to help in time of disaster or tragedy, the private groups concerned with alleviating social ills, the federal and state agencies which employ tax money for the aged, the delinquent, the out-of-work, the unwed mothers and their children—not to mention international agencies—are supported largely impersonally, the recipient seldom if ever seen, the organization through which the gift is made not really understood in its working. The charitable and kind act consists in sitting down and writing out a check, arranging for a payroll deduction, or dropping a coin in a collection container held by some individual we do not know. The social approval disappears unless the gift is so large that the press, radio, and television carry the story of our magnanimity—and perhaps our names are applied to the organization designed to carry on the good work. (The tax provisions regarding deduction of charitable gifts work as a kind of social approval also, but they, too, are impersonal in this regard.) Even when social approval is not desired, the individual is familiar with bureaucracy in all types of large organizations, and he very well may question if his contribution is going to be used for the purposes which the organization says it represents. He likely will never know how it was used; he likely will never be able to say to a person helped how happy he was to give; he likely will never be thanked, except through a formal token of acknowledgment (by a stretch of the imagination) or by a later request for another contribution.

The situation is clear. The inroads which can be made in bettering the lot of mankind through organized giving and specialized research and development are great. But surely there must be new attitudes and a new understanding on the part of the contributor, the person administering the funds, and the beneficiary of the funds.

Patriotism can be singled out as a special case of loyalty, but almost everything that was said about being generally loyal in a mass society can be said about patriotism: the cause to which one is dedicated increasingly seems remote in its effect on family and community, the forces which mobilize patriotic impulses seem increasingly impersonal, the mechanism and aims for making use of the impulses are not understood (nor can they be in critical times such as these, for to tell the citizen the key strategies of the government is often to tell the "enemy" also).

Further, given a society composed of large organizations frequently devoted to mutually inconsistent or incompatible aims, and a society in which the cry "patriotism" is one which can cause people to rally around widely divergent flags, it becomes unclear just what patriotism is. The patriotism of the conservative groups is surely not that of the liberal groups, and more obviously the patriotism of the radicals is not that of the reactionaries. Also, one can hardly blame people for being afraid to express their patriotism in other than the conventional ceremonies, for recent history has provided some excellent examples of an action lauded as patriotic in one decade becoming a conspiracy to be investigated and attacked during the next. Thus, there is a difficulty not only in understanding what patriotism means, but also in committing oneself to any nonconventional act of patriotism.

It certainly remains true that some of the techniques for teaching citizenship in small, personally oriented groups are still relevant. The purpose of these brief illustrations has not been to deny this, but to show that new techniques are necessary for areas of civic action which decidedly are not communally organized.

Vocational Competence

The shift from a communal to a mass society has also created novel problems for developing vocational competencies adequate for a person's career of work. The liberalisms of the seventeenth and eighteenth centuries placed great store by the dignity, and even the sanctity, of work. Work was made the justification of human worth and the individual's right to own and manage property. It was also conceived to be the basic mode by which the individual could express in this world the character and creativity which were uniquely his.

This was the ideological side of the picture: what the individual was, intrinsically, consisted in the worth and extent of his expression of himself through work which was personally and socially productive. The ideological perspective remains, most obviously among the older folk of our society, who continue to define their self-worth with respect to their productive work when the society as a whole has been cutting back the time per week, per year, and per useful lifetime devoted to productive work in every area except that of the professions. It is no surprise that the older people of today should feel themselves inconsequential and "in the way"; and, to the extent that the older generation has communicated its ideology, it is no wonder that the younger generations have been led to accept expectations which now produce anxiety with respect to maintaining continued self-esteem.

There was a cultural aspect which supported the ideology, for the doctrine of the nobility of work was plausible only insofar as there were tests of productive work which showed it to be truly noble. The social setting was fairly stable and traditionally organized: a fairly harmonious relation had developed over the two centuries preceding the Industrial Revolution to lend credence to the notion that the farmer-artisan-tradesman pattern was one which could be counted on to persevere. The acceptance of the pattern grew steadily and pervasively in this country, and, as it grew, the mobility routes to positions of status and power became as seemingly firm and obvious as did the ideology which was its corollary. Becoming an adult was reckoned to be a lockstep matter, with the rules clearly indicated even if seldom cognized or verbally expressed: one learned as a family member or as an apprentice merely growing up as a helpful participant in the chores of the farmer, artisan, or tradesman. Only later did vocational training and training for general membership in the community become differentiated.

The forces which were to challenge and disrupt this pattern, and which were themselves to establish a new one, did not by any means come into being overnight. Historical accounts of the growth of industrialization, technology, science, urbanization, and rapid transportation and communication show that these forces were not suddenly thrust onto the scene. However, it is doubtful that the cultural shock which they produced was anticipated in any detail. Writing as late as 1936, so perceptive a thinker as the late Alfred North Whitehead could remark only that "new methods of co-ordination are making their appearance, as yet not understood. These principles of organization are based upon economic necessities. That is about all we know of them; the rest is controversy."[1] What was not controversy, however, was the fact that the old modes of individualistic liberalism were being dealt a deathblow.

With respect to vocational competencies and work careers, this meant the demise of many ideals and practices previously assumed to be morally inviolate, considered by many to be sanctioned by the very nature of things. Thus, we are today asking some questions which would have been inconceivable in earlier years, and some of the answers suggest great readjustments in the schooling techniques which are a heritage from those years. A few examples are in order.

First, the traditional notion that the general socialization process of family and community can fully develop lasting vocational competencies obviously is not plausible. When it was plausible, it occurred in the context of the stable and well-organized communal pattern discussed above. But that type of social pattern—offering as it did constant and concerned overseeing of the youth—does not exist today. For some time, the traditional notion has not been plausible for another reason, one which led, around the turn of the century, to making the schools responsible for vocational programs: the knowledge, skills, and attitudes necessary for change in the modern era could not be inculcated via the general socialization process.

[1] "Memories," *Essays in Science and Philosophy* (New York: Philosophical Library, 1948), p. 25.

In many respects, we today find ourselves at a crisis comparable to the one which saw the introduction of vocational courses into the curriculum. Then it was the case that the family and community could not informally provide lasting vocational competencies. Now, as rapid developments in science and technology have made the requirements for continuing vocational competence still more exacting, it begins to appear that our present vocational programs are largely archaic.

We can only briefly indicate the nature of the problem. Invention and cultural diffusion are the two major sources of social change, and our society has shown itself to be very responsive to both, particularly insofar as they bear on scientific and technological developments. The new changes which are accomplished do not require the training of people in the hand skills of mass production, as did the early changes in the period of industrialization. Rather, the skills which are required today demand a prior, sophisticated, and general education, if there is to be uninterrupted mobility on the changing vocational scene.

This need and trend show no sign of slackening. We learn, for instance, that there are more scientists alive today than in all of previous history; that the number of scientific articles over the years has been increasing in the same fashion as money gathering compound interest, so that the plotted increase shows a curve approaching a vertical line; and that the time required to put radically new ideas and inventions into practical service is steadily decreasing. Thus, we have the picture of a steadily growing source of change, a source which requires more and more sophistication to understand and control, and one which more and more rapidly creates practical effects for all of us.[2] Given these things, it seems most improbable that we can trust either the general socialization process or the highly practicalistic

[2] See J. Robert Oppenheimer, "In the Keeping of Unreason," *Bulletin of the Atomic Scientists*, XVI (January, 1960), 18–22. Also see George E. Axtelle, "Technology and Social Change," *Educational Forum*, XXV, No. 2 (January, 1961), 133–40.

vocational programs of most schools to prepare students for lasting vocational competence.

Other questions face us. For instance, can the social order allow the youth to choose his occupation? This is another of the notions associated with traditional individualistic liberalism: what the individual makes of himself is up to the individual alone, and so it should be. The tenet has been honored more often in the breach than in the observance, but it retains its popularity. On the other hand, becoming increasingly popular is the tenet that society cannot afford to waste its talent. Doesn't this mean that we must put more effective strictures on the educational process, among other things, so that children become beneficial to both society and themselves?

The trend of government, business and industry, and education is increasingly toward guiding the individual toward the occupations which are significant and promise to be so in the future. Equally notable is the fact that individuals are making increasing use of such guidance. Does this imply an unhealthy coercion on the part of our institutions and a loss of individualism on the part of youth? Also, it should be noted that the training recommended is not based on the assumption that there is an equality of talent, for this assumption, too, is wasteful of talent, leading to placement of people in training programs and jobs too elementary or too difficult for them.

Thus, how far can we legitimately narrow the channels through which we send youth in order to develop vocational competencies which have an important and lasting place in the social order? One interpretation of the democratic creed would allow no channel at all, but only an ocean on which the individual charts his course alone. Another would make the channel quite definite and tailored to rather specific abilities and social needs. In the former case, we probably would get chaos in modern society, in the latter we might tend toward an autocratic social and educational system. There is little to choose between a bumbling, chaotic individualism and an efficient autocracy, for neither is desirable.

It clearly seems that there is a need for intensive grounding in general studies as a foundation for vocational preparation today, with specialization waiting for post-secondary training. This seems to be the case, at least, if we wish to provide a maximum of choice and mobility to the student in his life, and if we wish to avoid the specificity in vocational training which too often ends in early technological unemployment.

There is a sense in which we have already moved in this direction with respect to one aspect of education. It is a fact much overlooked that almost all liberal (liberal-arts curricula) education given at the secondary level is, in a broad sense, vocational in function, although perhaps not in intention. It is not needed for careers in hand skills or semiskilled and skilled industrial work, but it nonetheless commonly represents a program necessary for modes of employment that require collegiate training. As studied in college, the "liberal subjects" do not aim primarily at the Aristotelian ideal of self-cultivation, but rather at a career in teaching, writing, research, or advanced training and specialization of one kind or another. It was to this that Christopher Jencks referred when he commented that "undergraduate instruction at great universities like Harvard is primarily a device for training—or simply recruiting—academicians."[3] The promising programs of general education at the University of Chicago, the University of Minnesota, Harvard, and Columbia have been "emasculated" by the "specialists' scalpels," according to Earl J. McGrath and Charles H. Russell.[4]

It seems to be a hard fact that general education, if it is to be fully achieved, will have to be provided by the secondary school. With specialization and differentiation reaching down into the high school, the elementary school is destined to be the last

[3] "The Next Thirty Years in the Colleges," *Harper's Magazine*, CCXXIII (October, 1961), 123.
[4] *Are Liberal Arts Colleges Becoming Professional Schools?* (New York: Bureau of Publications, Teachers College, Columbia University, 1958), p. 12.

refuge of general education unless the secondary curriculum is rethought and restructured. And who would honestly contend that the elementary school can provide adequate general education for our times?

A second hard fact is that there is only one large group of people who are able to pursue a liberal education in the classic sense—solely for self-cultivation in order to realize and enjoy values at a high level in all aspects of life. This type of education is possible for those who have met their family obligations and made their "fortunes" secure. Except for the wealthy, these tend to be middle-aged and older people who have discharged the duties of parenthood, who have job security, and who are still free from the ravages of ill health, age, and excessive ambition. It is primarily they who have the time and the means for the cultivation of taste and intellect as such.

A second group has an opportunity for at least a rich general education: our youth. They, too, have a large measure of security, freedom, and health which allows them to develop perspectives and skills without immediate concern for earning a living in a job market in which only a few can survive without great travail. They are protected to some extent by the American family pattern, by laws which set school-leaving ages, and hopefully will be increasingly protected by the society's knowledge of the demands to be placed in the future upon their intellectual and evaluative abilities.

It is true that many slum and other youth do not have this protection at present, and it is true that time will be required to provide it. But it must be provided unless the curriculum is to remain, in effect, an institutionalized apologist for social neglect which is not really a product of educational or democratic ideals.

Self-Cultivation

Finally, let us turn more directly to the topic of self-cultivation as an aim of education in a mass society, meaning by "self-cultivation" the individual's use of his talents and his culture to produce a more civilized person and culture, so that he increases knowledge and value for both and promises to continue to do so. Equally important, the ideal of self-cultivation carries with it the notion of developing individuality and individual excellence.

One of the problems of encouraging self-cultivation, in this sense, is found in the description of mass culture. In the words of one writer, " 'Mass culture' refers to the production of synthetic, easily accessible amusements for mass audiences, as well as to the products themselves."[5] For a given population of low-level aesthetic tastes, such synthetic and easily accessible amusements for mass audiences might well constitute an upward step in taste even though they are not developed by the individual for himself. Nonetheless, the problems of self-cultivation in a mass society take on new dimensions. The new customer of art, music, and literature usually has only his own ill-formed taste to guide him; he no longer has to take what small groups of taste-makers prescribe as good and bad art. As a "mass customer," he commands the mass media to produce what his taste dictates, and thus he can prevent the production of that which might change his taste. Without the small, recognized group to guide, develop, and reinforce approved selective standards, how is the individual to judge whether *he* is producing genuinely unique and valuable works?

Self-cultivation, insofar as it connotes development of individual excellence, demands stable and defensible exemplars which both "lure" behavior and serve as standards against which behavior can be judged unambiguously. The exemplars furnished by communal groups may have left much to be desired aesthetically, but they did at least furnish stable standards for the members of the group. Today the standards not only leave much to be desired aesthetically, but they are also hopelessly confused.

The problem is great enough just as sketched, but its sig-

[5] Irving Howe, "Notes on Mass Culture," in B. Rosenberg and D. M. White (Eds.), *Mass Culture* (Glencoe, Ill.: Free Press, 1948), p. 503.

nificance becomes compounded when one thinks of it in relation to the ideal of American common education. The notion of common education forces one to consider such factors as the socio-economic background of the child, his ethnic background, aspiration level, preschool development and education, IQ level, and so on and on. Do we have the exemplars which can serve as standards and lures when this diversity is considered? Do the schools really seek such exemplars?

Common education is education for all of America's normally educable youth in all of its great diversity. If this is a purely utopian ideal for common education, then democracy in education is a farce.

There are indications that educators do regard the ideal as utopian. One of the most obvious examples is seen by looking at the educational programs provided and proposed for slum children. Given the fact that the dropout rate for slum children is high, can one expect them to master relatively high-level skills, knowledge, and arts, when it seems evident that their interest is solely in getting a job in the current labor market? Given the fact that many of these youth are thought barely educable and a drain on the resources which can be offered the schools' talented youth, why not train them in the hand skills which offer immediate opportunities for employment? So the reasoning of many schoolmen seems to proceed.

The premises of the argument are open to the questions raised in the previous chapter. The following related points might also be made. First, the fact seems to be that most hand skills learned in many vocational and industrial curricula are acquired by dealing with apparatus which is antiquated or fast becoming obsolete. The fellow who learns how to beat out the fender of a 1955 car in the school shop is going to have a fine time with the fiberglass fender of a 1965 model. The boy who handles traditional upholstery, whether in cars or on furniture, is going to have trouble dealing with preformed plastic and glass upholstery, especially when new units of the latter are likely to be more inexpensively replaced than can units of the former be repaired. The one who knows all about today's automobile engines still needs a training which will enable him to deal with the sophisticated devices of the future not anticipated in the work and materials ordinarily available in his high-school shop.

Second, it is true that slum youth of the type under consideration want and can have no more than simple hand skills as preparation for a livelihood? The research on enrichment programs would indicate not, and some sociological and psychological studies indicate that a large number of the problems of delinquent youth (for whom the same type of training is often recommended) can be explained by suppressed possibilities and frustration rather than by low ability or initially low aspirations. There are strong indications, for instance, that delinquents begin by aspiring to the conventional expectations of society, but gradually are led to develop deviant behavior patterns as social forces block the realization of those expectations.[6]

A number of astute critics of the American scene and American schooling in particular have commented forcefully on the fact that we are sitting on social dynamite in our handling of slum youth. Dr. James B. Conant, a rather mild-spoken critic of education and one of the most respected figures in American public life, drew great attention when he made just such a comment.[7] Now, *if* slum youth (among whom much delinquency occurs) do have conventional aspirations, and *if* technical developments require more general education in order to meet these conventional aspirations, is it not the case that those who argue for the traditional handcraft or skill programs are putting the match to the

---

[6] See R. A. Cloward and Lloyd E. Ohlin, *Delinquency and Opportunity* (Glencoe, Ill.: Free Press, 1960): "Our hypothesis can be summarized as follows: the disparity between what lower-class youth are led to want and what is actually available to them is the source of a major problem of adjustment. Adolescents who form delinquent subcultures, we suggest, *have internalized an emphasis upon conventional goals.* Faced with limitations on legitimate avenues of access to these goals, and unable to revise their aspirations downward, they experience intense frustrations; the exploration of nonconformist alternatives may be the result" (p. 86. Italics in original).
[7] *Slums and Suburbs* (New York: McGraw-Hill, 1961), p. 146.

fuse of the social dynamite? It is done with the best of intentions, perhaps, but done it is. At a time when an increasing proportion of high-school youth is college bound, the pupil who is not may find himself in a minority with much decreased status. Some observers have expressed the fear that this situation will grow and aggravate delinquent responses.

This leads again to the observation that schoolmen who advocate such traditional hand-skill programs are performing in some role other than that of educator. Specifically, except where they tolerate a bad educational program as a first step to its quick correction, they would seem to be apologists for economic, political, and social interests. The slum schools are the educational problems they are primarily because they are first of all economic, political, and social problems.

Another aspect of the situation concerns the education of the gifted. Here, too, we may have been missing the boat. In the case of the poor performers, the most that the school has been able to suggest is a program which at best prepares them for a low-grade contemporary job which, it is said, is mostly what they want and all for which they are obviously fitted. In the case of the gifted, the argument is that the country cannot afford to waste talent, and these children should be given special treatment so that they and society can have the benefit of those talents. When the gifted child does not respond, when *he* occasionally does not have high aspirations or want more than a low-level job, we respond in shocked indignation. But we do not criticize the child; our response is directed to the poor quality of his schooling. We seldom admit that the gifted child, like the slum-school child in the popular conception, may not want anything more than a job and to be "let go" by the schools, just as we apparently do not often realize that the slum-school child may have considerable talents which he would like to develop in support of both his and society's cherished ideals.

To state this contrast is to reveal that we are operating with a double standard which, like a double-edged blade, cuts both ways for good and bad. For the slum-school children, we allow and even encourage an education which gives them what we have decided they want and can handle, thus neglecting talent which could be utilized to promote their welfare. On the other hand, we have decided upon a forced draft of talent for the gifted, even if in some cases it is talent without high motivation or aspirations.

WHAT IS NEEDED

Thus, it is with a very complicated, even confusing, cultural and educational base that educators must work if they hope to meet the social and individual problems of the new era. All of the varied elements of education in a communal society remain; a seeming hodgepodge of new elements has entered upon the curriculum scene as a result of largely uncoordinated empirical studies of what can be taught or learned in various subject matters, particularly the sciences; and administrational innovations are further contributing to curriculum diversity.

What obviously is needed is a comprehensive and systematic view of the curriculum for common, general education—a view which allows us to organize our thoughts, our techniques, and our enormous energies and resources. Despite many of the heroic efforts of teachers and administrators to make do with grossly inadequate means, a lack of such a systematic view of the curriculum is bound to occasion tragic inefficiency and waste. More tragic will be a failure to meet our problems in time, knowing full well that the due date is fairly definite on some of them.

Basically, however, there is a need for a reassessment of what the outcomes and uses of schooling actually are in a society such as ours. It is to a discussion of this topic, and its relevance to the formation of a program of common, general education, that we now turn.

CHAPTER III

REASSESSMENT OF THE USES
OF SCHOOLING

Characteristic of educational literature is a dutiful listing of goals, objectives, and outcomes. Common sense tells us that a purposive enterprise such as education ought to map out its destination before undertaking its journey. What common sense sometimes overlooks is that maps can be of varying degrees of detail and size. Life maps are large, covering a long span of years. The destination of a lifetime is not a single location, but rather a whole area of experience to be traversed by a number of routes. It is to this broad area or region that one refers when speaking of the aim of life as growth, self-realization, and the like.

A school, on the other hand, can be compared to a small segment of the life map with fairly definite routes over relatively short distances. To be sure, these segments *should* lead to more remote destinations, and one designs them so that they will feed into many life goals. Nevertheless, the school must in the first instance be judged by how well it achieves the outcomes that make it a distinctive social institution. That a man ends his career as a forger in the penitentiary does not disqualify handwriting as a proper school outcome.

In trying to devise a curriculum that will connect life outcomes with schooling, several different approaches are possible. For example, it was fashionable in the twenties to make the connection by noting the skills, knowledge, and attitudes a person would need to hold a certain type of job. Later, one heard a good deal about a curriculum that would prepare the individual to carry out certain developmental tasks such as family membership, emotional maturity, vocational competence, and so on.

Such analyses tended to result in long lists of specific informational items, skills, principles, and attitudes. Does an auto mechanic, for example, need the same cluster of attitudes, skills, and knowledge as a dairy farmer? If not, then different lists must be made for auto mechanics and dairy farmers. And should they be the same for mechanics A and B? If this approach were to be followed to its logical end, all hope for common education would have to be abandoned, and, in practice, the schools, especially those which could afford a rich variety of course offerings, did abandon it.

The terms "general" and "common," when used to qualify education, are related but not synonymous. Whatever the total population of a school studies is common in the sense that it is shared by all pupils. In this sense, our elementary school curriculum is regarded as common, and the school has been known as the common school. "General," on the other hand, refers or could profitably refer to a characteristic of the subject being studied. The general is the opposite of the specific or of the particular and is therefore more likely to be abstract than concrete. In this sense, mathematics is more general than geography, and geography more general than corn agriculture.

This book sets forth a theory of the curriculum that is general, that is, made up of general studies, but it also urges that it be common as well. The writers believe that in the scientifically based mass society, vocational training increasingly presupposes thorough grounding in general studies. One can expect that with automation reducing the number of unskilled jobs, the cognitive component of job training will rise in amount and level. Even now, careers at the technician level in mechanics and electronics require a secondary schooling comparable to that needed for college entrance.

To be sure, not even automation will remove from the occupational market all low-skilled jobs, but the case for *common*, *general* education does not rest entirely, or perhaps even primarily, on vocational considerations. If the analysis of the new emergent mass society is correct, the needs of citizenship and self-development for general studies are even more urgent than the vocational needs. For, if the analysis is right, to exploit the possibilities of the technological civilization for a society that can in any genuine sense be called democratic will call upon a very large proportion of our people, not an elite handful, to think and feel as educated men and women think and feel. The enlargement of vision that this entails makes mandatory a common curriculum emphasizing the general studies.

Accordingly, cues as to the nature of the curriculum will be sought, not in the particular jobs that youth are likely to hold, nor in the diverse roles they will play in life, but rather in the ways that schooling or school learnings are used in modern life. In this domain, as in so many others, specialization and differentiation have created new educational problems.

The writers have distinguished four typical uses of knowledge or school learnings and have called them replicative, associative, applicative, and interpretive. The point of making such distinctions is not to multiply terms or to make the obvious seem esoteric and learned. The justification for distinctions among concepts and terms is that they denote processes that are more or less independent of each other or that cannot be substituted for each other. If such differences exist, the curriculum designer should be alerted, lest his efforts produce effects he did not anticipate and fail to produce those he had a right to expect.

We use school learnings in nonschool situations in ways that range from the apparently unconscious to the most deliberatively explicit use. There is the report of an experiment concerning the effect of reading Greek poetry to an infant on the child's ability to learn Greek poetry many years later. In the same vein, subliminal advertising on television has been banned, presumably because it effectively uses stimuli of which the viewer is not conscious. One can only speculate on the potency of "forgotten" learnings to affect adult behavior. Who knows how much of what we call "individuality," "creativeness," and "charm" is caused by learnings that operate at the unconscious or preconscious level? Various schools of psychiatric thought have capitalized on "forgotten" learnings and their role in neurotic behavior. The schools have not capitalized on them, partly because students of schooling have not taken the trouble to perfect methods for studying their effects.

ASSOCIATIVE USE OF SCHOOLING

Many learnings, while not subliminal or unconscious, have an air of the accidental about them, as when something we have learned comes to mind because it has something in common with what is before us. For example, we read the word "Greek" in the newspaper, and the thought of Achilles or Homer occurs to us, to be followed, perhaps, by the thought of rubber heels.

This is an example of the associative use of learning. When we are asked to respond to a question, we resurrect from memory something or other that the cue suggests. The laws of association —resemblance, contiguity, and satisfaction—purport to tell us what learnings the given cue is most likely to elicit.

Resemblance, contiguity, satisfaction, and vividness can determine what is associated with what, but these are not logical relations. "Red Square" and "redhead" are not related logically, although they have the word "red" in common. We cannot say logically that, given the stimulus "Red Square," the subject must respond with "redhead" or red-anything-else, but psychologically one might have expected something like this on the basis of what is known about people's speech patterns and the law of resemblance in association of ideas.

Nevertheless, the subliminal and associative modes of using what is learned in school are important, partly because many students and perhaps even some teachers mistake an associative response for a logical one. For example, if the teacher asks, "Why is the sun hot?" the pupil may reply, "Because it is round and bright." This is not a logical answer, although it is understandable as an associative use of learning, because the sun *is* round and it *is* bright.

Unfortunately, neither students nor teachers display adequate sensitivity to this distinction, as is made clear in subsequent chapters. Here, it may be remarked that many a conscientious student has passed high school courses by using learnings associatively in answering questions on essay examinations. In other words, students learn to respond with everything they can recall that is in any way related to some word or phrase in the examination question. Such an answer may contain nothing that is false and nothing that was not in the textbook and yet be completely irrelevant to the point of the question. If this answer is written in legible hand and with due respect for grammar and spelling, chances are better than even that the student will get a passing grade. Indeed, if there is anything that might qualify as a universal learning pattern in American schooling, it is precisely the method of using the instructor's questions as cues for the recall and statement of any and all associated materials. The valiant attempts of the Progressive critics to change this pattern unfortunately were in vain. The discovery that such responses will not earn passing grades for the student in college—although in many colleges they will—must be traumatic. Every time, therefore, an instructor accepts a psychologically relevant answer in place of a logically relevant one, he is an accessory after a pedagogical crime, and if in his teaching he ignores this distinction, he is an accessory to the crime.

Another reason for the importance of the associative use of school learnings is that it constitutes an important matrix of meaning for the appreciation of the arts. Much of the imagery in the reading of poetry, fiction, and drama depends on learned materials that cannot be recalled exactly as learned. Much of the effectiveness of figures of speech rests on comparisons once noted, now forgotten, yet still amenable to partial recall.[1] We perhaps have overlooked the importance of this use of school learnings because, as has been pointed out, we cannot trace their origins to particular school experiences.

Much of what has been called concomitant learnings by William H. Kilpatrick and others illustrates what is here meant by the associative use of schooling. The stress on this type of learning is justified both by the fact that it probably does occur and by its important effects. The difficulty in using it as a basis for curriculum theory arises because it makes too much depend on what, in the nature of the case, is highly idiosyncratic and uncontrollable. It should also be noted that associative uses of schooling do not all originate in the interpersonal relationships of pupils and teachers. Content, if rightly chosen, also teaches more than meets the eye or the test.

REPLICATIVE USE OF SCHOOLING

At almost the opposite pole of the unconscious and randomly associative use of learnings is the replicative use. When we read a newspaper, compute a sum, look up a word in the dictionary, read a map, or recite a poem, we repeat an operation performed many times in our school days and pretty much as we performed it in those days. The replicative use of schooling is most noticeable in the practice of the skills. Ordinarily we do not say that we

---

[1] See William York Tindall, *The Literary Symbol* (New York: Columbia University Press, 1955). Beginning the section called "Burial of the Dead," T. S. Eliot wrote in *The Waste Land* (*Collected Poems of T. S. Eliot, 1909–1935* [New York: Harcourt, Brace & World, Inc., 1936]):

> April is the cruelest month, breeding
> Lilacs out of the dead land, mixing
> Memory and desire, stirring
> Dull roots with spring rain.

What can we recall explicitly that gives these lines their haunting appropriateness? Grover Smith devoted twenty-six pages, in his *T. S. Eliot's Poetry and Plays* (Chicago: University of Chicago Press, 1950), to the sources of meaning of this section of the poem.

"apply" our skills of reading and writing in nonschool situations; rather we repeat the school performance in writing and reading situations, and such situations are virtually self-announcing in school and out. When does one write? When paper and pen are before him and when the situation says, "Write it down."

Attitudes presumably are instances of the same use, except that the triggering situations vary over a wider range. That neatness in school will transfer to tasks outside of the classroom is not so certain as that writing will take place in writing situations. Yet when the neatness attitude is instated in an unpracticed task, it is a repetition of much the same sort of experience that the learner underwent at the times when the attitude was formed.

We rely on the replicative use of schooling for those operations and contents that are used very much as learned in a wide range of frequently occurring situations. They are the most reliable type of school learnings precisely because life affords opportunities to overlearn them to the point of virtually faultless performance. Because the school can anticipate only a small portion of the behavior that is demanded by life, the replicative use of schooling is limited less in importance than in range.

The traditional emphasis on reading, writing, and arithmetic placed great reliance on the replicative use of schooling. Life was to make repeated demands on the individual to use these symbolic skills; hence, to overlearn them was the primary task of elementary schooling, whatever else might be added to garnish the education menu.

There is another ingredient of schooling that is sometimes used replicatively, the use of "facts" or, more precisely, statements of fact. If one is asked, "When did Columbus discover America?" the replicative response is "1492," a repetition of an oft-repeated response made in similar situations.

How many of the facts learned in school are used in this way is impossible to estimate. A repertory of facts is assuredly indispensable to life and thought. The building of such a repertory has been belittled first, because compared to the total stock of knowledge, any individual's stock is bound to be minuscule and second, because fact-storing is generally regarded as being of a lower order of mentation than thinking and reasoning. Yet all thinking requires facts as well as meanings and relations. Even in purely formal logical thinking one cannot wholly dispense with facts, for example, that certain symbols stand for certain logical meanings and operations, that there are logical rules, and the like. So in every thinking situation some elements are regarded as fact and when so taken they are used replicatively, that is, as given or as learned.

Thus, while it is admittedly futile to attempt to store all the facts one will need, the replicative use of facts is such that schooling should give attention to the strategy of fact-storage and retrieval, to use the language of the computer. Such strategy concerns itself, on the one hand, with selection of key facts to be stored, and, on the other, with conceptual nets or maps that facilitate both the storage of facts and their recall. These are the direct objective of general studies.

APPLICATIVE USE OF SCHOOLING

The most serious limitation on the replicative use of any learning is its lack of flexibility. It works best when the new situation is almost a replica of those in which the learning was acquired. We are told that whenever new materials or new designs are introduced in house-building, even master craftsmen are disturbed. This is so because well-established habits and skills can no longer function replicatively.

Our technological civilization depends on the application of knowledge to particular problems of practice rather than on its replicative use. Mathematics and physics *applied* to problems of mechanics give us the profession of engineering, that in turn solves problems of transportation, construction, mechanical toasters, and space probes. Hence the enormous importance of applying school learning, or the *applicative* use of learning. Here a learning—

usually in the form of some principle, generalization, or statement of fact—is used to solve a problem or to analyze a situation. The cues for what knowledge is needed and how it is to be used are limited and often hidden. Sometimes the situation is so unstructured and open that the bulk of the cues must come from the problem-solver himself (see Chapter VII). Accordingly, we rightly prize the applicative use of knowledge, for it greatly enhances our powers of understanding and control. The applicative use of knowledge is, however, more complicated than might first appear; otherwise we would not be so often chagrined that we had not applied knowledge that was in our possession all the time. If application of knowledge were a simple matter, would we not ourselves make those discoveries and inventions which seem so obvious after they have been made by others?

Knowledge is applied, of course, whenever one recognizes an object or an event as a member of a class or an instance of a generalization or a law. This is application by subsumption, and there is some justice in believing that it is a basic way of applying knowledge. In the more complex case one does not, as a rule, deal with one object or event. Rather, one deals with problems or problem situations, and to solve them one seeks some resemblance to a familiar problem or situation. This type of application may be thought of as filling in the missing terms of a proportional equation.

We have

$$\frac{\text{Familiar problem}}{\text{New problem}} = \frac{\text{Familiar solution}}{?}$$

As an example, we might consider the familiar situation of boys in slum neighborhoods resisting delinquency when an extensive recreational program is introduced. If another neighborhood is afflicted by a high rate of juvenile delinquency, it occurs to us to apply a familiar solution, namely, instituting recreational facilities.

This is, of course, an argument by analogy. Whoever first applied his knowledge of the power of an electric current to magnetize a bar of iron within a coil of wire, and thus to operate a bell, completed the analogy $\dfrac{\text{hand}}{\text{clapper}} = \dfrac{?}{\text{clapper}}$ and hit on the notion of using the magnetized iron bar to activate the clapper as the hand ordinarily does. Someone had to note the resemblance between the power of steam in a kettle and in an engine; between the phenomenon of parallax and the possibility of measuring the distance to inaccessible yet visible objects by sightings from differing positions.

Another example of applying knowledge is furnished when we work backwards and ask, "What will tell us how cold or warm it is?" In measuring other properties of objects such as weight or size, we often rely on pointers that move over a numerical scale. What in the temperature situation would move a pointer? If we know (or can use replicatively) the fact that heat and cold affect the volume of metals or liquids, we are on the road to completing an analogy and devising some kind of thermometer. One could illustrate the same sort of thinking process by raising a question such as, "What will turn salt water into fresh?" Here, knowledge about evaporation might furnish the clues to the solution, or knowledge about the chemical reactions that produce precipitates might be the starting point.

Applying knowledge is, therefore, not simply to recall it or to recite it. It is to use it for problem-solving, and, if we are not to use "application" trivially, we mean dealing with problems whose solutions are neither easy nor easily available from an expert or a handbook.

It is noteworthy that after we have solved the same type of problem many times, another problem of the same sort elicits a response that *replicates* at least part of the previous response. When this happens, one no longer applies knowledge, but rather uses a *skill*, much as one uses the skills of reading, writing, and spelling. In other words, even when we observe someone solving a problem, perhaps a difficult problem, we cannot be sure that he is applying knowledge; he may be merely replicating a skill. The human race has inherited the earth not because it can have knowledge or apply it, but primarily because it makes a habit of doing so.

For the curriculum designer, the important point is that in ordinary life the applicative use of knowledge is relatively rare. We do not solve many of our problems by thinking our way through them. On the contrary, we consult someone who has the solution for sale, or we look up the answer in some manual. Our behavior follows the law of least cognitive strain; we think no more than we have to.

As the next chapter explains more fully, it is the specialist in the exercise of his specialty who is most likely to use knowledge applicatively, and even he does so only when confronted with problems that are not routine. The highest applicative use of knowledge is to expand knowledge itself, as in the work of the scholar and researcher. The generalist is satisfying the requirements of thinking and intelligence when he uses knowledge interpretively.

Why do we stress the relative rarity of the applicative use of knowledge? Because in educational thinking it has generally been taken for granted that it is the applicative use of knowledge that justifies schooling in general and the teaching of any subject in particular. At times the schools have operated on the assumption that a large repertory of facts, rules, and principles learned for replication on cue would automatically be used applicatively when the life situation became problematic. At other times, disappointed that automatic application of school learnings did not occur, the schools urged that the pupil be given practice in application, so that applying a piece of knowledge became a standard part of a lesson. These Herbartian applications, usually practiced on problems within a given subject, served as an admirable test of the pupil's understanding, but they did not guarantee that the learning would be used to solve nonschool problems.

This was due partly to the fact that life problems are "molar," that is, more complex and massive than problems in a single discipline like mathematics or physics or chemistry. It was also due to the technological complexity of our culture. In such a culture, one depends more and more on specialized problem-solvers who have the knowledge, tools, and skills required. In such a state of affairs, to justify a curriculum on applicative uses is neither practically nor theoretically defensible, unless it is the curriculum for the training of specialists.

INTERPRETIVE USE OF SCHOOLING

Much of what in ordinary language we call application of knowledge is better regarded as interpretation, a process related to application but far less specific and detailed.

Experience becomes intelligible only as we categorize it, conceptualize it, or classify it. In other words, experience becomes intelligible and intelligently manageable insofar as we impose form upon it. But which forms, and from whence do they come?

The ultimate answer to this question is still a profound philosophical mystery, but for our purpose it is safe to say that every intellectual discipline, every science, every poem, and every picture is a source of forms or molds into which experience must flow and be shaped if we are to understand it at all. Our language is the great prefigurer or premolder of ordinary everyday experience; the sciences use molds or categories that allow us to understand our world in terms of atoms and electrons, galaxies and solar systems, acids and bases, causes and effects; our works of art enable us to feel the world as pervaded by human values.

Whenever we use our school learnings in these areas to perceive, understand, or feel life situations, we say that we are using our learnings primarily for interpretation, and not replicatively, associatively, or applicatively, although, strictly speaking, these uses do not necessarily exclude each other. There is a sense, however, in which the interpretive use of knowledge is the most fundamental of all, for without a prior interpretation of the situation we are not sure what we shall replicate, associate, or apply.

The interpretive use of schooling, accordingly, is primarily for orientation and perspective rather than for action and problem-solving. Although interpretation is a necessary preliminary to all the other uses of knowledge, there are many situations in which orientation toward a problem is as far as we can go, that is, in virtually all of the situations in which we cannot function as specialists.

CRITICAL THINKING

What about critical thinking? Is critical thinking an interpretive or an applicative use of schooling? Is it confined to the specialist, or must we all make use of it? There is little doubt that all citizens are expected to think critically and to be good at it in all domains of life. By critical thinking, we mean the scrutiny of discourse for truth and validity. We think critically when we attend closely to such questions as, "Is this statement true?" "Does this statement follow from the evidence presented in its behalf?" "Is this statement more or less probable on the evidence than alternative statements?"

Good thinking has both form and content. The form is provided and regulated by logic, or the rules for correct definition, classification, and inference. Good thinking or critical thinking also involves knowledge *about* the field in which the thinking is being done. It is this content that enables us to judge the truth and relevance of the alternatives presented to us in life situations. But it is precisely with respect to content, that is, with respect to knowledge about situations, that the citizen is not a specialist.

It turns out, therefore, that although content is used applicatively only by the specialist, logical form is the same when used by specialist or nonspecialist; it must be used applicatively if used at all. This means that all subjects, if logically organized, must be studied with respect to both their logical form or structure and their specific content. Except by the specialist, the content is used interpretively and associatively, but the logical form of the subject (mathematics, chemistry, physics, history) is used applicatively, and this means only that the logical form of a subject matter is used applicatively to regulate our interpretations. When this occurs, we are thinking critically.

The discussion of the various uses of school learnings has been admittedly schematic and abstract. It may be helpful, therefore, to examine in some detail a task that confronts us so commonly that we forget its importance as a test of schooling—the task of reading a newspaper or magazine.

Suppose that the task is to read the following excerpt from the *Saturday Review:*

> In a few weeks, Albert Schweitzer will have completed fifty years of service at the jungle hospital bearing his name in Lambaréné, now part of the newly independent state of Gabon, in West Africa.
>
> In establishing a medical center in the heart of Africa, Albert Schweitzer subordinated careers as organist and organ builder, musicologist, theologian, philosopher, and historian. His initial funds came from his book on Johann Sebastian Bach. Much of the carpentering he did himself. What he built was not a "hospital" in the Western sense; he built an African village in which medical care was available to people most in need of it. He knew that Africans would be apprehensive about coming to a frosty white modern clinic. He wanted to meet the Africans on their own terms. He had a concept of human purpose that didn't permit a life of comfortable theorizing—even about matters of the gravest importance for renowned philosophers or theologians. He also had ideas about the nature of Christianity that didn't completely coincide with what he had been taught as a student. These ideas were related to a concept of the indwelling God and the way the reality of human brotherhood asserted itself. Rather than teach other students what he himself could not accept, he decided to leave the seminary and make his life his argument. If what he believed had genuine validity, it would be proved in his work.[2]

In this quotation from a Norman Cousins editorial, there is a typical cognitive task for modern man. The article assumes that the reader has some knowledge about Albert Schweitzer. In response to the name Albert Schweitzer, one typical ten-year-old boy

[2] March 16, 1963, p. 30.

gave the following associated items: "missionary," "mustache," and "doctor."

Although a specialist could give a precise definition of "musicologist," "theologian," and "philosopher," this youngster could not. He made a stab at "musicologist," but a "theologian" was defined as a man "interested in theories," and a philosopher was "you know, a sort of brainy type."

The following few sentences were adequately interpreted, but when he got to "These ideas were related to a concept of the indwelling God . . .," the task of interpretation was too severe, and a vague "it has something to do with religion" was the best he could manage. "To make his life his argument" also gave trouble, requiring, as it did, some understanding of an unusual metaphor.

How was the youngster using schooling in this reading situation? Replicatively, he was using skills of pronunciation and syntax as well as visual habits involved in reading. Associatively, his previous learnings were functioning well enough that the words had sufficient meaning to give sense to most of the sentences. He had enough knowledge to interpret a good portion of the passage. He could say what it was about. Roughly, he could set the scene of a doctor in an African jungle, a learned man who gave up life among learned men because of some difficulty with religious belief. In the terminology of this book, the young reader had cognitive maps on which these sentences could be plotted.

The plotting, however, was exceedingly rough. What would refine it? More knowledge about Schweitzer and Africa, to be sure, but also a clearer notion of the subject matter of philosophy, musicology, and theology. Note, however, that there is no problem to be solved by the reader. He does not need to "apply" his knowledge to solve any problem. He uses some of his schooling to interpret these paragraphs; this particular boy achieved a marginal interpretation.

What in this example would be an applicative use of knowledge? A theologian might scrutinize the article for accuracy of statement and cogency of argument, and so might a student of the emerging new countries. A specialist in these fields would apply his theoretical knowledge and practical experience to evaluate Mr. Cousins' analysis and perhaps to suggest an alternative analysis or solution. An expert editorial writer would examine the passage for details of literary construction and rhetorical effect.

It will be pointed out that in applying knowledge, the specialist uses knowledge replicatively, associatively, and interpretively as well. Of course this is true, inasmuch as the applicative use of knowledge is the most highly developed use. The difference between the interpretive and applicative uses is that application carries interpretation to the degree of detail and precision needed to deal with a problem; it does not simply identify the focus and nature of the problem. Interpretive use leads to meaningful discourse and understanding; application is aimed at problem-solving.

Clearly, interpretation is a necessary condition for application, but not a sufficient one. Schooling that is adequate for interpretation may not be adequate for application, while some applicative study may be too narrow for adequate interpretive use. General education has for its goal the interpretive rather than the applicative use of schooling, whereas special schooling has the applicative use as its ultimate goal.

In terms of logical operations, interpretation can be achieved when a given cognitive task is subsumed under a class of cognitive tasks. For example, "This material has to do with chemistry," or "This is a sample of English poetry." More concretely, the test of acceptable interpretation is translation of the material to be cognized into roughly equivalent terminology, or giving an example. Thus, "gravitational field" is acceptably interpreted when the respondent says, "the pulling of the earth on things" or "it's what keeps people from flying off the earth." Definitions need not be precise nor explanations adequate; minimal interpretation is satisfied when identification is correct.

It follows that interpretation can be made highly precise by appropriate study, but it does not follow that it will automatically shade into application. Thus, a philosopher of science can be highly precise about the nature of scientific method, but remain helpless before a bubble-chamber problem in physics. One can become highly precise in interpreting number theory and yet be awkward in solving quadratic equations or translating problems of mechanics into mathematical terms.

Application presupposes interpretation but logically goes beyond identification. The whole series of acts—formulating a problem, observation, hypothecation, experimental imagination and design, verification procedures and criteria, judgments of adequacy—is involved in applying knowledge. Clearly, it involves a degree of detailed knowledge of fact as well as of theory, experience as well as adequate conceptual frames.

In subsequent chapters it will be indicated that such detailed knowledge is often mistaken for general education. As a result, unless the student completes a long array of courses within a domain, he is qualified to use his learnings neither applicatively nor interpretively. His studies in chemistry are in great detail, but being incomplete, may not give him a cognitive map large enough to interpret ordinary experience or complete enough to solve problems in chemistry. It will be argued that chemistry for general education should provide for interpretation of experience, as precise an interpretation as one can make it; and although this chemistry will lay a cognitive foundation for the applicative study of chemistry, the latter is not a responsibility of the secondary school.

From what has been said in this chapter the following observations are in order:

First, in a society in which vocational specialization in a narrow sector of life is the rule, the difference between schooling for specialization and nonspecialization is of the first importance to the design of the curriculum. If secondary schools have been ignoring this distinction, it may account for their chronic failure to provide for general education. The importance of this distinction leads to discussion in the next chapter of the specialist and generalist uses of schooling.

Second, if certain psychological and logical operations constitute a more-or-less constant factor in the uses of knowledge and schooling, a more detailed account is needed of these operations and their relations to the curriculum. This is given in Chapters VI and VII.

CHAPTER IV

SCHOOLING AS USED BY THE SPECIALIST AND NONSPECIALIST

It cannot be repeated too often that in modern society every man's vocation requires specialization, while his roles as citizen and person demand that he be a generalist. Significantly, specialist and generalist roles in such a society (for reasons adumbrated in Chapters I and II), both look to cognitive products and processes of a quality hitherto expected from only a small minority of the population.

Because so much more in the way of schooling is demanded of so many more of our citizens, it becomes imperative to ask, How can the secondary school of our time most economically deploy its resources? Can we fashion a curriculum that provides adequate basic education for both the specialist and the generalist roles? Can we avoid the waste inherent in overschooling and underschooling for these roles? Clearly, a further exploration of how schooling is to be used in these roles is needed before one can answer these questions.

HOW THE SPECIALIST OR PROFESSIONAL USES SCHOOLING

The most usual, although not exclusive, meaning of the term "specialist use of schooling" is vocational use, inasmuch as it is with respect to vocation that most of us are likely to be specialists. How, then, do we use schooling on the job? Do we use it associatively, replicatively, interpretively, applicatively? How frequently is schooling used in these ways? Which use, if any, is the distinctive use? Does the level of occupational role affect the uses?

With respect to all four uses, schooling enters into the specialist's work from general and special education. General education provides the store of ideas and images from which some may be summoned for vocational purposes or in relation to vocational activity. For example, an architect's thoughts as he muses over the design for a nightclub might be affected by a long-ago reading of "In Xanadu did Kubla Khan/A stately pleasure-dome decree. . . ." Replicatively, the same architect uses his school learnings of reading and writing, and interpretively and applicatively, he uses some of his general education. Precisely because the studies are general, does this type of schooling have reverberations in all occupations or in the preparation for them. Special or vocational education, on the other hand, contributes knowledge and skill that are used almost exclusively on a particular set of behaviors required by a particular vocation or, at most, a small family of them. One of the problems we face is that some elements of general education, especially some of the content, can be taught with primary emphasis on only one of the four uses. When in general education we stress a use that is characteristic of the work of a specialist, we may be defeating the purpose of general education.

For example, the technical or the professional school tries to introduce into its curriculum tasks that the trainee can replicate on the job. This is the practice phase of the curriculum. Thus, in a school for draftsmen, the drawings assigned may closely resemble the drawings to be done on the prospective job; an auto-mechanics' school requires practice on automotive problems no different from those to be found in the contemporary repair shop. Professional schools devote a smaller proportion of time to tasks for replication than do technical schools. Only a small proportion of legal education, for example, is given over to the writing of briefs, courtroom procedures, and so on.

However, items of knowledge, rules, and even modes of speaking and writing are included in legal training that presumably are to be used replicatively, that is, just as learned, and if one does not perfect these habits in school, one has to do it by practicing on one's clients.

General education in the secondary school cannot include practice on sample tasks of this or that occupation or of any set of occupations. Yet, we hear the argument that certain subjects should be taught in high school because they will be used in certain vocations, for example, mathematics in engineering, history in the teaching of the social studies, logical thinking in law, chemistry in medicine, and so forth. Presumably, they will be used replicatively (as taught) or applicatively (to guide the prospective practitioner in solving the problems peculiar to his job). But suppose such subjects are not so used by generalists, or even by specialists under ordinary circumstances, or in either case not so frequently as one might expect. Would this not make a difference in the way we organize these subjects for instruction in a program of general education?

One can begin the inquiry by noting that knowledge, as used vocationally, can take several forms. For example, one can teach it, as a teacher of chemistry uses chemistry to teach chemistry. An industrial chemist uses chemistry to solve industrial problems, making a new synthetic fabric, for example. A physician may use chemistry to understand the literature on a new drug. A research chemist may not teach chemistry or apply it to industrial problems; he may use it primarily to further chemical knowledge. Nevertheless, these people and others *might* use certain chemical apparatus or procedures in exactly the same way, for example, test tubes, Bunsen burners, wash bottles, and the like. In other words, their use of chemical skills may be the same, replicative, but their uses of the content can vary, even when used in relation to vocation.

An important characteristic of the specialist's use of a given segment of knowledge is its high selectivity. What is selected is dictated by his daily work. What is not relevant to it is not used and often forgotten; what is retained is retained as used. We are often ruefully surprised at how little of our schooling we actually use "on the job." For this reason, conscientious schools that follow up their graduates to inquire what courses helped them most in their work are usually disappointed or baffled by the responses. Either the number of courses mentioned is very small, thereby casting doubt on the value of the bulk of the curriculum, or many courses are cited as valuable but not by any sizable percentage of the graduates. Worse still, graduates impute to this or that inspiring teacher the reason for their success, although what he taught has no discernible or conceivable connection with what the graduate is now doing. We would avoid this disappointment if we realized that by its very nature specialization has to be narrow, that the direct use of "general" studies by a specialist in his specialty is always small in volume and narrow in range, and finally that content is not all that is learned in school. Associative and unconscious uses of schooling defy easy identification by recall, but may operate powerfully nonetheless.

Thus, the expert may get by with a restricted set of symbolic skills. The reading, the mathematics (if any), drawing, note-reading, and so on, he uses are highly specific to the specialty. A first-rate chemist who cannot read Shakespeare or Proust might surprise us, but not very much, and surely there are many good auto mechanics to whom algebra is not even a meaningful word. This does not mean that as citizens the chemist or auto mechanic can get by without these items of knowledge or that having them might not affect their *interpretation* of their activities, even as specialists. It merely means that it is unlikely that these specialists make an applicative use of them.

Similarly with the conceptual store of content. The research or theoretical chemist, one would suppose, knows the basic conceptual structure of chemistry, and nowadays he had better be on reading and speaking terms with the basic concepts of physics and mathematics. Yet, in many chemical specialties, one can be ignorant of biology and economics with comparative safety. The modern surgeon likewise is probably more sophisticated in the sciences than were his forebears, but even so, the margin of tolerable ignorance is wide indeed. What one does not have to know about science to be a good surgeon would fill a large book.

On the other hand, the relevant knowledge is cultivated in as great detail as practice dictates. A professional chemist, for example, needs to know almost all there is to know about what has been done, what is being done, and what might be done within the bounds of his chemical specialty. He knows his field in detail and depth; he knows "who's who" in it, and how to appraise the import of every new piece of research. He himself may or may not contribute by research to the chemical domain; this depends on his chemical specialty.

To what extent is this theoretical competence required of the chemical laboratory technician? Or of the man who works on the control panels of an automated oil refinery?

A theoretical grounding in chemistry is desirable at the technician level, but it need not be as detailed or as sophisticated as that required of the research chemist. The knowledge needed by the technician is that which enables him to learn *about* the operations he is to perform in his work. These are guided by rules of procedure and manipulations with specific apparatus in specific situations. He uses courses in chemistry to *understand* what he is doing and why he is doing it. He does not use them to solve problems or to extend chemical knowledge. The technician uses his knowledge of *rules* applicatively but his knowledge of *chemistry* interpretively.

The specialist at all levels uses knowledge as a source of rubrics that enable him to classify a problem, to identify the causes of the difficulty, and to select a remedial procedure. One learns in school—usually at a professional law school—that a given client's trouble with the law can be classified with other legal troubles that have similar features. One also learns that in such a class of cases the difficulties of the defense are such and such, and that there are more-or-less standard gambits to over-come these difficulties.

The practicing physician and the auto mechanic operate no differently. Their specialized schooling enables them quickly to classify the usual problems of practice, and the usual remedial procedures are reduced to technical rules. In standard cases of measles, do this and this; when the car won't start, do this and this. That is why the depth and narrowness of specialized train-ing are so valuable. The narrowness permits depth, and depth permits rapid and accurate classification of a wide variety of cases within the limited domain. That is why, also, students in professional schools are so often impatient with courses that do not contribute to this facility. They want knowledge for appli-cation, not for general interpretive use. General education, how-ever, provides the initial gross interpretive framework within which the specialized curriculum is taught and learned.

When, however, the specialist is asked to justify his rules of procedure and operation; when, for example, a case turns up that does not respond to the standard treatment for the class of cases to which it belongs, then the classificatory use of knowl-edge by itself is insufficient. He then has to turn to an explana-tory use of knowledge. He has to back up into a more general set of concepts. If the observed symptoms—fever and rash—do not signify measles, then what else can cause such symptoms? The physician can go through the catalogue of diseases and their symptoms, or he can try ruling out one alternative after another, but if these means fail, he has to fall back on his knowledge of how the various organs of the body work and what happens when they fail to work. He must fall back on his knowledge of the action of microbes, viruses, the blood, the other body fluids, and the nervous system.

As long as his practice was proceeding happily according to rule, this knowledge remained latent. Once the specialist is chal-lenged to explain why he did what he did, once ordinary rules fail, the knowledge comes into active use as a source of new hypotheses and new suggestions for experiments and trials. To explain and justify, he has to consult the theory from which the rules were originally derived.

At this stage, general interpretive use of knowledge is insufficient. Knowledge now has to be precise, detailed, and sophisticated in order to function applicatively. A general familiarity with basic theory is not enough; only a thorough familiarity with the problems under investigation, the issues under controversy, and the research in progress will do. When, for example, the telemetry system of an orbiting satellite goes awry, the specialist cannot rely on his introductory courses in physics to solve the problem.

An account of how such a situation was dealt with in the case of Telstar illustrates this. Several times before failing altogether, Telstar obeyed commands only after they had been repeated several times. It was as if passage of a signal through the malfunctioning decoder tended to cure it, at least temporarily. What would account for this?

The specialists on the job knew that transistors ceased to function properly after being subjected to powerful radiation, but they also had to be in a position to know that such powerful radiation could have been released by a nuclear test bomb near Johnston Island.

Now imagine the uses of knowledge represented by the following reasonings and operations: (1) tracing the trouble to a single transistor called the "zero gate" designed to react to short impulses in the command signals; (2) figuring out how to shut off the power from Telstar's storage battery when the satellite could not hear commands; (3) devising a new code language; (4) testing both the theory and the device designed to test the theory.

The specialist, the physician, for example, uses knowledge of different degrees of generality at different times. At one level are such basic sciences as physics, chemistry, biology, and mathematics. At another level he uses such sciences as physiology, anatomy, bacteriology, and pharmacology; at still another are pathology and diseases of the various organs; still closer to practice are courses dealing with methods of surgery and other therapy.

The particular problems of a profession draw to themselves as nuclei the knowledges and skills relevant to these problems. As a rule, these knowledges do not all come from any one discipline but from a number of them. New disciplines that organize this knowledge in terms of professional problems help the practitioner identify and treat his problems more rapidly and more accurately. These new disciplines are not so general as the basic disciplines from which they were assembled, but they are more directly applicable to the problems for which they were designed. Sometimes they come from "interdisciplinary disciplines," such as biochemistry or astrophysics.

In other words, there are layers of knowledge, each descending layer being closer to the problems that the practitioner encounters every day. Pharmacology is closer to the problems of the general practitioner of medicine than chemistry; anatomy and physiology are closer than biology; blood-pressure readings and electrocardiograms are closer than physics. Each rule of practice which says, "In this kind of situation, do thus and so," if it is theoretically valid, can be deductively traced back and back through the layers of knowledge until it rests cognitively in the principles of such basic sciences as physics, chemistry, biology, economics, and psychology.

Here is the reason for the peculiar nature of a professional curriculum. It is ordered by problems of practice rather than, as in a standard discipline, by the homogeneity of ideas or objects of study. Not everything in professional education is for application and replication; not everything has to be taught as if it were to be so used either in preprofessional training or during professional training. Certainly, the general education of those who may enter professional fields need not operate on these assumptions. Nevertheless, the upper limits of expected applicative use do prescribe the minimum level of theory required for professional competence.

Although the medical practitioner uses many disciplines, his knowledge does not have to be equally minute in all of them. He has to know enough about pharmacology, for example, to understand and appraise the claims made for drugs, but it is not often the case that he himself does the research on the basis of which he judges the value of a drug. He has to know enough about physics to understand the working of X-ray machines and the interpretations of the findings of the roentgenologist, but he himself is far from being a physicist or even a student of physics.

As the practitioner acquires experience in which the rules are used and tested, and as his problems fall into a few major classes, his knowledge of the basic sciences and of the more remote layers of the applied sciences becomes *perspectival* or interpretive. That is to say, only the most general features, terminologies, and methods of inquiry remain functional. He might have trouble passing even an elementary examination in them. Yet they do function in helping him structure every problem— even the most unfamiliar ones—in terms and in ways dictated by the categories or concepts of these disciplines.

Little more need be said about such theoretical specialists as, say, the research chemist who intends to devote his life to learning more and more about chemistry. For him, the basic conceptual structures and methods of inquiry, the history of his subject, its relations to other disciplines are central and continue always to be directly functional, not merely perspectival. For him, particular technological applications may become perspectival. For example, he may know about the application of chemistry to modern steel production in only the most general way and nothing at all about the particular procedures used to produce high-carbon steel. Analogously, some distinguished medical research scientists might be put to shame by an Eagle Scout in applying splints to a broken leg.

The discussion of the specialist's use of knowledge may give rise to two related objections: first, it gives the impression that science and mathematics are the only types of learnings useful for specialization, and, all secondary-school pupils are destined to work at jobs that require school learnings at a high theoretical level.

It is true that some specialties, for example, the writing of poetry, the painting of pictures, the winning of elections, do not require the application of science, mathematics, or indeed of any well-developed body of knowledge. One can operate by inspiration and hunches, but the moment the practitioner formulates a rule or rules for his practice, he is subject to the demand for the justification of these rules.

If one asks a politician why he always refers to mothers in his speeches, and why he prescribes this for his followers and apprentices, he may reply in one of two ways. First, he can say, "All men have a soft spot in their heart for mothers, and all men look kindly upon anyone who feels as they do about mothers. Hence, they will feel kindly toward anyone talking as if he had a soft spot for mothers and motherhood." Or he might say, "I don't know why it works, but I know from experience that it does help win elections, so I make it my rule always to talk about motherhood, mother love, and so on."

The first answer exemplifies a rudimentary justification by science in that the politician is basing his rule on a generalization about human behavior. The second does not, unless it be on the generalization that future political behavior will resemble that of the past. That many people practice their specialties at these levels of justification is not to be denied. This fact does not change the way the specialist uses school learnings (applicatively), but it does affect the kind and amount of school learnings he so uses.

The objection that not all of our citizens, or that a large proportion of them, do not use theoretical learnings in their work raises doubt as to the advisability of using high-school time for this kind of vocational training rather than about the importance of theoretical learnings. The writers can only re-iterate that they do not look on the secondary-school curriculum as a means for job training, that is, for the applicative use of knowledge, but rather as the means to general education which exemplifies the interpretive use of knowledge primarily and its applicative use only indirectly.

HOW THE NONSPECIALIST USES SCHOOLING

The perspectival or interpretive use of knowledge has not been investigated as thoroughly as the applicative and replicative uses. For example, watching water boil, a child asks, "Why does the water bubble?" Father uses his schooling interpretively when he classifies the question as one to which two items he has re-membered from his schooling are relevant: (1) molecules move faster when heated, and (2) water contains air. He may never have practiced or read the explanation he now devises; he can-not in all likelihood calculate or "do" problems involving heated liquids, although Boyle's Law might recur to him as of possible relevance. He cannot, on the spot, "apply" his knowledge to problems that require precise, detailed information. Yet he can fol-low such an application if made by someone else. This often is what we mean by "understanding," that we see how something to be explained (the boiling, seething of water) follows as necessarily true if a general principle (the molecular theory) is true. Why does a satellite have to attain a critical velocity to enter and stay in orbit? When does it pay for a prosperous corporation to buy up a company that is losing money? Why is it so difficult to solve the problem of agricultural surpluses? The well-edu-cated citizen, as will be seen, uses his schooling *interpretively* in responding to these questions; the specialist uses it technically and theoretically to give precise and detailed solutions. He applies it in a sense and degree that a generalist does not.

As nonspecialists, however, we all use the results of schooling in other ways. Much is used associatively, as has already been pointed out, to supply a source of images and meanings that give to experience richness, variety, and no small amount of spontaneity. In the field of our specialties, we do not rely on associative hunches as a regular thing, although there are numerous occasions when we are grateful for their occurrence. A curriculum that treats the associative use of schooling with condescension is likely both to impoverish experience in general and to dry up prematurely the wellsprings of creativity. Testing procedures that disvalue the associative uses of learning affect the curriculum indirectly, insofar as they determine what is stressed in teaching and learning.

Some school learnings, especially those involving symbolic and manipulative skills, are used replicatively and are discussed in some detail in Chapter X, but they do not exhaust the replicative use of school learnings either for the specialist or the non-specialist. Some content is used replicatively to anchor the interpretive frames that are used for orientation and perspective. Certain statements of fact ("There are fifty states in the Union."), certain generalizations ("Water freezes at 0 degrees centigrade."), certain hypotheses ("The universe is expanding."), and certain well-established theories (the atomic structure of matter) are all used replicatively as true assertions, even though the maker of these assertions has only the vaguest notions of how they were discovered or validated. A great deal of what John Dewey called "funded knowledge" is used by specialist and non-specialist, but especially by the latter, in a replicative way.

Finally, the nonspecialist's way of using logical operations, as in critical thinking, differs in no significantly formal way from that of the specialist. The difference lies rather in the wealth of content each can summon to supply instances, counterinstances, alternatives, and distinctions. An astronomer might not think with better or different logic than the layman, but he has so much astronomical content with which to think and reason and the layman so little that conversation between them about matters astronomical is embarrassing to both.

The coming chapters discuss two major types of perspective needed by the nonspecialist. One is for cognitive interpretation, the other for evaluative orientation. There will be occasion to speak of cognitive and evaluative maps, the construction and use of which entail certain specific kinds of content and certain specific kinds of operation.

CHAPTER V

OUTLINES OF A DESIGN FOR SCHOOLING

The preceding chapters have distinguished four uses of schooling and shown how these are related to the activities of the citizen and the specialist. These uses have been viewed against a social background that increasingly reflects the growth of mass democracy, with its promises and its threats, and the breakdown of the educational ideas rooted in the individualistic world view of the last century. In the present chapter, two topics are discussed. First, certain conceptions of the uses of schooling which stand in sharp contrast to those already set forth are explored. Further discussion will help to make clear the crucial importance of the writers' conception of the uses of schooling in curriculum development. Second, a synoptic view of that conception is set forth in order to indicate the focal points of discussion in subsequent chapters and to give a context within which discussion of details can be carried on later without loss of perspective.

THE CURRICULUM AND USES OF SCHOOLING

Any conception of the curriculum consists of certain component elements. It includes some notion of the nature of content; it provides for categories of instruction; and it ordinarily includes reference to modes of teaching. What makes one conception of a curriculum different from another is not so much variation in component parts as how those parts are conceived

And the way these components are thought of is in any case, consonant with the conceptions of the uses of schooling and of learning outcomes held by those who design the curriculum. The way the uses of schooling are perceived is therefore crucial in any theory of curriculum development. For this reason, it is well to distinguish the uses of schooling set forth in the preceding chapters from those which are being discarded.

Ever since the theory of formal discipline was repudiated at the beginning of this century, there have been two conceptions of the uses of schooling that in one way or another have left their imprint upon the educational program. One stems directly from the connectionist theory of learning and the other from the pragmatic conception of thinking; but the latter did not escape the pervasive influence of the connectionist theory.

The connectionist theory of learning, as taken from Edward L. Thorndike, assumed that for each learning there is a corresponding connection or chain of connections in the nervous system. Furthermore, each connection relates a specific stimulus to a specific response. Thus, learning is not only quantitative—differing from one person to another only in the number of connections—but also is specific. Each stimulus has its corresponding response. Moreover, the difference in achievement between one person and another is simply a difference in the number of synaptic connections developed within the nervous system. The fact that A has achieved more than B is reducible to the fact that A has developed a larger number of synaptic connections than B.

According to this view, school learnings and the uses of such learnings are specific and coterminous. Behavior outside of the school is specific, just as learning in school is specific. To be useful, school learnings need to be the same as those which life behavior requires. Thus, words commonly written by adults should be the words taught in the school. If words in common use are learned, then the student is able to meet spelling demands made on him in life. Similarly, if the historical facts occurring repeatedly in newspapers, magazines, and other media of communication are taught in school, the learnings thus acquired are directly used in life as the individual reads and listens to various communications and otherwise engages in out-of-school activities. By the same formula, all learnings in geography, arithmetic, English, and other studies are useful. This conception of the uses of schooling is based upon the well-known theory of transfer by identical elements, which holds that learning in one situation is used in another situation only to the extent that there are identical elements in the two sets of circumstances.

This leads to the second conception of the uses of schooling —one which borrowed heavily from the pragmatic theory of thinking—the view that learning is situational. The individual learns by thinking his way through situations for which he has no ready-made way of behaving. Hence, the curriculum should be made up of a series of situations falling in various areas of experience and calling for different kinds of subject matter. As the individual deals with the situations, he draws subject matter from various domains in an effort to cope effectively with the difficulty. From using the subject matter in these circumstances, the individual learns. But these learnings are within and for the specific circumstances. This notion of specificity came from the influence of the connectionist theory of learning upon the interpretation of the pragmatic theory of reflection. Accordingly, the utility of school learning depends upon whether or not school situations are comparable to life situations. A curriculum based upon life situations therefore generates the maximum utility of schooling, because the learnings acquired are those which the activities of life demand. Thus, this view of the utility of schooling also is based upon a sort of one-to-one correspondence between the content of school situations and the content of activities performed by people in life generally.

The curriculum theory which grew out of the first of these two conceptions of the uses of schooling—the theory involving specificity—may be characterized as follows. If the curriculum designer construes the uses of schooling as direct application of what the student learns in school to out-of-school situations and circumstances, based upon the theory of identical elements, he thinks of the content of instruction in terms of specific elements of experience which can be identified and dealt with in the classroom. The curriculum emphasizes specific objectives and specific outcomes expressed in behavioral terms. The subject matter of instruction is reduced to atomistic bits of information. The prototypes of such bits consist of number combinations in arithmetic, certain factual elements of history, geography, and so on. Conceptions and generalizations are minimized, while factual learnings are intensified. Furthermore, the theory of transfer involved in this conception of the uses of school learnings assumes that the maximum use is attained only if application of learning outcomes is directly provided for in the curriculum. Thus, a great deal of emphasis is placed upon the application of learning to situations comparable to those occurring out of school. Children are required to study arithmetic in connection with budgeting, buying, and more technical matters such as stocks and bonds. The curriculum in science is developed so as to emphasize the uses of scientific knowledge in dealing with practical situations at home. Such topics as "Science in the Home" were until recently found over and over again in general science books. Likewise, the subject matter of biology, chemistry, and physics until the 1950's was oriented to practical and technological problems.

The second conception of the uses of schooling—the theory involving similar situations—led to a theory of the curriculum which stressed the development of programs emphasizing life situations. For example, one proposed curriculum was made up of such situations as those involving selecting clothing, balancing bank accounts, making floor plans for workshops or clubrooms, and so on. This conception, as can easily be seen, is one which attempts to make situations in the classroom as comparable as possible to those encountered in life.

In sharp contrast, the uses of schooling set forth in this book involve a one-to-one correspondence between school learn-

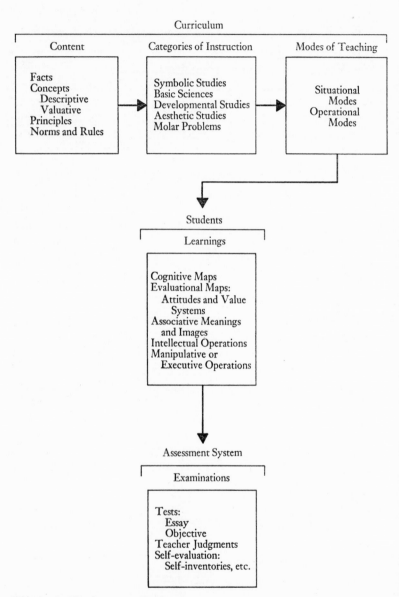

Figure 1. SCHEMA FOR SCHOOLING

ings and the uses of schooling only in the *replicative* sense of use. And here, as has been indicated, the school learnings pertain primarily to the domain of skills and specific factual information. In applicative and interpretive uses, it is assumed that the cognitive structures which are built up are so comprehensive as to subsume a great number of situations and experiences. By such subsumption, a large part of the world becomes intelligible because of its relationship to a few basic elements of knowledge. Thus, the mastery of basic concepts and intellectual operations, together with mastery of the symbolic skills, promises a high degree of utility as one interprets and deals with his world. This conception of the uses of schooling also leads to a particular way of thinking about the curriculum. The remaining sections of this chapter indicate in general terms some of the curriculum implications of this view. The following chapters deal with these implications at length.

THE CURRICULUM AND SCHOOLING

The curriculum may be viewed as a part of a total influence system directed toward the student. This system is called schooling. As can be seen from Figure 1, the total plan of schooling includes three sets of components: a curriculum, an assessment system, and student learnings.

The curriculum consists primarily of certain content organized into categories of instruction. Although modes of teaching are not, strictly speaking, a part of the curriculum, for practical purposes it is not useful to ignore them entirely in curriculum theory. Hence, in subsequent chapters attention is given to this aspect of schooling, although emphasis is placed mainly upon content and its grouping into basic strands of instruction.

The content, organized into categories of instruction and handled in certain ways, brings about changes in students. These changes are called learnings. The following changes can be thought of as taking place in a student's mental repertory: cognitive maps, attitudes and value systems, intellectual operations, associative meanings, and skills of manipulatory and executive operations. As is indicated below, these are not necessarily manifested in changes of behavior. They are changes in dispositions. They may be manifested in behavior, but they are not to be equated with the medium of their expression.

The assessment of instruction is not really a part of the curriculum either, but it is shaped primarily by the curriculum and by the way learnings are conceived. It is dealt with only incidentally in the treatment of the curriculum in the chapters that follow, but if assessment procedures are not consonant with the proclaimed outcomes of instruction, the consequences for the curriculum are clearly bound to be bad.

CONTENT COMPONENTS OF THE CURRICULUM

In the schema of Figure 1, content is considered as kinds of propositions. When thus conceived, elements of subject matter can be separated from a consideration of the situations and circumstances in which they are learned. They can be thought of as elements of knowledge expressible in verbal forms. Facts are thus conceived to be singular propositions such as "This automobile is red," "That table is five feet tall," and "Isaac Newton was born in 1642." Principles are general propositions such as "Water boils at 100 degrees centigrade," and "If the pressure is kept constant, the volume of a gas is proportional to its absolute temperature." Similarly, concepts are treated primarily as definitions. For example, the concept of dew point is reduced to the following sentence: "The dew point is the temperature at which the water vapor in the air begins to condense." Norms and rules are prescriptive principles or statements such as "One should always drive on the right side of the road," or "One should always treat others as he would like to be treated."

Content thus conceived is consistent with the uses of schooling set forth in the preceding chapters. This can be seen by noting briefly how a person interprets his world. Any new event or happening in one's experience is understood as he relates it to what he already understands. The logical machinery for relating new things to old is that of classification. We have understood a new element of experience when it is classified in accordance with our conceptual systems. In other words, our concepts enable us to divide our world up into categories and to name them. As new and unfamiliar things come into our field of view, we understand them by finding the class of things to which they belong in our conceptual system. Concepts are taught in an elementary sense through the use of perceptual material and in a more advanced sense through symbols. The more abstract the concepts are, the more we must rely upon symbolic means of explicating the concepts through definitions and their analysis. What has just been said about the use of concepts illustrates the *interpretive use* of knowledge.

The same thing can be said in a little different way regarding the *applicative use* of what one has learned. To deal with difficulties in one's environment is to go back to some general principle which relates elements within one's conceptual system. Thus, when we speak of application, we are thinking primarily of the use of principles in a deductive sense of explanation as, for example, when a specialist applies to some new set of circumstances a principle of chemistry or of physics which enables him to deal successfully with difficulty.

CATEGORIES OF INSTRUCTION AS CURRICULUM COMPONENTS

The composite of offerings from all secondary school programs now includes over 350 subjects. This multiplicity of subjects is, of course, due in part to the increase in knowledge that has come about during the last hundred years. But it can be attributed even more to the fact that a conception of the uses of schooling that assumes specific and direct uses of school learnings in life situations leads logically to the conclusion that whatever is needed in life must somehow be taught directly in school. When the teacher or the curriculum-maker believes that all subject matter is of equal importance logically, differing in value only as it differs in its direct utility in life, he will have no adequate basis for choosing from among the subjects those most important for an instructional program. He is thus driven to add course after course as specialized activities out of school increase. This is just what has happened, and only the traditional college requirements and specific job demands made by society have prevented the numerous subjects of instruction in the secondary school from being considered of equal worth. Except for these limitations, there would be no grounds for distinguishing among them in terms of educational importance.

The view of the uses of schooling developed in this book makes it possible to differentiate among subjects in terms of their *educational* value. This can be seen from a consideration of the nature of knowledge and systems of knowledge. It is possible to consider the structure of knowledge only briefly at this point, its fuller treatment being reserved for later chapters. But it should be noted here that the uses of schooling emphasize the control and interpretation of one's environment by reference to the basic elements of knowledge. And the basic elements of knowledge are precisely those facts, concepts, principles, norms, and rules that give the broadest and most comprehensive interpretation of the world. The concept of deficit financing, for example, is more important than the concept of par value of stocks precisely for the simple reason that the deficit financing concept explains more of the economy than does the concept of par value. If one understands the concept of deficit financing, he is able to understand an aspect of one of the most significant political and economic issues of our times, as well as many of the economic policies and political moves of the federal government. There is in a rough sense a hierarchy of knowledge such that some concepts and principles explain far more than other concepts and principles, and, in some cases, the less powerful concepts and principles can be derived from the more powerful ones. The subjects which embrace the most generally explanatory concepts and principles are the ones which are basic to *any* education. The question of whether these subjects prepare a student for college is not relevant to the question of their general utility.

Relying upon this general consideration of the differences among the elements of knowledge and their relation to the interpretation of the world, for the purposes of general education, one can reduce the multiplicity of courses to five basic strands: symbolic studies, basic sciences, developmental studies, aesthetic studies, and molar problems. These are analyzed and described in later chapters from the standpoint of the nature of their content and the uses to which their learning outcomes may be put in life activities. It is believed that this way of looking at school subjects brings order into the educational program and gives a unified view of the curriculum.

MODES OF INSTRUCTION

The replicative use of schooling requires that the person do tasks out of school that he did at school. To spell "cat" in life activities is the same as to spell the word in school. Although associative uses do not require that the connections which a word, say, calls up in school be the same as those it calls up out of school, mechanisms of both associations are the same: it is psychological conditioning in both instances. No special operation beyond that of psychological association is required. Interpretive and applicative uses, however, invoke such operations as defining, designating, classifying, valuing, explaining, and conditional inferring. To interpret is to classify, to define, to evaluate, and to perform other logical operations with respect to a novel event, object, or experience. To apply is to make conditional inferences, to show that some relationship is a special case of a more general formulation; or it is to use the machinery of logical inference to formulate and establish a new principle describing a set of relationships.

In short, these uses of schooling entail the application of logical operations to the content of experience.

To acquire facility in the use of these operations, the student must have some opportunity to use them again and again in school. From one standpoint this condition is not hard to satisfy, because the content of instruction is manipulated and controlled during instruction by recourse to operations, except, of course, in drill and other repetitive forms of behavior. Unless the content of instruction is handled logically, the manipulation and control of the content in the process of instruction become somewhat of a mystery. For, in the final analysis, the content can be manipulated and controlled only by relating its elements logically to one another. This is the case regardless of whether the subject matter is being dealt with by the teacher or by the student. Of course, the logical processes employed may be performed elliptically and often at a low level of sophistication. Nevertheless, the subject matter of instruction comes to the student through the performance of such operations.

Where the use of schooling is conceived in terms of comparable elements of school and out-of-school situations, and where learning is thought to result from the individual's being involved in unsettled situations, the mode of teaching consists of ingratiating oneself with students, enlisting them in activities, and cooperating with them in ventures jointly worked out. To teach, one must be on the alert to identify challenging situations and be able to use materials to frame situations that will involve students. In this view, to manipulate and maneuver students so as to involve them is more important than to know how to handle the subject matter of instruction. The subject matter is introduced into the situation by students, who bring it from reference materials and are responsible for its manipulation and organization as they themselves deal with the situation. To be sure, the teacher is expected to introduce and control the use of subject matter at points where the situation is too difficult for students. But it is often assumed in the training program that the teacher needs no special work in the control and manipulation of subject matter itself. Rather, the training is to emphasize the teacher's understanding of students and how to work with them.

This is a partial view of teaching; it is not the whole picture, and it emphasizes factors that are not unique features of teaching. Teaching behavior may be interactive, it may be ingratiating, it may involve individuals and situations, it may be attended by a wholesome social atmosphere, it may eventuate in learning, but these are not uniquely characteristic of teaching. These features are to be found in political, economic, and administrative behavior as well. Were these factors to constitute teaching in its entirety, there would be no reason for a theory of teaching nor for a program of teacher education as such, for teaching behavior would then be the same as any social behavior. All that would be required for teacher education, in this view, would be a general theory of social behavior and a program to train the teacher in its patterns and techniques, with slight adaptations to the classroom. Basically, the training of the teacher would be the same as that of the politician, the commercial worker, or any other individual whose work requires him to engage cooperatively with others at an interactive level.

While the foregoing factors are certainly involved in teaching behavior, teaching is more than a way of working with students. It is also a way of working with the subject matter of instruction. Behavior is didactic to the extent that it is determined by considerations of the subject matter of instruction and by what the concepts, principles, norms, and facts of that subject matter require for their explication. What distinguishes teaching from all other forms of social behavior is that teaching behavior is controlled by the requirements of the body of knowledge and by the commitment to develop cognitive and valuative structures coordinate with that knowledge. While the behavior of the teacher is influenced by his understanding of the student—by his perception and diagnosis of the student's behavior—still, the determining factor is not his understanding of the student but rather his own cognitive preferences, his knowledge, and the demands which clear instruction in it makes upon him. The instruments through which these demands of his knowledge are met, at least in the content fields, are precisely those by which meanings are clarified, principles and norms are explicated, and the objects and events of experiences are classified and interpreted, predicted and controlled. These instruments, in the final analysis, are the logical operations which teaching entails and which, as is discussed in later chapters, become apparent in a rudimentary form in every individual during his early development.

The writers' view of instruction, as well as of the uses of schooling, includes a necessary reference to situations in instruction. But there is a fundamental difference between their view of the bases on which situations are selected and the notion which holds that the curriculum is but a series of lifelike situations. The writers would select situations primarily in terms of the logical requirements to be made upon the student. In the other view, the selection of situations is determined by the belief that they should be as nearly as possible like those to be found in life. In other words, the selection of instructional situations in the writers' view is determined largely by logical considerations.

STUDENT LEARNING

If the content of the subject of instruction has been properly dealt with in the course of instruction, certain learnings probably accrue to the student. These are represented in Figure 1 under the heading "Learnings" and are referred to more specifically as cognitive maps, evaluative maps—attitudes and value systems—intellectual operations, associative meanings, and skills. These learnings, of course, are not part of the curriculum. They are the effects upon the student of his going through an educational program such as that described in this theory of curriculum development. Although not discussed as such, they are dealt with incidentally throughout the chapters that follow.

These learnings are not behaviors. They are dispositions to

behave in certain ways in certain circumstances. If one's attitude system enables him to enjoy music of a certain quality, he can enjoy it when the music is accessible and he wishes to do so. But the fact that he is not enjoying music at a particular moment, or that good music is available to him and he is making no effort to enjoy it, cannot be taken as evidence that he is unable to do so. He does not go around enjoying music all of the time. All that is called for in this example is the recognition that the individual has the ability to enjoy music when he wishes to do so. The same can be said for one's ability to perform intellectual operations. Although such operations develop partly as the result of maturation, they are refined and perfected through instruction. But even so, one does not use intellectual operations on any and every occasion. He does so only when the conditions require him to think in certain ways. He seldom would use logical operations while listening to music or looking at a painting. Nor would he necessarily use them while listening to a speaker discuss a political issue. But he has the disposition to do so if something is said which he thinks is important and which he is inclined to consider. The point is that learnings as conceived in this book are fundamentally dispositions rather than ways of behavior. They are exhibited in behavior, but no particular behavior ever exhausts or completely expresses a particular learning.

THE ASSESSMENT SYSTEM

What is learned in school is manifested in at least two ways. In the first place, it is exhibited in student performances on various tests. Tests may be designed to exhibit the cognitive structure of the student, his ability to handle logical operations, his various skills, or the content of his memory. If he performs well on such tests, it is assumed that the desired dispositions have been built into his personal structure. If he performs poorly, it is assumed that personal adaptations have not occurred, or at least have not occurred in sufficient degree.

The second way in which learning may be manifested is

through the uses of schooling in ordinary daily activities. These uses have been discussed at some length in preceding chapters. At this point only the relationship between the assessment system and the uses of learning should be noted. It is not possible to go directly from performance on school tests to the conclusion that one will use the learnings exhibited in the tests in the actual activities of life. But it is a fair assumption, and one not without some support, that in most cases one will make use of the cognitive maps, the attitudinal systems, and the skills in intellectual operations which he has acquired through schooling. The uses of schooling described above may be found also, in a limited sense, in the tests which students are required to take, of course. It is possible, for example, to test for the associative uses of knowledge, and for the replicative, applicative, and interpretive uses. There is, therefore, a similarity between performances that may be required on school tests and those involved in the uses of schooling. But the similarity is still no guarantee that in any particular case the schooling will be so used.

The assessment system of a particular program of schooling is, of course, no more a part of the curriculum than is the learning of the student. The assessment system is simply a means of checking upon the effectiveness of the curriculum: it enables us to ascertain whether or not the objectives for which a curriculum is designed have in fact been realized in the learnings of the students. In the final analysis, the items of an assessment instrument are determined by the content of the curriculum. In this sense the curriculum itself shapes the program of evaluation. The next four chapters are devoted to a discussion of factors relevant to content selection.

---

PART TWO

*LOGICAL AND PSYCHOLOGICAL
DEMANDS ON THE
SECONDARY-SCHOOL CURRICULUM*

CHAPTER VI

A NEW LOOK AT READINESS

To be effective, a curriculum must provide learning tasks that students can perform. But the tasks must not be so easy that they offer no challenge, nor so difficult that they are overwhelming.

Today, we are being told, as though it were some new and bold idea, that any subject can be taught effectively and in an intellectually honest fashion to any child at any age. The controversy over what children can learn is an old one. There was a time not so long ago when children were thought to be miniature adults with adult minds on a small scale. Rousseau was one of the first of modern theorists to come to the child's rescue, claiming for him characteristics of mind and body that set him apart from adults. The fallacious tendency of adults to overlook the abilities of the child while imposing their image of the world upon him is, and has been, common. This tendency becomes especially strong in a national crisis when adults are anxious to speed up the production of trained brains. When the future of a nation itself appears to depend upon more training for more individuals in less time, the natural tendency for adults to overcrowd the child's mind with their own intellectual products and concerns can easily get out of hand.

As a nation, we are now in such a crisis. We are opposed by a group of aggressive nations whose ideology makes education a principal feature of their programs. We no longer feel that learning can be taken leisurely. The schools, like the country as a whole, challenged by a group of nations in a hurry to complete the task of world subversion, are now faced by pressures from every direction to speed up their programs of instruction. So we are now trying to settle the age-old question of how much and how fast the young can learn, not in the quiet of the laboratory or in the classroom, but in the halls of debate and controversy, and sometimes in classes being taught by learned individuals who only recently have discovered that children can learn very complex things indeed.

TWO VIEWS OF DEVELOPMENT

The notion that instruction should be coordinate with the child's development, that is, geared to his readiness to learn, has been part of pedagogical lore at least since Rousseau. During this time, two theories of such coordination, one stemming from psychology of development and the other from associative theories of learning, have influenced curriculum planning and development.

Perhaps the oldest view of the individual's development is that based on the notion of progressive emergence of inherent abilities. According to this view, there is latent in the individual at birth all that he is later to become. In its extreme form this doctrine holds that development is independent of instruction. The child's development will run its natural course and reach its highest point independently of adult efforts to instruct him.

As the individual grows older, his potentialities for learning are both extended and actualized. What he learns is simply a veneer overlaying the substructure of his development. In this view, learning depends entirely upon the maturation of the individual. The child cannot learn anything until he has reached the stage of maturity necessary for its attainment. While learning depends upon development, development does not depend upon learning. For development is something which takes place within the organism and is governed by its own laws and conditions, quite apart from outside influences.

Of course, common experience bears out the fact that certain learnings cannot be acquired at an early age. A child six months old does not ordinarily learn to walk or talk. A one-year-old child does not learn to read, and it is quite unlikely that effective methods of teaching him to read will be devised. No one supposes that algebra can be learned by a child three years of age. The child at this age could not learn algebraic operations, or the rules of order and addition which such operations presuppose, in any significant sense.

These common observations give rise to widespread belief that a fixed degree of development is a necessary condition of certain types of learning. Thus, some recent pedagogical views hold that the child is to be taught reading beginning at six years of age when he enters school. He is to be taught to count and to do the simple combinations of arithmetic in the early elementary grades. But, as everyone knows, common observations often lead to erroneous conclusions. It may turn out that some skills and concepts now taught in certain grades will be found to be improperly placed, when all factors are taken into account.

A second view reduces learning and development to one and the same thing. This, too, is an old notion, dating back to the beginnings of the associative school of psychology. According to this school, the development of the individual comes about through an increase in the number of associations among ideas built up through experience. Perhaps the clearest statement of this position has been given by Thorndike. He said that the difference between one individual and another, or between one period of an individual's growth and another period, is simply a difference in the number of synaptic connections which become established. Accordingly, there are no stages of development, but rather a gradual accretion of learnings. Thus, the difference between what an individual is at one chronological age and another is purely quantitative. There are no qualitative changes, no stages of development, but only changes in quantity as measured by the number of synaptic connections. Development is an additive process.

This same view of development is also found in that form of associative psychology based upon the theory of conditioned reflex. Differences between what an individual is at one time and what he is at another are measured in terms of the accumulation of conditioned responses. Again, there are no stages in the growth of the individual, but only a gradual increase in the number and kind of responses he acquires.

All forms of the associative school of psychology rule out stages of development. Any change in the individual is a result of learning, and anything can be learned, provided instruction in it has been prepared for by prior learnings. The problem of meshing instruction with the individual's growth is reducible to the question of what learnings are psychologically prerequisite for new conditionings.

Neither of these views of development is entirely correct. The ability to learn to do certain things is obviously dependent upon the maturation of neural structures. But at the same time, the behavior which the individual takes on is not entirely determined by the development of such structures. For example, no matter how mature an individual's nervous system may become, he would never learn to think mathematically without the influence of a social environment in which mathematical knowledge was present. Maturation and learning are both necessary factors in the growth of the individual, and acquired behavior consists in the coordination of these two factors. Neither by itself is a sufficient condition of human development.

SYNCHRONIZING INSTRUCTION AND DEVELOPMENT

The way in which these two factors may influence curriculum decisions can be seen by exploring them in relation to two topics: (1) the sequential ordering of materials of instruction and (2) the individual's ability to handle materials by progressively more complex operations.

Consider first the ordering of materials of instruction. There can be no quarrel with the view that what an individual can learn is dependent in part upon what he has already learned. But it is often difficult, if not impossible, to specify exactly what must be known already in order to learn a particular concept, generalization, or set of related ideas. One must be able to add and subtract before he can learn to do long division, because these processes are part of the process of doing long division. But it is more difficult to specify what elements of grammar one must know before he can learn to tell whether the subject and the predicate of a sentence agree in number. And it is still more difficult to tell what one must know about history in order to understand the Crusades. For this reason, arguments for prerequisite courses, or for necessary sequences of subject matter for the purpose of instruction, are often difficult to uphold.

Nevertheless, it is possible to arrange concepts, principles, and other sorts of content in a rough order such that they parallel approximately the capacity of the individual to learn them in terms of what he has already achieved. Furthermore, concepts and principles as well as other sorts of content can themselves be expressed in varying degrees of difficulty. For example, it is quite possible for a child at a very early age to understand in a rudimentary way the concept of the atom and the molecular structure of matter. As he acquires more and more learning, he becomes able to grasp the atomic concept in its more complex forms and finally, even as a young adult, to become immersed in the learnings possessed by the specialists in theoretical physics. Almost twenty-five years ago John Anderson, appraising the research on child development and the curriculum, said that scientific concepts can be introduced into the curriculum at any point provided the concepts are presented in appropriate form to younger children. He then went on to point out that the time had come to place emphasis upon determining the methods and materials appropriate for teaching the same concept at various age levels, rather than upon attempts to locate particular skills and concepts in terms of age or maturity.

It is important to note here that no stages have been found in the development of the individual's capacity to acquire information. In learning the atomic concept, as noted above, the individual may begin in his early years with a very rough notion of an atom and little by little add increments of learning until he has acquired an understanding of the atomic concept in its more complex form. There is no marked qualitative difference in the individual's understanding from the beginning until he has acquired the fuller comprehension. He simply understands more and more of a given concept and of its relations to other concepts. Granting that a minimum amount of inherent development is necessary to learn anything at all, one can say that increases in the acquisition of information beyond this point do not seem to be contingent upon some sort of development controlled by laws of its own, but rather upon prior learnings.

COORDINATION OF INSTRUCTION WITH GROWTH IN LOGICAL OPERATIONS

But the story is different when one looks at evidence bearing on the development of the individual's ability to deal with logical operations. The primary logical operations performed by the individual upon the content of his experience are those of classifying, ordering in serial relations, and numbering.[1] As the individual deals with his environment, he classifies the things that make it up. He groups certain objects as chairs, others as tables, and so on. He arranges things in order. He says, "This table is larger than that

[1] Since this discussion is based in part upon the works of Jean Piaget, it is important to note that his concept of logical operations is not entirely clear. One interpretation holds that such operations consist in certain fundamental processes of thought: combinativity, reversibility, associativity, and identity. Another interpretation claims that these fundamental processes are the psychological factors necessary to such logical operations as classifying and fitting classes together, serializing or relating asymmetrically and transitively, and so on. The second of these interpretations appears to be more plausible and is the one which is here accepted. See *The Psychology of Intelligence*, trans. by M. Piercy and D. E. Berlyne (London: Routledge & Kegan Paul, 1950), pp. 139–50.

one," and "This one here is still larger." And then he can go on to say, "We shall call this table 1, this table 2, and so on." **Of** course, the individual is able to perform most of these operations, in at least a rudimentary sense, by the time he enters school, and the teacher ordinarily takes the ability for granted.

These are the elementary operations upon which are erected the more complex ones that have to do with the handling of propositions and their relations to one another. For example, the deductive operation is based either upon class relationships or upon relations of order. Thus, it follows from the fact that all presidents of the United States have been males that Woodrow Wilson, who was also a president of the United States, was a male. We know this from the proposition that a class contains its members. By a similar deductive operation, we know that if A is taller than B, and if B is taller than C, that A is also taller than C. In this case, the deductive relation depends upon a serial order of height, rather than upon class relations of inclusion. There are many complex operations based upon the simpler operations of classifying and ordering. Many of these do not seem to be within the grasp of the elementary-school child, and even the high-school or college student often performs them very inadequately.

It is evident from the investigations of Piaget and others that it is possible to identify stages of development with regard to these operations. Such stages seem to be relative to the interaction of the child with his environment, and they vary to some extent from one individual to another; but, on the average and for a given social environment, it is possible to identify stages of individual development. Furthermore, transition from one stage to another is gradual. The individual does not go to bed in one stage of development and wake up in another.

Piaget's investigations showed that until approximately two years of age the child is able to perform only overt activities. The child draws objects to himself or moves in the direction of objects which he desires to obtain. At this stage the child has not internalized his actions; he cannot think about them. He apparently cannot think to himself, "Now I will move in the direction of the object." The child simply performs the activity somewhat at the same intellectual level as Köhler's famous chimpanzee, which was able to obtain food outside of his cage and beyond his reach by joining two sticks, thus enabling him to rake the food within reaching distance.

The preschool period of two to six years of age represents the preoperational level. In this age range, the child has learned to use language, although in a very limited degree. He is able to think of his actions; not only can he perform them, but he can also imagine them. Thus, he is able to picture to himself the actions which he wishes to perform. And he can think about actions which he has already performed as well as listen to stories about actions performed by others remote in both space and time. But at this stage, the child cannot express his actions in words, or at least if he attempts to do so, he finds it to be more difficult than to carry out the actions himself.

It is significant that, during this period, the child believes that the amount of a thing is changed as operations are performed on it. He does not grasp the idea that certain features of a thing remain the same through change. If one pours a liquid from one container into another of quite a different shape, the child believes that the amount of liquid has been increased or decreased. He believes that two sticks unequal in length are in fact equal if an end of one stick is placed even with an end of the other; but if the sticks are then placed in such a way that their ends are no longer even, he thinks that the lengths of the sticks have been changed. The child at this age is unable to see that the whole of anything remains the same when its form is changed, when it is displaced in space, or when its parts have been rearranged.

From about seven years of age to about twelve, that is, during the elementary-school years, the child is in what Piaget has called the concrete operational stage. In this stage the child can perform certain operations with concrete things that he can later handle through symbols alone. For example, he can classify actual objects. He can also arrange them in a serial order such that if A is greater than B, and B is greater than C, A is greater than C. The arrangements of things into classes and into a series are logical operations, and in this stage of development the child is able to perform them with concrete things but not with symbols. Of course, he can use symbols. He can represent objects by means of symbols; he can use numbers and perform arithmetical processes. But he cannot perform classificatory and relational operations symbolically. Nor is he able to think in terms of possibility. He cannot take a set of conditions, either formal or concrete, and think systematically of the various possibilities to which they may lead. He seems tied to what is.

The child structures his experience by performing logical operations on various materials as he works in different spheres of activity. He learns from these operations, but he cannot abstract the operations from the concrete context in which they are used: thus, he has no generalized formulation of operations developed in the different areas of his experience.

The child at this stage cannot engage in systematic thinking. He cannot grasp a set of definitions and postulates and then derive propositions from them, nor can he cast them into a pattern of proof after the fashion of proof in plane geometry. He cannot develop a systematic explanation of an historical event or the empirical proof of a proposition in science. As mentioned above, he can grasp intuitively some aspects of these systematic processes, and he can understand almost any part of them that can be represented concretely. For example, he can readily grasp the congruence of triangles when paper models are superimposed upon one another, but he cannot follow the proof of such congruence.

At this stage the child usually has achieved the notions of invariance and reversibility. He sees that a given object remains constant even though it is changed in shape, in space, or in arrangement of parts. If he is presented with a group of objects, say, marbles, and they are divided into two subgroups, he knows that the number of marbles is not changed by dividing them. He knows that there are as many marbles in the two subgroups combined as there were in the total group before dividing them. And he knows also that when the two subgroups are put together, the total group will contain as many marbles as before.

Since mathematics and science are based upon the notions of classification and order, and upon the equally fundamental ideas of invariance and reversibility, the child is at this stage of his development able to learn procedures basic to these fields of knowledge; among others, he can grasp intuitively and concretely some aspects of set theory, traditionally restricted to advanced mathematical study. But, again, he can neither follow nor give a theoretical formulation of the ideas he intuitively grasps. Thus, the effort to move some aspects of higher mathematics into the elementary school is not incompatible with the child's development at this level, as long as he is not required to think systematically. But it should be understood that such curriculum change represents no new knowledge about the intellectual abilities of children, but rather a reassessment of the content itself—a reconsideration of it from the standpoint of its teachability.

At the beginning of junior high school, most individuals enter a period of formal operations. At this point in their development, they are able to manipulate symbols in various logical ways. The average individual is now able to perform with sentences and words the very operations which earlier he could perform only with things. He can now deal verbally with ideas without having to resort to concrete materials, and he can go from a less to a more abstract idea without any intervening manipulation of physical objects. In other words, he is now in the stage at which abstract theoretical thought is possible, and for the most part he is freed from the necessity of working with concrete things. The individual has reached the point at which he is capable of thinking in purely abstract terms, systematically using the sorts of formal operations characteristic of scientists, mathematicians, philosophers, and others who engage in rigorous intellectual work. That the student often fails to think systematically and to perform the intellectual operations of which he is capable is perhaps due more to the failure of curriculum workers and teachers to understand the structure of systematic thought than to the nature of the content of the educational program or to the student's lack of either experience or ability.

During childhood, both content and form are interwoven in the experience of the individual, and he is unable to separate them. But the educative process, from its beginning to its advanced phases, can profitably move in the direction of abstracting the forms of operations from their content. At present, however, the educational program places greater emphasis at all levels upon the concrete rather than the abstract side of operations and content. Consequently, the individual gains little experience in dealing with operations *as such*. He does not reflect upon the operations he performs, or, for that matter, upon those performed by others. Nor is he ordinarily aware of these operations in either high school or college. Although he is capable of doing so, he seldom generalizes these intellectual operations beyond the context in which they are used. Partly for this reason, instruction in one subject probably facilitates the use of higher mental functions in another field only occasionally. Were logical operations to become abstracted from the content of a particular field and understood in their own right, the individual would be more adept at dealing with the great variety of problems and contents that exemplify them. It would appear that as much improvement in the educational program at the high-school level is to be gained by proper instruction in logical operations as in changing the nature and grade location of content.

It is generally held that the individual learns through problem-solving to perform the logical operations that rigorous thought entails. Problems are defined in terms of barriers to action in concrete situations. How to deal with a given barrier is the problem. The solution consists in finding a way of overcoming the barrier and thereby reinstating the impeded action. Considerable research has been carried on to discover ways of increasing the chances that an individual will find a way of dealing with the difficulty when his actions have been blocked. Thus, among other things, it is clear that reduction of fear and inflexibility increases the individual's chances of solving problems.

Problem-solving carried on in strict conformity to logical requirements will doubtless go a long way in the direction of developing a generalized ability to deal with problematic situations, provided the individual is made aware of the methodological and logical elements in his behavior. But the current version of problem-solving has ruled out any explicit reference to the methodological and logical controls of behavior, so that the governance of the individual's thought is reduced to psychological considerations. And, unfortunately, psychology, being a descriptive science, supplies no norms by which to evaluate either the process by which an individual reaches a conclusion or the conclusion itself.

Moreover, the psychological version of problem-solving leaves out the fact that there are many problems in the symbolic as well as in the empirical domain. In other words, not all the significant problems the individual must deal with are those which have to do with concrete situations. The individual is also required to clear up the meaning of expressions, justify decisions, examine arguments, and decide upon their soundness. Analysis of typical contexts calling for thinking reveals a number of distinct kinds of tasks which thinking discharges in the normal course of experience. Among these are deciding upon the meaning of a word, phrase, or statement; deciding upon the soundness of an argument; deciding upon the acceptability of a proposal or proposition; and judging the value of something.

CONTENT AND OPERATIONS IN THE CURRICULUM

It should be clear from the foregoing analysis that the curriculum is comprised of two strands extending from the early grades through the high school, college, and university. One of these strands is the content—factual information, concepts, principles and laws. Certain problems in connection with the determination of the content of the curriculum are considered in later chapters. These problems have to do with the way in which concepts and principles function in human behavior and the further question of whether, and on what basis, some elements of content are more important than others.

The other strand in the curriculum consists in the logical operations which are to be found in behavior generally. Logical operations constitute the rational means by which the individual manipulates content. The intellectual quality of his behavior is dependent not only upon the accuracy of the content which he employs, but also upon the skill with which he performs the various logical operations by which he handles the content itself. By these operations he makes his concepts clear, he puts them into relationship with one another by eliciting laws and principles, and he orders definitions and principles in such a way as to enable him to draw conclusions and make predictions. All of these tasks, together with others too numerous to mention here, the individual performs by means of logical operations.

It has been argued that logical operations develop in the individual progressively, beginning at an early age and extending up to the beginning of the high-school years. By this time the inherent ability of the individual to perform logical operations has been fully developed. But this does not mean that the individual is able to perform these operations adequately at this time. It only means that he is now at the point in his career at which he can begin to refine and perfect the use of these operations in behavior. If the curriculum is to be made more adequate from an intellectual standpoint, it is necessary that the logical operations possible for the individual, at each stage, be identified and adequately catered to by instruction. This also means that content should be properly selected, with emphasis upon more important elements of it, for the purpose of highlighting operational excellence.

This chapter has attempted to show that readiness for learning must be considered with reference to two aspects of the educational program: the subject matter and the logical operations by which it is manipulated. It seems apparent that subject matter can be adapted to the level of the individual's ability to learn it by controlling such factors as vocabulary, complexity of sentence structure, and the rate at which information is given to him. But it is different with logical operations. Here, the range of adjustments is not as clearly discernible. Apparently, the logical operations the immature person can perform depend more upon his level of development than the degree to which they can be simplified. It would therefore seem to be inefficient to attempt to adjust these more complex logical operations to his level of development. On the contrary, it would appear to be wiser to let his development catch up with the particular level of logical performance we may wish to demand of him.

These observations about readiness for learning are important in the placement of such materials of instruction as fundamental concepts of science and mathematics. They are also important in connection with the adjustment of instruction to different levels of ability within the same age group. As is discussed in a later chapter, the writers' view of the curriculum calls for children progressing through the educational program at different rates and at different levels of performance. In adjusting the instructional program to differing ability groups, it is important to recognize that there is a rather wide range of adjustments demanded in concepts, principles, norms, rules, and factual information. That is to say, it would be possible to present the same concepts and principles in different ways so as to bring them within the experience of children of different abilities. But the amount of refinement and complexity which a child can take on with respect to logical operations appears to depend less upon his fund of information than upon his level of development.

The readiness factors in learning are extremely important

in curriculum development and underlie any and all efforts to improve the educational program. But there are other factors that must be taken into account, such as our conception of the instructional process and the nature and structure of the knowledge to be taught. The next three chapters explore these additional factors.

CHAPTER VII

STRATEGIC DETERMINANTS
OF THE CURRICULUM

What an individual learns depends, among other things, upon the situations he is placed in, the operations he is required to perform in dealing with them, and the information available to him. An effective curriculum must therefore provide adequately for these three factors. This chapter explores these elements of the curriculum and how they are related to one another.

TYPES OF SITUATIONS

Teaching situations can be distributed on a continuum or scale according to their structure, ranging from those situations which are completely open to those which are completely closed.

A completely open situation is unstructured. Although there is a vague goal, the features of the situation have not been identified, and no problem has been formulated. There is a predicament but as yet no problem. There is relatively little information available in the situation, and the individual is uncertain how to proceed. This sort of situation is relatively fluid and calls for adventurous thinking. Such situations may occur in fields of scientific endeavor, in the arts, or in the sphere of everyday responsibilities. In the sciences and the arts, they sometimes encourage creativity; in everyday life, wisdom.

Perhaps a few brief observations should be made here about creativity and wisdom. It is generally said in educational literature that creative ability can be cultivated. Waiving the question of what is meant by creative ability, it is now generally supposed that creative behavior involves divergent thought. The individual is creative if he responds with a large number of varied and perceptive ideas about a situation. For example, in a history class a teacher asks, "What would have been the future course of Western civilization had the Saracens won the battle of Tours?" The student who can come up with a large number of meaningful and insightful responses to this question is considered more creative than one who comes up with a small number of such ideas.

It should be noted that this is a psychological rather than a social criterion of creativity. Socially, an individual is creative if he comes through with some idea or invention or work of art that is both novel and outstanding. But psychologically, the individual is thought to be creative if he suggests a wide range of ideas about any given situation, whether these ideas prove to be socially fruitful, and whether they are ideas of which no one else has thought.

An individual cannot be taught to produce new and diverse ideas. He does not learn to create by creating as he learns to type by typing. What, then, is meant by cultivating the creative ability of an individual? Although one cannot learn to be creative, he may learn to overcome his fears and inhibitions and to be more flexible and versatile in his thought. In other words, he learns to establish and maintain the conditions under which his thinking can be most free and most productive from the standpoint of the range and number of ideas which come to him. Open and partially structured situations provide the conditions under which such learning is encouraged.

What about wisdom? What is it? How is it developed? To define wisdom is no less difficult than to define creativity. We ordinarily think of a wise person as being one who makes his judgments in terms of anticipated consequences of the widest range of possibilities. But there is also a temporal factor in wisdom. The wise person is not one who feels compelled to decide an issue apart from timing. He attempts to keep the situation from closing and puts off decisions and actions until the time is propitious. Knowing when to say or do something is as much a part of wisdom as knowing what to say or what to do.

Wisdom in the modern world is perhaps as important as creativity. Insofar as the education of people in general is concerned, it is perhaps more important for the schools to develop wise men than creative men. Fortunately, it is not necessary to make the choice, because open and unstructured situations, especially if they involve broad problems such as those discussed in Chapter XIV, may be used to encourage the development of wisdom no less than creativity. For in such situations the individual must learn to make the widest possible assessment of the various factors involved, to consider the courses of action that are possible, and to exercise his sense of when it is appropriate to render decision and take action. Wisdom, like creativity, cannot be learned by practice as one learns to spell or to read. It comes from a wide range of experience in a variety of open situations from which the individual may develop a sense of timing and an appreciation of the importance of surveying all the possible ways of dealing with the circumstances.

A closed situation is one which is already structured, so that the response called for is implicitly indicated in the situation itself. In its purest form, the end result is given, and so much information is made available that almost anyone would be able to supply the correct response. For example, in discussing the question of the annexation of the Hawaiian Islands, the teacher asks, "Did the people of the islands become citizens immediately upon annexation, or was it several years afterward?" A student says, "It was two years." The teacher then says, "All right," and further asks, "If it was two years and they were annexed in 1898, then when were they admitted to citizenship?" A student says, "It was 1900," and the teacher says, "Okay." Both information and logical structure are so compelling in this case that it seems quite appropriate to call it a completely closed situation.

Between the completely open and the completely closed situations—the extremes of the continuum—are three other types that allow varying degrees of freedom, depending upon the amount of information given and the logical operations required.

In one of these types, a result is given together with a certain amount of information, and the individual is required to fill in the gap between the information and the terminus of his thought. In the teaching process, the situation is usually introduced by a verbal formulation of evidence that requires the student to give further information leading to the event, outcome, or result. For example, in discussing the nervous system, the teacher gives the following information: "Suppose we take the impulses carried by the auditory nerve, the optic nerve, and the olfactory nerve, would they all be the same impulse as far as what the nerve is carrying is concerned? Yes, these are all identical. But what is the difference? Why do they bring about different results?" A student responds, "Because different things strike them or set up the impulse." The teacher replies, "Different things might set them up, but we say they are all identical. So what is the difference?" Another student then answers, "Isn't it where the impulses are carried in the brain?" The teacher then says, "Yes, where they are carried," and then he goes ahead to elaborate the point. It is easy to see that the students are given certain information—impulses go over different nerves, and impulses just as impulses are all qualitatively the same. They are also told that the results of these impulses are different: one arouses the sensation of smell, another of hearing, and so on. The students are then required to fill in the gap with information that accounts for the apparently anomalous result.

The second type of situation consists in setting up a set of conditions, either manipulative or verbal or both, and then asking the individual to tell what will result or what may reasonably be inferred. The structure of these situations is less definite than that of closed situations. Some evidence is given pointing in the general direction that thought is to move, but the terminus of thought is to be worked out together with the steps leading to it,

Situations of this type bring the instructional program nearer to thinking as it occurs in scientific work, in the arts, and in the more taxing situations of everyday life. Here is an example of this type of situation: A class in physics is studying friction. The teacher sets the situation as follows: "Before going any further, let's try this. Let's just keep the block in position (block on horizontal plane). Now, the width of the block this way is 800 millimeters; this way is about 400 millimeters. In other words, this width is just about double this width. So, if I set the block up on this edge (sets block up on narrow edge), I'd just be halving the surface area, wouldn't I? I'm going to put this one-kilogram weight on there (placing weight on block). So we again have 1,260 grams resting on the horizontal surface. And let's see now what force is required to overcome friction. Anyone want to make a prediction on this?" Here, the teacher has set a situation by giving a quantum of information, and then asks the students to go on from there to further information leading to an outcome that is barely suggested.

The third situation to which a student may be required to respond is one in which all the information is given. The individual is asked to examine the given data from a particular standpoint, or from some novel viewpoint, and then to interpret or reorganize the evidence. An example of this sort of situation is as follows: An English class is discussing a novel—*Cry, the Beloved Country*—and the teacher reads this passage:

There is a man sleeping in the grass . . . and over him is gathering the greatest storm of all his days. Such lightning and thunder will come there as have never been seen before, bringing death and destruction. People hurry home past him, to places safe from danger. And whether they do not see him there in the grass, or whether they fear to halt even a moment, but they do not wake him, they let him be.[1]

Then the teacher asks, "What is the author comparing this man to? What is the metaphor here? Who is the man?" After much

[1] Alan Paton, *Cry, the Beloved Country* (New York: Charles Scribner's Sons, 1948), p. 125.

discussion a student says, "The people of South Africa." In this case students are asked to reinterpret the information given, to put it in a broader context, and thereby to recognize its social significance.

One of the effects of programmed instruction and teaching machines is to reduce the instructional program to a system of closed situations. The frames in programmed instruction are so structured as to reduce the chances of incorrect responses. This effect is accomplished by reducing the size of the learning step to be taken, and by feeding in so much information that hardly anyone can respond incorrectly. Whether or not this tendency to shape the individual's response completely is an inherent feature of programmed instruction is an open question. But it cannot be denied that the outcome of this form of instruction is to reduce the number of possible responses an individual can make.

KNOWLEDGE:
ITS SOURCES AND STRUCTURE IN LEARNING

As the student deals with a situation, he resorts to three sources of information: the teacher, the situation itself, and his own fund of knowledge, images, and meanings. In open or relatively unstructured situations, information may also be sought in books and other reference materials.

The amount of thinking the student does depends in part upon the amount of information available to him. It has already been seen that if the teacher provides a very full pool of information, the proper behavior in a situation is almost completely determined, provided the logical operations are simple. By the same token, if the information available in a student's repertory of prior learnings fits the requirements of a situation, he may be able to fill the gap by the simple process of recall. In either case, thinking of any serious kind is precluded. This is the result that often obtains in the classroom where the situations set by the teacher call merely for the replicative use of information recently acquired from textbooks or other sources. On the other hand, when the teacher provides a minimum of information and the student does not have appropriate images, meanings, and knowledge in his storage, he may be required to do a great deal of thinking. This often happens in open and near-open situations.

The completely open situation is one which taxes the student in quite a different way. The teacher may give very little information because he does not possess the relevant evidence, or because he has not structured the situation in his own thought so as to give proper information. Too, the knowledge already possessed by the student may not be appropriate, or it may be so deficient in amount as to make it impossible for him to fill in the gaps. All of this means that in an open situation a great deal of evidence must be gathered in the situation itself. This task requires the student to make observations, to look for additional information in various sources, and to organize this information for proper use in the situation. In other words, in free and open situations, the student has the opportunity to engage in those intellectual processes and techniques which are found in mature and responsible thought such as that which occurs in the fields of science, in the arts, and in politics. Whether he takes advantage of the opportunity depends upon the teacher's alertness and understanding of the logical operations which such situations call for.

His intellectual content—images, meanings, knowledge—and its organization are of the utmost importance in an individual's education. Curriculum development has seldom given adequate attention to this point. In the first place, the nature of knowledge and how it functions in behavior has not been understood; and it is too often forgotten that hunches and interpretations frequently go back to meanings and mental imagery. In the second place, pedagogical thought has been dominated by a behavioristic psychology that reduces learning to responses to specific stimuli.

Prior to the rise of behaviorism, pedagogical thinking was very strongly influenced by Herbartian psychology. According to this psychology, what the individual is able to learn is in large measure determined by his apperceptive mass, that is to say, by the knowledge that has already taken shape in the learner's experience. Furthermore, apperceptive mass is not an aggregate in which one learning is as important as another, and in which each item of learning rests on a separate footing; it is endowed with order because the mass is formed according to an inner logic of its own.

Behavioristic psychology completely undercuts the notion of apperceptive mass. It reduces learning either to a connection of a response to a stimulus through a synapse, or else through conditioning. Between the stimulus and the response, nothing of any consequence exists or takes place insofar as learning is concerned. Educationally speaking, the individual responds to a stimulus, practices the response, and receives reinforcement designed to strengthen the association of the response and the stimulus. In this view, there is no such thing as content of mind, mind being either eliminated entirely or reduced to a system of responses. The only way in which prior learning influences current learning is through transfer. What the individual has learned at some prior time influences his learning in a current situation if the prior learning is similar to that which is now being acquired. Furthermore, according to behavioristic theory, organization of learning is unimportant. The order of responding and relations among responses make no difference in learning. For example, in learning nonsense syllables it makes no difference whether the individual learns the syllables in one order or in another. And the structure of what is learned—the logical relationship between one item and another—in no way influences subsequent learning.

We are now beginning to see that the behavioristic theory of learning is inadequate for curriculum development, for the curriculum worker must take into account facts about the structures of the various fields of knowledge. By "fields of knowledge" is meant the conventional school studies such as history, mathematics, physics, chemistry, biology, and the like. Of course, this is a rather loose meaning of the expression, because, obviously, a field of knowledge may be thought of in either a general or a highly specialized sense. For example, we can think of physical science as being a field, and then we can think further of physics, chemistry, and geology as being fields within the more general domain of physical science. For purposes of discussion here, "field of knowledge" ordinarily means the general areas included in the school's program—namely, history, the fine arts, chemistry, physics, mathematics, and so on. When referring to fields of knowledge in which the material is logically organized, the more specialized label of "discipline" is often used.

The structure of knowledge may take many different forms, depending upon the nature of the content of a given field of knowledge and the ways in which the elements of content are related. The content of the field of literature, for example, consists of statements of belief, evaluations, generalizations, and so on; but, these elements are woven together in such a way as to depict incidents, describe characters, and so forth. Obviously, these various elements of content may be related temporally, logically, causally, spatially, and so on. In contrast, the content of physics, for example, is made up of concepts, theories, and laws together with statements of factual observations. These elements, of course, are related primarily in a logical sense involving deductive and inductive orders.

The sequential organization of knowledge can be seen in the field of history. For example, if we answer the question of how Lincoln was assassinated, we recount the events leading up to his assassination. We tell the story about his going to the theater and about what happened on that tragic evening. In our description, one item of information is as important as another, and, with respect to their explanatory power, one fact in our description is as important as any other. This is true if the organizing principle in the account is that of a temporal pattern such that each statement of fact fits into the sequential arrangement leading up to and culminating in the act of assassination. This type of sequential ordering of knowledge helps us to understand how things came to be as they are now, and it affords a background from which to view the present and the future in perspective.

While logical relationships are to be found in almost every field of knowledge, the logical structure of knowledge is most clearly illustrated in those fields which are highly developed, such as the disciplines of physics, chemistry, and mathematics. In these domains the most fundamental elements are definitions and postulates based upon the definitions. These are the most fundamental because all other propositions making up the field of knowledge are derivable from these more primitive elements. A classic model of this type of organization is, of course, plane geometry; the physical sciences evidence greater complexity, but it is still fair to consider them as being roughly of the same general type.

Within such a system of organized knowledge, some ideas are more important than others. This is the case for the simple reason that some ideas include other ideas. If this were not the case, deduction would be impossible, because logically one cannot draw a conclusion when its elements are not in the premises. It is not useful, therefore, in a logically organized field of knowledge to think of all ideas as being on the same plane of logical importance. Some ideas have greater explanatory power than others, that is to say, a larger number of events, objects, and other ideas are subsumed by those having the greater power. For example, the molecular theory of matter is more fundamental than Boyle's Law or any of the other gas laws. It is more fundamental in the sense that the molecular theory includes the elements of knowledge from which the gas laws may themselves be derived. Suppose we wish to explain how it is that an inflated tire is able to support the weight of an automobile. We may attempt to do this by appealing to the gas laws, but if we wish to explain the gas laws themselves, we show that they represent special cases of the molecular theory of matter. The molecular theory of matter is more inclusive than the gas laws, not only because the theory explains the gas laws, but also because it accounts for the behavior of solids and liquids as well as gases. The late Boyd Bode used to illustrate this point dramatically by putting the following questions to his classes: "The earth is round and Italy is shaped like a boot. Which idea is more important and why?" Obviously, if we are aiming at general education, the answer is that, it is more important to know that the earth is round than that Italy is shaped like a boot, because more commonly important facts can be interpreted by the idea of the earth's roundness than by the concept of Italy's shape.

The notion that some ideas, because of their logical scope, are more important than others is fundamental in curriculum development. Of course, we have always held that ideas are not equally important, and we have attempted to use this notion in selecting content. But it is only recently that we have come to see that the importance of an idea can best be determined by a logical criterion. In the recent past, we have tended to decide the importance of the content of the curriculum in terms of its practical utility as measured by the frequency of its use, however trivially. Thus, for a Mediterranean fisherman it might be as important to know that Italy is shaped like a boot as that the earth is round. When we have not resorted to the criterion of frequency or immediacy of use, we have appealed to the social significance of ideas. Although these criteria cannot be completely dismissed in curriculum-building, as is evidenced in Chapters X and XI, they do fail to take account of the relational aspects of knowledge and hence of the structural features of the disciplines. The criterion of logical significance takes the curriculum-builder into the intellectual disciplines themselves, and requires of him that he understand the logical structure of these fields. He must know not only the facts and ideas, but also the logical relations among these elements of knowledge. Within the basic concepts of the disciplines, it becomes appropriate to impose the criterion of what is most generally and significantly useful. There is more on this subject in later chapters.

The emphasis being placed upon logical relations among the elements of content, and upon the strategic importance of certain ideas within various fields of knowledge, represents one of the distinguishing features of the new curriculum programs now being encouraged in various subjects, such as Max Beberman's work in mathematics and other work to be mentioned later. These programs tend to emphasize the general concepts which enable the individual to handle a wide range of data. Since they also stress the logical relations within a field of knowledge, they in consequence emphasize inquiry in depth. The student comes to see that ideas can be fruitfully arranged in a hierarchy, and that the further he goes into the hierarchy the deeper he gets into the field of knowledge.

The individual's personal organization of knowledge can be similar to the logical organization of knowledge within the various fields of learning. With proper instruction, the individual builds guiding ideas. These ideas function in his thought as schemata, that is to say, they bring together in one comprehensive view many otherwise disparate and completely unrelated elements in the experience of the learner. These ideas give a sense of direction to the student's activities in the process of learning; they help him to organize the facts and ideas that come to him; and they confer meaning upon those aspects of his experience which he finds difficult to grasp. When these guiding ideas are clear and well understood by the student, he is better able to learn new and unfamiliar ideas and to retain them for further use. These are the ideas of greater logical inclusiveness discussed above, and they are the basic constituents of the cognitive frames or maps typical of persons who have a good general education.

It therefore makes a difference what materials we choose to teach. The curriculum has to include materials that exemplify the major ways in which experience can be ordered and has been ordered. It is insufficient to prescribe a few solid subjects or a rich variety of interesting topics.

LOGICAL OPERATIONS AND CONTROL OF CONTENT

We are beginning to see also that the behavioristic theory is inadequate in another sense. The individual does not learn merely responses; he does not learn to do or say something as a mere sequence of responses to stimuli. Rather, he handles and organizes content in certain ways, and from such manipulations and arrangements of content he acquires concepts, principles, operations, images, and so on.

It has already been mentioned that the development of the individual entails the emergence of the capacity to perform certain operations of a logical character. He arrives in his development at the point where he is able to classify and arrange in a series the objects and things about him. He also becomes able to perform certain formal operations upon symbols. The content of the individual's experience is organized and tested through the performance of these operations, and a curriculum which neglects them is inadequate. Furthermore, if they are ignored, the individual fails to learn the potential relationships in the content of his experience, because these can be made evident only through the analysis and manipulation of the content in accordance with these logical processes.

Studies of classroom discourse have demonstrated that certain logical operations are being performed by both teachers and students in even the most routine question-and-answer procedures. In other words, when we speak of logical operations, we are not thinking of what teachers ought to do, but rather of what they actually do, no matter how they teach. In dealing with classroom learning situations, the students therefore engage in logical operations, and these operations are determined in part by the amount and kind of content given and in part by the sort of questions they are attempting to answer in the situation. For example, in one situation the student attempts to *define* a term. In another situation he attempts to *explain* an event or to account for a given result. In still another he tries to *assess* the worth of something, to decide its value. Altogether, one can distinguish some twelve different sorts of identifiable logical operations performed by teachers and pupils in the classroom. In addition to those already mentioned are the following: conditional inferring, classifying, comparing and contrasting, designating, reporting, stating, substituting, opining, and describing.

It is quite natural to ask why one should consider these operations if they are performed in the classroom anyway. Of course, it would be useless to point out their occurrence if the level of their performance were satisfactory. But the fact is that the degree of refinement, the rigor and clarity with which these operations are handled in the classroom, does not exceed that ordinarily found in daily conversation. Current programs of instruction seldom provide for an improvement in the performance of these operations beyond that found at a common-sense level.

Certain consequences flow from this fact. In the first place, instruction is far less challenging intellectually than it could be. Since the teacher seldom handles these processes with any marked degree of understanding, he is often unable to follow up points made by students in such a way as to challenge their thinking. If their explanations are inadequate, he does not know how to pry into what they have said so as to bring out the inadequacies. If their definitions are inappropriate or unacceptable, or if the class becomes engaged in a discussion of definition, the teacher ordinarily does not know how to handle such discussion, nor does he know how to point out the inadequacies of the students' defining procedures.

In the second place, one of the chief consequences of the failure to deal adequately with these operations is a rather low level of intellectual rigor. There is a sense in which we can say that intellectual rigor does not consist in the amount of information an individual retains and recalls, the number of problems he can work in a given domain, or his persistence in pursuing a task. Rather, intellectual rigor consists in the ability of the student to handle logical operations with marked precision in any domain of information with which he may be required to deal. The educational program only accidentally engenders the ability to think clearly and consistently, unless the curriculum of the school makes provision for these operations to be performed in a more adequate manner than is now the case, and unless it also provides for the student to become aware of what these operations are and to understand their structure and the rules by which they are themselves assessed.

The role of logical operations has already been noted in relation to the uses of schooling. For both the interpretive and the applicative use of schooling, the student requires cognitive maps and evaluative maps. As the next two chapters show, these maps are constructed out of key concepts or ideas in such a way that one can orient himself by logical operations. The key concepts are drawn from certain intellectual disciplines; the operations are elicited from and practiced in these disciplines. Yet the concepts and operations are not so distant as might first appear, because the key ideas of a discipline were arrived at by the use of logical operations.

CHAPTER VIII

CONTENT AS DESCRIPTIVE CONCEPTS AND PRINCIPLES

Intelligent behavior is prefigured by the individual's scheme of concepts and their relationships. An effective curriculum therefore includes concepts and principles which are basic to intelligent behavior. It also takes into account both the logic and psychology of concept formation and the relation of concepts to principles and their use.

From a psychological standpoint, a concept can be defined as consisting of the abstracted characteristics common to a group of objects, events, and the like. It is also defined by some psychologists as a common way of behaving toward a group of objects. But these two views overlook the role of concepts as nodes in the development of cognitive networks. Concepts are foci of organization in the mental make-up of the individual, focal points in the organization of experience. In this sense, they are to be thought of as intervening conditions lying between stimulus and response. Concepts are, therefore, not linguistic; they are not symbolic, nor are they operations. But they can be expressed either symbolically or operationally. When expressed in either of these two ways, they are called definitions.

Strictly speaking, the curriculum does not contain concepts, but rather their symbolic and operational expressions. Nor does the teacher work with concepts as such. Instead, he deals with definitions and other verbal formulations, together with materials and instruments which build concepts into the student's experience. But for convenience in this discussion, the terms "concept" and "definition" are ordinarily used interchangeably.

KINDS OF CONCEPTS

Concepts may be classified in various ways. For the purposes of curriculum development, perhaps the most basic classification is that which distinguishes descriptive from valuative concepts.

Descriptive concepts are neutral with respect to our preferences or our picture of the world as we would have it. For example, our concept of a meter is free of preferential elements. Of course, it can be argued that no concept is ever completely devoid of affective tones of pleasantness or unpleasantness. But at least we have concepts in science and often in common experience which, if they do embody preferences, embody those which are so uniformly held that they give rise to no controversy and give us no concern.

Valuative concepts by their very nature embody preferences. We ordinarily include in our concept of democracy whatever we think a society ought to be and have. The liberal concept of democracy embodies preferences not to be found in the conservative concept, and the preferential aspect of the Communist concept of democracy differs radically from that of either the American liberal or the conservative view. We often engage in similar preferential loading when we entertain such concepts as those indicated by the terms "patriotism," "nationalism," "conservatism," "liberalism," and any number of ideas which we use in the social studies, literature, and in common parlance.

In this chapter the discussion is confined to descriptive concepts and principles, reserving the exploration of valuative concepts for the next chapter.

Three types of descriptive concepts are especially important in curriculum theory and practice—classificatory, relational, and operational concepts.

A classificatory concept is based upon a group of objects or events having certain features selected as characteristic of the group in common. For example, when a whale is classified as a mammal rather than a fish, it is because we select the fact that it gives birth to and suckles its young as its defining characteristics rather than the fact that it swims and lives in water.

A relational concept is one which includes reference to a relationship between two or more attributes. The relationship may be expressed either as a ratio or a product. For example, the concept of speed may be expressed as a ratio between distance traversed and the amount of time required to negotiate the distance, and force is expressed as the product of mass and acceleration.

An operational concept consists in a way of doing something—a "know-how." It is an idea consisting of an awareness of an order of operations that when performed lead to a particular result. For example, our concept of weight may consist in a set of ideas which refer to a set of operations leading to the reading of a number on a scale, a number thus designating the weight. Hence, we may take a spring balance, place an object on the hook of the balance, and read the scale. We then say this is what we mean by weight. At a more naive level, we could say, "Lift this object. Do you feel the resistance? Well, that is what we mean by weight." These concepts may also refer to various forms of order, such that we can say of a given attribute that a is greater, less than, or equal to b with respect to it. For instance, "harder than" may be defined as "x scratches y, but y does not scratch x."

THE LOGICAL STRUCTURE OF CONCEPTS

Although the psychological version of a concept is essential to curriculum development, it is not sufficient. For one thing, it does not reveal the structure of concepts in such a way as to indicate the materials and operations which must be used in teaching, except perhaps at the perceptual level of experience. For another thing, the teacher, as already pointed out, does not work with concepts but with operations and linguistic expressions through which concepts are built. Therefore, a way of looking at concepts more nearly in line with pedagogical requirements is needed. This way is to be found in the logic of concepts, and the discussion begins by considering the classificatory concept.

The logical counterpart of such a concept is a classificatory definition. This type of definition is made up of a class term and a further statement of characteristics which distinguish the group of things to be defined from other members of the class. In other words, if we look at the logical structure of a generic concept, we see that it is made up of two parts, a class of objects and a set of criteria by which to decide which objects are to be included in the class and which are to be excluded. Consider the term "tax" as a word which stands for a concept. A tax is defined in the *Dictionary of American Politics* as follows: "A tax is a compulsory payment made to a government for its support or for the regulation or promotion of certain social purposes and levied according to law uniformly upon all taxpayers of a given class." The logical structure of this concept may be illustrated as in Figure 2.

Category	*Criteria*
	1. Payment made to government
	2. Levied according to law
	3. Levied uniformly upon all payers of a given class
	4. Purpose is to support the government or
	5. to regulate social purposes or
	6. to promote social purposes

Figure 2.

In the structure of this concept, "payment" is the class term, and a tax is classifiable as a member of a certain subclass of payments. The criteria specify the characteristics which a payment must have in order to be called a tax. To tell whether or not a given payment is a tax, the criteria must be applied to the payment. If the given payment meets all of the criteria, it is a tax. If it does not, the payment is not a tax, even though it may be made to the government. For example, an installment on a debt is a payment, but it meets none of the criteria and hence is not a tax. But what about fines, fees, and tariffs? These are all payments to government. Are they to be called taxes? It depends upon whether or not they satisfy the remaining criteria. And of course they do not. A fine is exacted as punishment for violation of the law and is not a tax. A tariff is designed to protect domestic industry and agriculture, and a fee is paid in return for services rendered directly to the individual. Neither meets the criteria and hence is not a tax.

Note that criteria in a classificatory definition may be conjunctive, that is, they may constitute a set all of which must be satisfied by an exemplar of the class. For instance, an acid is a compound which tastes sour, turns blue litmus paper red, and produces free hydrogen ions. Any acid satisfies all of these criteria. Criteria may also be disjunctive. In this case, the criteria are alternatives, and it is sufficient that the exemplar satisfy any one of them. For example, a citizen of the United States is defined by disjunctive criteria. An individual may be a citizen if he is born in the United States, or if he is born in a foreign country to parents who are citizens of the United States, or if he is born of foreign parentage and in a foreign country, provided he lives in the United States for a specified time and his application for citizenship is accepted. If an individual meets any one of these criteria, he is a citizen. The criteria for deciding whether or not a payment is a tax are both conjunctive and disjunctive. The first three criteria above are conjunctive, the last three disjunctive.

Classificatory definitions are used extensively in biological sciences, where they are basic to the whole system of classification. They are used also in the social sciences, where the disjunctive form is found in abundance, and in grammar and geometry. Of course, classificatory definitions are found in all subjects. But in the natural sciences they are being supplemented and often replaced by operational definitions.

In a relational definition, the characteristics are usually compared and expressed quantitatively. And, as pointed out above, these characteristics are then related to one another as a ratio. Density in physics is defined as a ratio of mass to volume, mass being one characteristic of a substance and volume another. Mass is described by a set of operations, usually those involved in the ordinary measurement of weight, and volume is determined by measuring special dimensions and performing the usual calculations. The ratio of the measured weight to the calculated volume is taken to be the density of the substance. It is so much mass per unit of volume.

It should be noted, however, that the concept is not the actual quotient in any given case, but rather results from the insight into the relationship between the mass of a sample and its volume, as in physics; or between the new and the familiar words per page, as in vocabulary density; or between area and number of persons, as in population studies. If we were to say that the density of water is one, thinking that we had thereby fully conveyed the idea of density, we should be in error. For, as just said, density, in whatever domain of experience, is not the numerical outcome of a calculation. It is, as exemplified by the concept of density in physics, an insight into the relationship such that one is able to see that if the mass of a sample of wood were to be the same as that of a sample of iron, their volumes would be quite different; and if their volumes were equal, their masses would be unequal.

Relational definitions yield constants which are extremely useful in science. The intelligence quotient—the ratio of mental age and chronological age—is repeatedly used in educational research. These sorts of definitions are found in all fields that have achieved the level of quantitative studies—physics, chemistry, psychology, economics, to mention a few.

It is often thought that clarity is gained if a concept is expressed in words that refer to observable things wherever possible. Terms such as "mass," "force," "elasticity," and "conductivity," as used in physics, and "nationalism," "national income," and "democracy," as used in social science, represent neither observable processes nor entities. If we define the term "force" as meaning the same as "a cause of motion," our definition is couched in terms as abstract as the word "force" itself. For the expression "cause of motion" is just as far removed from what can be observed as is the term "force." This need for concreteness is satisfied by operational definitions.

To see how a concept may be treated operationally, consider the concept of force as it is used in physics. Begin with the anthropomorphic formulation of the concept. Force is, in this view, a push or a pull. It relates kinesthetic sensations to objects. The teacher can say to a student, "Push or pull this table. Now what you exerted when you pushed or pulled is what we mean by force." This way of defining the term "force" leaves the definition at a very low operational level. One can take another step toward a more sophisticated definition by defining the term through the use of devices such as a spring balance. He pulls the spring and says that it exerts a force in proportion to its extension. He can also place a scale over the spring, and by providing the spring with a pointer, he can describe the force quantitatively. A more sophisticated approach defines "force" by reference to the relationship between two variables, namely, mass and acceleration. In this definition, he enters into the processs of determining the mass of an object and its acceleration in quantitative terms. He would then use the formula, force $=$ mass $\times$ acceleration, and by calculation arrive at a value which he would call the amount of the force. These operations and calculations would constitute the meaning of the concept of force. The foregoing description represents steps leading from a rather naive to a rather sophisticated operational definition.

Although there are certain criticisms of operational definitions, they are nevertheless extremely useful when the purpose is to reduce concepts to as concrete a form as possible, that is, to operations that can be observed. They are used extensively in the natural sciences, in economics, and in psychology and related fields.

In their more sophisticated form, operational definitions tend to be similar to relational definitions. The difference appears to be the amount of stress placed upon the performance of operations with actual materials. There is less reference to concrete manipulation of materials in a relational definition than in an operational one.

SPECIAL CASES AND PROBLEMS OF DEFINING

Although they present no departure from the logical patterns discussed above, some concepts nevertheless present special problems. These are concepts which are difficult, if not impossible, to define, such as those for which criteria tend to be vague or ambiguous or for which data are difficult to obtain, and those which are "open ended."

Some concepts, such as the notion of importance, cannot be formulated, at least not in a strict or complete sense. Yet terms representing them mean something to us. When someone says, "This is important," we know we are expected to give it special attention. Ordinary discourse is filled with such terms—specific, general, individual, concrete, to mention only a few examples. And it is ordinarily useless to try to reach a level of clarity beyond our common-sense understanding of them.

Some concepts cannot be clarified except very arbitrarily. For example, most of us use the term "rain," and we ordinarily understand what it means. But if we are to issue rain insurance or purchase such insurance, we want to know more specifically what we are talking about. Does one drop make a rain? How many drops make a rain? We can know what is to count as a rain only by stating precisely what is to be meant by the term "rain," and this requires that we state precisely the criteria for using the term. In this case, an insurance company specifies that the fall of moisture must amount to such and such a quantity in a specified time, if it is to be called "rain." Such definitions are sometimes called *stipulative* definitions. But their logical structure may often be found to be similar to one or another of the definitions discussed above.

There are other sorts of definitions which are unclear, even though we may know the criteria for deciding what is covered by the concept and what is not. Such cases as this arise when the criteria themselves are unclear, or when it is difficult to decide whether or not the given instances satisfy the criteria. Suppose we define "society" as "a group of individuals united by common interests, possessing a sense of corporate unity and discipline, and organized to promote common aims." The criteria—"common interest," "sense of corporate unity," "sense of discipline," and "organized to promote common aims"—are vague. If we were given a large number of social groups and were asked to decide whether these aggregates were societies or not, it would be almost impossible to know whether or not the given aggregates satisfied these criteria. If a number of persons were attempting to decide independently whether these aggregates of individuals were to be called societies or not, the amount of agreement among them would probably be very low. The small amount of agreement would indicate either lack of clarity about the criteria, or inability to determine whether or not the criteria apply in particular cases. By the same token, were we to try to decide which among the nations of the world are imperialistic and which are not, it might turn out to be extremely difficult to do so even if we had clear-cut criteria. This would be the case for the simple reason that the data suggested by the criteria might not be available to us. Nevertheless, we would understand what we were talking about if our concept of imperialism were identified by clear-cut criteria. Many social-science concepts are unclear in this sense.

Finally, some concepts are undefinable in a complete sense because all of the criteria can never be specified. Definitions of this type of concept are "open ended." Although they present no new problems of logical structure, they do present a unique problem in discussion.

The social sciences appear to have an abundance of these open-ended definitions. For example, "democracy" may be defined with reference to a particular set of criteria, but it is easily possible to add additional criteria and thus to open the question of whether or not a given society heretofore excluded from the category of democracies is to be admitted. The concept of murder illustrates this point very well. From the standpoint of a court of law, murder is not an act committed by an individual. To kill someone is an act. To class a killing as murder is to make a judgment of the act. If we try to specify the criteria by which the act of killing would be decided to be a case of murder, it is found that the list is theoretically interminable. We now know, for example, that if x kills y, it is murder provided x was not insane at the time of the act, or he did not commit it in self-defense, or it was not done accidentally or incidentally to the performance of some duty, to mention only a few of the criteria by which a court may rule the act of killing out of the category of murder. Even were we to extend the list to include all criteria previously used, theoretically the list would still be incomplete. It is possible that some astute attorney would come forth with an argument giving rise to some new criterion.

USES OF CONCEPTS

It has already been noted that concepts organize our experience. To say that concepts are centers of organization in our cognitive structure is to say that they are used in identifying and classifying the objects, events, and the like, of our environment. They determine how we see the world. As Kant noted long ago, we depend as much for our understanding upon our concepts as upon our percepts.

There are many things which we experience through our senses and for which we seek interpretations and explanations.

Concepts and conceptual systems enable us to understand these features of our environment. In common sense, we assume that we explain that which is strange and new by reference to that which is familiar; the abstract is explained by the concrete. But to understand the role of concepts in helping us explain the features of our environment is to see this whole process in reverse. For when we use concepts in this fashion, we explain the more familiar things of the world by reference to the things that we know least about. We account for what is observed by reference to that which is unseen, that is, explain the concrete by the abstract. For example, we observe that a child resembles its parents. We explain this similarity by saying that it has been inherited. We then go on to explain inheritance by reference to the genes and to other aspects of genetic structure not immediately visible to us. In like manner, we explain the hotness of an object by reference to molecular motion; the greater the speed of the molecules the higher the temperature. Similarly, we interpret the world of social behavior, the story of man's doings, and the world of art with the concepts we bring to those domains. Concepts are the media not only for bringing the world to us, but also the instrument for sorting out and giving meaning to our experience.

We also use concepts, as has already been indicated, in the formulation of principles. The principle or law of gravity says that any two bodies will be attracted to one another by a force directly proportional to their masses and inversely proportional to the square of the distance between them. The concepts in this statement are given by the terms "body," "mass," "distance," "directly proportional" and "inversely proportional," and "square of the distance." The law in this case is simply a statement relating these concepts.

A law, as someone has said, is an inference ticket. It tells us that if such and such conditions are present, then such and such consequences may be safely inferred. If we know that an actual state of affairs corresponds to what the law prescribes, we know from the law what to expect. The law also suggests what condition must be brought into existence if we want a given result. A basic science such as physics or chemistry is not primarily concerned with the task of bringing about the state of affairs essential to a practical result. It is the business of a technology or of an applied science to work out the ways by which the conditions specified in scientific laws may be realized in a practical situation. Back of all of this—laws and their application—is the conceptual system which comprises the basic elements in the intellectual organization of scientists and technologists, and, in verbal form, makes up a large part of the content of the curriculum.

CRITERIA FOR SELECTING CONCEPTS

Curriculum development with respect to concepts involves two basic tasks. The first is to determine what concepts to teach, and the second is to decide how they are to be taught.

It is not possible in the present chapter to deal with the question of what particular concepts to include in the curriculum. This question will be taken up in a later chapter. But it is feasible to suggest certain criteria for their selection. Other things being equal, basic concepts should be emphasized. But how is the basic character of concepts to be ascertained? There are two criteria which may be given in answer to this question. The first of these is that those concepts which are most widely instrumental are basic to the behavior of an individual. These are concepts used by the individual no matter what content he deals with. Such concepts as these are usually acquired in the fields of mathematics and languages—the symbols of information—although other subjects do contribute to their development. One or two examples are appropriate. Direct and indirect proportion are concepts which are used repeatedly by the individual in a great variety of fields. A rudimentary concept of direct proportion is acquired from daily experience. An individual learns that if he buys one apple for ten cents and another at the same price, the amount which he pays for apples is directly proportional to the number of apples he purchases. He may not articulate the concept, but it is implicit in his behavior. The concept of direct proportion is used over and over again in the sciences as well as in everyday life.

The concept of inverse proportion, although encountered in everyday experience, is more difficult for the student to grasp. It is difficult for him to see that there are some relationships such that the more of one thing he has the less he has of something else. He can see clearly that if he spends money for amusement, say, his money decreases as his time in recreation increases. But when this concept is brought into problems involving data in the natural and social sciences, the student has difficulty in understanding it. When he is told that the volume of a gas varies inversely with its pressure, and especially when this idea is expressed in mathematical terms, the idea often seems strange and unfamiliar to him. Partly for this reason, this concept is often dealt with explicitly and at considerable length in beginning sciences.

These two concepts, as already indicated, are useful in any field where variables are related to one another. They are in a sense without content; that is to say, they can be used in dealing with almost any sort of content. They are modes of operation generalized from a broad base of experience.

The concept of truth is another idea which has general instrumental value. In ordinary experience everyone knows what truth means. But in the domain of history, physics, or mathematics, for example, the individual is very often unable to give the grounds for believing what is claimed or asserted to be true. There are several different ways of defining the term "truth." It may be defined one way in religion, another way in mathematics, and still another way in science. And since the student's thought, at least a great deal of it, presupposes some conception of what it means for a statement to be true, we can say that the various concepts of truth have wide utility and should perhaps be dealt with explicitly in the educational program.

The concept of equilibrium is another case in point. It is used in chemistry, physics, psychology, social sciences, and in ordinary experience. To be sure, there is a difference in meaning from one of these fields to another, but still there is a root meaning of the term "equilibrium" that holds roughly from domain to domain. In all of its uses, the term means a balance of forces. In the final analysis, it reduces to the simple notion that the resultant of all the forces, whatever be their character, is zero.

The second criterion by which to decide upon key concepts is that the concept be logically basic to a given field of study. These concepts do not cut across subject fields but are restricted to a particular domain. In physics, the concepts of time and motion are basic ideas, and it is important that they be thoroughly understood, if the student is to grasp even the elementary aspects of physics. The concept of valence in chemistry is likewise a basic notion.

Effective curriculum development requires that these basic notions be identified in each field of instruction, and that instructional materials be prepared to teach them effectively. As will be seen in later chapters, this is one of the characteristics of the new programs in physics, chemistry, biology, economics, and other fields.

HOW CONCEPTS ARE LEARNED

There are at least three related ways in which concepts are acquired—incidentally, by instruction, and by discovery.

Perhaps most concepts are acquired through ordinary experience and without the individual being aware that he is learning them. An individual may be able to identify a giraffe when he sees it and to pick it out from among all other animals. But if he were asked to state the characteristics which distinguish it from other animals in an unmistakable fashion, he might be unable to do so. This is especially likely to be the case when dealing with abstract concepts such as tax, patriotism, and nationalism. The individual may act as if he understood the concept of a tax without being able to state the characteristics that distinguish a tax from a duty, a tariff, or a fine. Indeed, an individual acquires many concepts in the course of his daily experience without clearly understanding the concepts themselves, even though they operate in his behavior and shape his thought. But when he is in a situation that requires that he make distinctions among concepts, and especially if the concepts are very similar, he often finds himself unable to think and express himself clearly with ideas that have been acquired incidentally.

In much the same way, most of the concepts which are learned in school are taken on incidentally in the course of classroom discussion and reading. The student acquires the meaning of symbols from the context as he reads or listens. He is able to acquire concepts in this way partly because he already knows the structure of the language. There is a meaning which he acquires merely from syntax itself. This fact was made abundantly clear by Ogden and Richards many years ago by means of a sentence without semantic content: *The Gostak distims the doshes.* Although the words in this sentence have no meaning, the sentence itself does mean something to us. We know that reference is made to a class of things called gostaks and to another class of things called doshes. We know also that a gostak is doing something to the doshes—distimming them. And we know that at least some, perhaps all, of the doshes are receiving the effects of the doing. We know all of this from syntax. The structure of the sentence is the same as that of the following: *The man paints the houses.* From this sentence, we know that there is a class of things called men and a class of things called houses, and that the men are doing something to the houses. If we know English, we know also what men and houses are and what activity the word "paint" refers to.

Many sentences that students hear or read in their schoolwork contain symbols which stand for concepts that they do not understand, and, in some cases, know nothing at all about. But if they know the syntax and most of the words that appear in the sentences, they can often infer from the context the rudimentary meanings of the concepts symbolized by the unfamiliar terms.

Probably most of our concepts are come by in this way. If this is the case, it would account for the fact that words which stand for concepts are often vague and ambiguous. In short, the concepts which we acquire in this way are ordinarily not analyzed and verbalized as definitions. Rather they remain at a rather rudimentary level. Although they serve the purposes of ordinary parlance, they are often inadequate where clear and concise thought is required. In the course of instruction, a teacher often needs to select certain of these concepts which are key points in discussion and open them up for more thorough consideration.

This leads to the second way in which concepts are learned—by direct instruction. In direct instruction, the structure of the concept *is* laid out so that the various elements of its verbal formulation are clearly indicated. If it is a classificatory definition, the student comes to see the class term and the criteria by which those things which are to be either put into the class or excluded from it are themselves judged. If the formulation is not to be merely rote, the teacher must present a number of cases, some of which would be excluded by the criteria and some of which would be included by them. For example, if the teacher were dealing with the definition of a tax, as discussed above, he would give cases which are very similar to taxes but which are in fact not so—duties, tariffs, fines, and so on. As the student examines each of these in terms of the criteria, the concept itself becomes clear, because its meaning boundaries are made more definite.

In dealing with operational definitions, the teacher would, of course, either indicate or perform the operations entailed by the concept, or better still have the student do the operations himself. The sorts of operations chosen depend upon the level of the student's maturity. If he is in the elementary school, operations in the field of science, for example, might begin with those which are somewhat anthropomorphic and move on to those which are more sophisticated. But at the high-school level, the teachers would use operations that have been employed in the more developed stages of the science.

It is important to note that the operational mode of teaching has its weakness. This defect is best illustrated in the social sciences. We have attempted in recent decades to define democracy operationally and to teach the individual to act democratically by placing him in situations that elicit democratic behavior from him. He learns to behave democratically under these circumstances, and perhaps to like this way of doing things. But what he fails to acquire is a clear verbalization of the concept of democracy. Consequently, he is often unable to hold his own in discussion with those who have a different view of democracy or who wish to deny democracy altogether. Young people as well as older ones are often unable to meet Communist and fascist ideological arguments. In some cases, of course, this is due to the fact that the individual does not possess the information needed to answer the criticisms being made of democracy. But it is also due to the fact that he does not understand at the verbal level what democracy means. He cannot analyze the concept into its elements and make them explicitly clear, nor is he able to meet the cogent arguments of those who hold a contrary view. Nevertheless, he can behave democratically in all sorts of situations. It therefore seems desirable that operational definitions be supplemented by clear verbal formulations, especially in the social domain, where one is frequently called upon to defend his beliefs by arguments and where empirical demonstrations are not readily available. Indeed, such demonstrations are sometimes wholly incongruous. For example, what democratic behavior is appropriate when a totalitarian advocate attacks democracy? If one were to rely on overt behavior alone, he could applaud the speaker's right to his opinion, display disapproval, or leave the scene altogether. But none or all of these behaviors prove the speaker's argument to be false; they merely exhibit an "attitude," and none too clear a one, toward the speaker or what he is saying.

In the discovery method, the teacher presents a quantum of information and the student is asked to extend it so as to indicate whether or not he grasps the concept. Consider the case of a teacher who is trying to develop a concept of an imperialistic nation by the discovery procedure. He might begin by describing the act of a nation and then ask the students to indicate whether or not this action is imperialistic. He would then describe the behavior of another nation, or a different behavior of the same nation, and again ask the students to decide whether or not the behavior indicates an imperialistic country. By thus presenting case after case, it is hoped that students will be able to formulate the criteria by which nations are judged to be imperialistic or not. They would thus arrive at the structure of the concept inductively; that is to say, they would have worked out a definition of "imperialistic nation" for themselves.

What has been said in this chapter points up the curriculum-maker's concern with the attainment of those concepts and combinations of concepts by which we expect the student to map his world for correct description. Part of the strategy of the curriculum is to figure out what types of school materials, organized in what ways, serve to enlarge and refine the conceptual store. Are there some materials and modes of teaching them that are better than others for making pupil and teacher aware of both the structure and the importance of concepts? Another focal strategy of the curriculum consists in determining what types of school materials, organized in what ways, serve to enrich and refine the valuative store. It is to a discussion of this topic that the next chapter turns.

CHAPTER IX

CONTENT AS VALUATIVE CONCEPTS AND NORMS

We not only arrange our world into classes and relationships and explain and interpret events in it by reference to laws, but we also express our attitude toward events and evaluate them in many different ways. We deal with such questions as: Was Wilson a strong President? Is Mr. X a good governor? Is that a good novel? Is it true that Mr. Y lost his job? What should Mr. Z have done? In dealing with questions of this sort, we make use of valuative concepts, attitudes, and norms or rules of conduct. Just as descriptive concepts and principles are the building stones of our cognitive structure for analyzing, describing, and controlling our environment, so valuative concepts, attitudes, and norms are the basic elements of our mental organization for rating the things of our environment and for judging the actions of individuals and social groups. To prepare the individual to deal with broad questions of social programs and policies and to find his way among the conflicting views and opinions to which he is exposed, the school must emphasize valuative concepts and norms no less than it stresses the concepts and principles by which the objects and events of our world are ordered and controlled.

NEGLECT OF VALUATIVE CONTENT

A half-century ago, a great deal of emphasis was placed upon the valuative and normative content of education. Stories in elementary-school readers were selected because they illustrated moral lessons. Copybooks were based on maxims. Moral notions made up a great deal of the content of English and social studies, and even the natural sciences were tinted with moral views.

A revolt occurred against this direct way of teaching valuative content. For one thing, it was alleged that such instruction tended to be merely verbal—mere rote learning. For another, as behavioristic psychology gained ascendancy, emphasis was placed more and more upon the development of attitudes and overt ways of behaving instead of on ideas. This meant that in the realm of moral conduct it was conceived to be far more effective to develop right attitudes and habits of behavior than to deal with the concepts and rules of such behavior.

As a result of these counterforces, the curriculum came to be stripped of much significant normative and valuative content. Activities of a gross sort, designed to develop in the individual both moral and democratic ways of behaving and to induce the attitudes appropriate to them, became the major emphasis. Student government and other sorts of extracurricular activities were justified on the grounds that they developed proper attitudes and democratic behavior. In this view, it was hardly necessary for the individual to develop *concepts* of right conduct and to learn the norms of such behavior; it was only necessary that he learn to behave in approved ways. Or, it was believed that such concepts would be acquired incidentally but nonetheless effectively as a by-product of the behavior.

This way of handling problems of moral conduct and civic behavior has tended to develop individuals who are unable to give justifications for their behavior, except, of course, those derived from common sense. Youth as well as adults are conservatives without knowing why, or liberals without knowing why. They believe democracy to be the best way of life, but are unable to defend it effectively when challenged by those who hold contrary views. Indeed, they are often unable to tell whether or not another view affirms or denies democracy. It seems clearly evident that the time has come for the curriculum to give primary consideration to the study of the values and norms by which individual and social conduct is regulated and justified.

VALUATIVE CONTENT

The preceding chapter noted the distinction between descriptive concepts and valuative concepts. It will be recalled that valuative concepts contain both descriptive and preferential components. They are heavily weighted with preferential or attitudinal elements of experience. This fact is reflected in linguistic behavior. It is possible to think of verbal expressions as being on a continuum from attitudinal expressions at one end to those which are descriptive at the other. If one were to say, "Good old teacher," we would understand him to be expressing his attitude toward the person in question, to be expressing some affection or some sort of approval of the individual, unless, of course, it were said in a sarcastic tone. But even in the latter case, the expression would still be attitudinal. At the other end of the scale would be such an expression as, "The teacher is six feet tall." We would ordinarily understand this sentence to be saying something about the teacher and little, if anything, about the attitude of the speaker.

Between these two extremes are such expressions as the following: "These are wonderful apples," "That is a fine automobile," and "Mr. X is a good teacher." In these sentences, we would understand the individual to be saying two things. Consider, for example, the last sentence. He would be saying something about the teacher and he would at the same time be expressing his attitude toward the teacher. When he says that the teacher is a good teacher, we understand him to be approving the teacher. If he were to say, "Mr. X is a good teacher, but I would not employ him," it would seem rather odd to us. We would expect the speaker to give some special explanation of why he would not employ Mr. X after having said that he was a good teacher. But the speaker is not only approving the teacher, he is also claiming that the teacher meets some sort of standard. Were we to ask the speaker his reasons for saying that Mr. X is a good teacher, we would expect him to say that Mr. X does so-and-so with his students in the classroom and that that is what he means when he says Mr. X is a good teacher.

There is also another sort of expression which falls between the two extremes of the continuum. Suppose a speaker utters the old adage, "Honesty is the best policy." We would understand him to be expressing a positive attitude toward honesty. Were he to say, "I do not think one should be honest," after having said, "Honesty is the best policy," we would think it rather odd. We would probably ask him to justify his claim that one should not be honest when it is the best policy to be so. But the speaker would be expressing more than an attitude. For when he says, "Honesty is the best policy," we would also understand him to mean that, in the long run, if one pursues the policy of being honest, he will have less trouble in life and be happier than he otherwise would be. This example approaches a norm of conduct in contrast to a valuative concept. Like descriptive principles, a norm is comprised of concepts; in this case, the valuative concepts of *honesty* and *best*.

ATTITUDINAL ASPECTS OF CONDUCT

The rest of this chapter takes up each of these elements—attitudes, valuative concepts, and norms—in greater detail. Attitudes are psychological structures. They may be defined as states of readiness that influence the action of an individual toward objects and events. Although they are not a form of subject matter, but positive and negative dispositions, attitudes are expressible in emotive language. Words such as "enjoy," "want," "accept," "desire," "fond of," and the like, express positive attitudes, and words such as "hate," "disapprove of," "detest," "aversion," and "dislike," express negative attitudes. Furthermore, they are expressed as components in valuative concepts such as "desirable," "good," "efficient," "beautiful," and their antonyms. Many of the adjectives in our language, habitually used to describe inanimate objects, betray our inveterate tendency to see the world in terms of human attitudes. Such phrases as "lonely road," "angry sea," and "cheerful melody" attach attributes to roads, seas, and melodies that only metaphorically belong to them.

Most attitudes are formed by unconscious association or conditioning. The individual becomes loaded, so to speak, with attitudes without knowing their origin or without being aware that he has acquired them. For example, one may be afraid of the dark because in his early childhood some frightening experience happened in connection with darkness. The stage of fright is thereafter evoked when the individual is alone in darkness. In like manner, an individual becomes positively oriented toward a political party, a particular type of political leader, different kinds of food, subjects taught in school, teachers, parents, and so on. As has already been indicated, we probably underestimate the influence of this mode of acquiring attitudes, simply because there is no way of estimating the associative and unconscious uses of schooling. The world of the individual is filled with many objects toward which he either has a positive feeling or a negative feeling. Attitudes also become organized into systems in such a way as to focus on clusters of events and objects. A conservative has many attitudes characteristic of his conservatism, and these focus upon a great variety of features of his environment.

Since there is no verbal content corresponding to attitudes, it is often claimed that they can neither be taught nor included in the curriculum in the same way in which norms and valuative concepts are included. According to this view, the readiness of an individual to act in a particular way cannot be taught by the use of a specific content. The individual's likes and dislikes, his desires and aversions, his approvals and disapprovals, his acceptances and his rejections can only be induced by environmental circumstances. For this reason, it has often been argued that the best way to lead a person to enjoy music or painting or reading is to surround him with good music, good paintings, and good books. To live with these materials, to hear them talked about in approving ways, and to partake of them at moments most conducive to the enjoyment of them is to acquire a taste for them. In this view, no rational processes and no analytic procedures are necessary for the acquisition of proper dispositions. Indeed, too much emphasis upon analysis and reasoning in the study of the arts is likely to build negative rather than positive attitudes.

If this view is correct, there is much to be said for the school of thought which emphasizes the creation of an aesthetic environment in the school. The display of good paintings and the playing of good music at opportune moments in the school without calling attention to the quality of the paintings or the music is, in this view, the proper way to engender the enjoyment of such aesthetic objects. By the same token, to place an individual in a group characterized by certain attitudes and to let him participate in the group as a member is to build into him those attitudes. He will not know how he came by them, nor will he know how to handle them when they come into conflict with other attitudes which he himself holds or which are held by others. Nevertheless, these attitudes will influence his subsequent behavior.

Of course, this is not the complete picture. Attitudes are also acquired and refined through analysis and argument. The individual's cognitive structure often exercises a controlling influence over his attitudes. It may be difficult for an individual to maintain an attitude toward an object or event after learning that he has misunderstood the facts or has been in possession of misinformation. And even though he may continue to hold an attitude after he has been correctly informed, he will not hold it with the same conviction and tenacity. An individual may have negative reactions toward deficit financing by the government. He may believe that the budget should be balanced annually, and that any government which fails to balance its budget is in some way basically inadequate. But if he comes to understand the theory of deficit financing and sees that it can be related positively to the problem of maintaining a growing, healthy economy, his attitude toward the whole matter may be modified. In other words, when his cognitive structure changes, there may be corresponding changes in his attitude toward the things embraced by the cognitive outlook. Furthermore, the more extensive one's cognitive structure and the more adequate it is from a factual and theoretical standpoint, the less likely he is to be influenced by unfounded claims and outright appeals to his emotions. At least the discrepancy may, as Gunnar Myrdal has argued, create a need for restoring consistency between beliefs and attitudes. Perhaps one of the best means of insuring against the effects of purely emotional appeal, against the individual's succumbing to mere propaganda, is the development of his conceptual system in the various domains of experience. To point out interesting features of good examples of literature, music, or any other art form is to enrich the individual's enjoyment of these examples, if it does not actually shape his attitudes toward them. A teacher who points out the imagery evoked by Browning's "My Last Duchess" is likely to build positive attitudes toward the poem and probably leave a lasting impression with many of his students.

DEALING WITH VALUATIVE CONCEPTS

It was seen in the preceding chapter that concepts are reference points in the individual's behavior, and when they are organized into systems they constitute the individual's cognitive maps. Valuative concepts are those which have become suffused with attitudes. They not only help to categorize events and objects, but they also shape actions toward them, in the sense that they embody one's readiness to be either for or against something, to think it desirable or undesirable, good or bad. To classify a person who takes property belonging to someone else as a thief is to evoke disapproval of him, but to classify him as a sick person arouses sympathy.

To teach valuative concepts is to deal with their verbal counterparts. When we begin to deal with these counterparts, it soon becomes evident that we are again involved in the task of definition. For example, in a history class the question arose as to whether or not Andrew Jackson was a strong President. Some students held that he was a weak President, while others maintained with equal enthusiasm that he was strong. The words "strong" and "weak" in this context are expressive of attitudes. Persons are usually for strong Presidents and against weak ones. But the expression, "Andrew Jackson was a strong President," purports to say something about Jackson and not merely to express the attitude of the speaker. In the course of the class discussion, it was said a number of times that Jackson was a strong President because he got his programs through. At the same time, it was maintained by other students that he was a weak President because he was an opportunist, basing his decisions on circumstances rather than principle.

To decide this question it is necessary to agree upon some set of criteria by which to rate a President as either strong or weak or somewhere in between these two extremes. The criteria being used by the students were as follows: (a) A President is strong if he gets his programs through. (b) A President is weak if he acts on principle and fails to get his programs through. (c) A President is strong if he acts on principle. (d) A President is weak if he bases his action on circumstances, even though he may get his programs through. The first and second criteria are incompatible with the third and fourth. Students holding to the first two criteria were insisting that Jackson was a strong President. Those insisting on the last two criteria claimed that Jackson was weak.

It is clear from this analysis that the students in the class were using two different sets of criteria to rate Jackson as a

President. So long as they disagreed on criteria, it was impossible for them to give the same rating. The criteria embody preferences of the students, and this is characteristic of all criteria that have to do with the use of valuative language. That is to say, valuative concepts are expressed in such symbolic forms as *strong* or *weak*, and when we try to define such expressions, we state criteria which embody our preferences. Issues arising from differences in preferences cannot be squarely faced, let alone effectively dealt with, until the differences in criteria are explicitly recognized.

Suppose that students come to agree on a set of criteria, and assume that they agree upon the first two in the list above. Their next task in the process of evaluating Jackson as a President would be to determine whether or not he was successful in getting his programs through the Congress. If he were successful, he would be judged by the criteria to be a strong President. But to the degree that he was unsuccessful in getting his programs adopted, he would be a weak President.

This analysis demonstrates that the process of evaluation consists in at least four things: first, there must be an object, event, or something to consider; second, there must be a set of criteria which incorporate the preferences of the individual or group involved in the consideration; third, there are facts about whatever is being evaluated which indicate that the criteria are applicable to it; and finally, a judgment is rendered and a rating is made of whatever it is that is being evaluated.

If evaluation in the aesthetic domain is considered, it becomes clear that the process just described holds there as well. If we want to decide whether or not Georgia O'Keeffe's "Pinons with Cedar" is a good painting, we have to decide upon the criteria by which it is to be rated. Suppose that it is agreed that a painting is good if it has a center of interest, perspective and depth, proper color harmony, and other criteria which we may also agree upon. The task then is to see whether or not the painting by O'Keeffe has the properties prescribed by the criteria. If it does possess these properties, then we rate it as being good. Preferences with respect to what constitutes quality in a painting will have been incorporated in our criteria. If persons disagree with us as to whether or not the painting in question is a good piece of work, they have to go back to our criteria in order to locate the real points of difference.

It is worthy of note, and of considerable significance pedagogically, that our rating of a work of art and our enjoyment or cherishing of it may be two quite different things. We may believe that a given painting is of high quality according to certain criteria and yet feel that we do not like it. It would not be odd to say that we do not like the work even though it is good. Nor is there anything unusual in saying that we like a painting though it is not a good piece of work. This is possible when the criteria by which judgments are made are not those of the individual, but of a reference group. One may use the criteria developed by art critics to decide whether or not a painting is good. If these are not the criteria that incorporate his own preferences, it would then be quite legitimate for him to say that the painting is a good one, but he does not like it.

Truth and falsity, correctness and incorrectness, dependability and undependability, are all matters of value definition no less than beauty, strength, goodness, and the like. If someone says that a statement is true, he is giving the statement a rating. We do not know the bases of the rating unless he gives the criteria that he is using. Suppose, in the discussion of a novel, one of the characters is pointed out as having been brought up in underprivileged circumstances, and it is also noted that this individual is unusually sympathetic and understanding of the troubles and difficulties of others. Suppose that a student asks, "Is it true that individuals who are brought up in this way are more sympathetic and understanding of other individuals than people brought up under more favorable circumstances?" To answer this question is in part to ask what sort of criteria of truth the class is willing to accept. If they accept the criterion that statements which correspond to observations are true statements, then the truth or falsity of the claim can be established. In this case, it is necessary to study people who were thus reared and to determine what sort of attitudes they have toward other people. It is also necessary to study similar attitudes of individuals brought up under more favorable circumstances. From a comparison of these two sets of facts, the class is in a better position to decide the truth value of the statement.

On the other hand, if the students assert that their criterion of truth is that any statement is true which expresses their intuitions, it is necessary to follow some other procedure. The class wants to know, for example, how to tell whether or not a given claim was a reflection of their intuitions. And in this case one supposes that the unchecked testimony of individuals concerned would be taken as prime evidence.

There can be any number of criteria by which to judge the truth of what is said, and the decision of what criteria are to be used in any given case depends upon the individual or the group. For example, the criterion of truth in the domain of religion may be different from the criterion of truth in the domain of science. And the criterion of truth in the domain of history for those teachers who hold to a subjective interpretation of the past may be different from that of those who hold a scientific or objective view of history.

NORMS IN THE CURRICULUM

It was noted in the preceding chapter that descriptive principles are used in the interpretation and explanation of factual aspects of the environment. Even the small child wants to know the causes of events. He wants to know why the leaves fall, or why the clouds move. It is the role of descriptive principles to provide answers to such questions. In the domain of human conduct, where the action of an individual influences the life of another, the individual may want to know what is the right and proper thing to do. He may wish to know what is his duty; what under the circumstances he ought to do. Or he may wish to know what the proper rule is for attaining a given end. Answers to questions such as these are to be worked out in terms, not of descriptive principles, but of valuative principles or norms. If the curriculum is to be designed to make individuals as intelligent about their social conduct as about their behavior toward the material world, the content of the educational program must consist in part of valuative principles and concepts. It must also include experience in handling such concepts and principles at the verbal level. For, as has been seen, it is not sufficient that an individual behave in right and proper ways, but he also must be able to verbalize his behavior and to examine it critically, offering such justification of it as seems desirable. An unexamined and uncritical enjoyment may be worth having, but the decision as to whether it is or is not is never justified by the enjoyment alone.

Three kinds of norms should be taken into account as the content of the curriculum is selected. These are the norms of efficiency or prescriptive rules, regulatory norms, and moral norms.

From time to time, each individual is engaged in activities which require that he perform in specified ways in order to attain certain ends. A housewife bakes cakes; a gardener grows flowers; a carpenter squares corners; a mechanic replaces a tire. Each of these tasks is performed in conformity with some sort of procedural rule which we call a prescription or recipe. The rules for baking a cake tell the housewife the ingredients to include, the order in which they are to be mixed, and so on. The midwestern gardener knows that he should not uncover his roses until the forsythia blooms in the spring.

The educational program contains a large number of such prescriptive rules. Thus, the rules of rhetoric and grammar tell how to attain certain effects in written expression. The same thing can be said of rules having to do with how to achieve certain effects in painting or in music.

It is characteristic of rules of this sort that there is an end to be attained, and that the rule tells the individual how to attain the end in the most efficient way. There are no penalties for failing to follow such rules, save that the individual may fail to achieve the result he desires. But the consequences are of his own doing.

The individual is often involved in situations in which his conduct is expected to conform to certain regulations. In such situations he is bound by what may be called regulatory rules. If he is driving an automobile on the highway, his behavior must conform to the traffic rules. If he is taking a test, he must conform to rules governing the examination. There are rules for classroom behavior, for behaving in the school, and in society generally. Some of the latter are laws, or legal regulations. These rules are not designed for the attainment of some particular end, as in the case of prescriptive rules. Unlike prescriptive rules, they are put into effect or enforced, and there are penalties for breaking them.

Many of the individual's activities are controlled, in one way or another, by regulatory rules. In fact, the individual lives and carries on his ordinary activities within a system of such rules. Every institution with which he is associated has its own set of rules governing the activities for which it is responsible. And what is called bureaucracy in modern society is little more than institutions in which the behavior of individuals responsible for carrying on the work of these institutions is thoroughly and systematically governed by certain regulatory rules. To understand social institutions is in large measure to understand the different activities which these institutions carry on and the rules by which they are governed. Partly for this reason, some critics of the school claim that the curriculum has given too little attention to those rules of conduct established and enforced by authority.

Finally, there are the rules of morality and prudence. The individual is often in situations in which the question of what is the moral thing to do arises. Over the centuries mankind has worked out certain norms of conduct to which men are to conform in their dealings with one another. These rules make up perhaps the most basic elements of human culture. They lie at the base not only of social institutions, but ultimately of regulatory rules themselves and of the choice of ends which are served by prescriptive rules. They have to do with such virtues as honesty, sincerity, justice, charity, fairness, and brotherhood. Moral rules are not put into effect and enforced as are regulatory rules. Neither are they passed and put into operation by convention or authority. They cannot be rescinded. Nor do they provide formulas for attaining given ends. They rest in man's higher conscience and are not capable of proof by empirical procedures.

The curriculum must be designed to teach the student not only to conform to selected sets of these three types of rules, but also to be aware of the rules themselves. To attain these ends, the school curriculum should contain selected examples of human behavior which can be analyzed and studied from the standpoint of the norms which they involve.

Moreover, the student needs to be taught in such a way that he understands the nature of these rules. He should see clearly that the criteria of acceptability for such norms are quite different from the criteria used in deciding the acceptability of descriptive statements and principles.

It is one of the tasks of the schools not only to teach the individuals to do that which is right and wise, but also to know why it is right and wise. The school cannot teach choices and decisions, but it can teach the facts, the value definitions, and the valuative principles on which right and wise decisions are based. It can, of course, inculcate habits of behaving in certain ways. But on analysis, even these habits turn out to be incipient principles as well as ways of behaving. This can be seen from the fact that habits are always exercised in certain conditions and in certain times and places. When the conditions are specified verbally, together with the mode of action appropriate to them, the whole formulation is a principle. The trouble with sheer habit is that the individual does not understand the circumstances under which it is performed, and this may easily render it outside the range of his intelligence and so not subject to deliberate modification.

Moreover, valuative principles can be taught by example and reinforced by sanctions for replicative use. But this, too, is inadequate, because it results in individuals who behave in proper ways without knowing why they do so. In a stable society in which there is little fundamental change and where the norms of conduct remain stable throughout an individual's lifetime, instruction in proper conduct by example and precept may be sufficient. But in a society in which the valuative principles themselves are in controversy, and where the society is itself broken into many groups giving allegiance to conflicting norms, something more is needed than the mere conditioning of behavior. In such circumstances, the individual needs to know the valuative principles at the verbal level. He also needs to know how to examine these principles in terms of the valuative concepts that make them up and the consequences to which they lead in action. He also needs to be able to relate one valuative principle to another and even to see them in their systematic relationships, because if he is unable to do this, the individual will fail to note inconsistencies and thereby be unaware of the source of conflicts that arise in action.

Furthermore, at a time when the valuative principles of the social system are themselves in conflict, it becomes necessary to reconstruct them, to reshape them to meet new conditions. This requires of the citizen a fairly high level of logical ability to handle concepts and principles charged with strongly held preferences. It is a major task of the curriculum-builder in these times not only to work out the ways individuals should behave, but also to formulate the content which is entailed by such behavior. This is a task which falls upon the entire teaching staff, but primarily upon those who are concerned with the social sciences, with the arts—especially literature—and with those aspects of the language arts which have to do with the role of language in human conduct.

The question of what norms should be given special attention is one which cannot be answered specifically in a general discussion. Ultimately, the question is perhaps best answered by individuals who have expert knowledge in the fields of art, social science, and areas of practical activity. Nevertheless, it is possible to suggest criteria which concepts and norms should satisfy if they are to be included in the educational program. In general, only those concepts and norms basic to individual and social conduct should have a place in the curriculum. The question, of course, is how to decide whether or not a given concept or norm is basic. This may be answered differently for each of the three types of norms. One thing seems to be clear: the logical criterion which is readily applicable to descriptive concepts and principles is not as useful when it comes to the selection of valuative concepts and norms. In the domain of valuative concepts, there are few ideas logically prior to others, though some are certainly more logically inclusive than others. Too, the logical relations among prescriptive and regulatory rules are of little consequence, although this cannot be said of moral norms. The main question in the case of prescriptive rules is whether or not the given end is attained efficiently by following the particular norm. Furthermore, the justification of the rule is one which requires no great amount of logical manipulation. If one wishes to know why roses should be uncovered when the forsythia blooms, he need only be told that experience has shown that it pays to do so; that if one uncovers his roses before that time, they are likely to be harmed by frost. In the case of regulatory rules, the important consideration is the extent to which persons are mutually protected and benefited by the rule.

The criterion for selecting prescriptive rules would seem to be tied to the question of what practical activities, deemed important in the ordinary affairs of the individual, the school should incorporate in its program. This question comes down to being one of what sort of utility the school wishes to serve. Apparently, the vocational fields such as agriculture, commerce, and the various industrial occupations are replete with activities which would require a mastery of certain rules of procedure. Likewise, the arts are areas in which the mastery of such rules seems to be uppermost.

What about regulatory rules? Naturally, those rules which have to do with the operation of the school itself are to be learned. But beyond these are the norms of behavior which are ordinarily considered to be legal matters. The task facing the curriculum-builder is to decide what set of legal and institutional regulations should be taught to students as part of their general knowledge. At the present time, of course, traffic rules are taught as part of driver-training programs. But this is only a small part of the total range of activities in which citizens are engaged and about whose regulations they need to be informed. There is no clear-cut guiding idea as to what content the curriculum should emphasize in this domain. To select for study sample regulatory situations deemed to be significant to people generally is perhaps as near as one can come to laying down a criterion as to what is basic in this sphere of social behavior.

Turning now to moral rules, it is easy to see that the school is always in danger of treating the more superficial aspects of morality at the expense of the more basic concepts and norms upon which the whole social system ultimately rests. In the recent past, the schools have tended to deal with minor morals and manners, such as how an individual should conduct himself in a theater, at the dining table, at social gatherings, or in dating. These are secondary in importance to such questions as how an individual should behave when he is confronted by someone trying to prevent another individual or group from participating in the cultural advantages to which they are entitled as human beings. The question of morality involved in the practice of preventing individuals, because of their membership in certain groups, from being admitted to theaters or dining places or public schools on an equal basis with other persons, overshadows completely any moral issue that could be involved in such matters as proper conduct at a social gathering or in a theater. It can be said that such concepts as freedom and equality and the norms which are based upon such concepts are so basic to our cultural system that a denial of them would completely alter the nature and character of our institutions and social, political, and economic practices. The question, therefore, of what moral concepts and rules to include in the curriculum is settled in part by an examination of our institutions from the standpoint of what basic concepts they rest upon. This, of course, is primarily the task of persons who are competent in the various disciplines having to do with the social and moral sciences.

This chapter has tried to present some of the considerations that have led to the organization, in Chapters XIII and XIV, of those portions of the curriculum called exemplars and molar problems and provides some of the reasons for organizing the developmental studies to be discussed in Chapter XII.

PART THREE

A CURRICULUM RESPONSE TO
THE NEW DEMANDS

CHAPTER X

USE AND DEVELOPMENT OF SKILLS

The previous chapters have laid the theoretical groundwork for the organization of content into subjects of instruction. From a consideration of the educational demands made by the mass society upon the school, the discussion passed to a study of the way school learnings are used by the specialist and nonspecialist. From this was derived a schema of schooling distinguishing contents, subjects of instruction, modes of teaching, student learnings, and evaluational procedures.

The contents and operations that make up the curriculum were then discussed in detail, stressing the ways in which concepts and logical operations are learned and used to make experience more intelligible and more manageable.

It is time to translate the arguments and observations into subjects of instruction. How are the facts, principles, rules, and norms to be presented in the classroom? From what disciplines shall they be drawn? How are the choices of materials and their arrangement justified by the arguments in the previous chapters?

These questions are taken up in the next four chapters, dealing with curriculum provisions for skills, the descriptive use of concepts, and their valuative use. In the final chapter, a possible program of studies to illustrate the curriculum design is presented.

Figure 3 may be helpful in clarifying the topics and their relations. The upper part of the diagram indicates in summary form the topics discussed thus far; the lower part indicates the

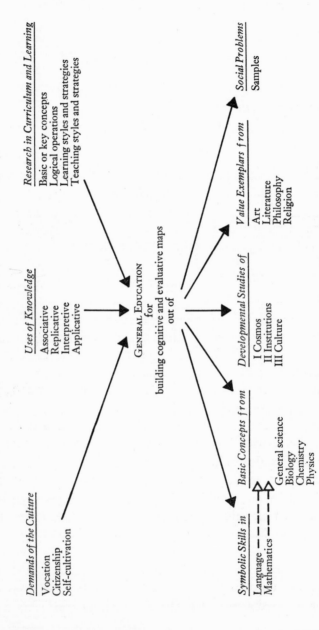

Figure 3. DESIGN FOR COMMON CURRICULUM IN GENERAL EDUCATION (GRADES 7–12)

topics which are dealt with in the next four chapters. It should be remembered that the final chapter is designed only to illustrate how an actual program could be constructed on the basis of the discussion of the various topics.

SYMBOLIC SKILLS

Before beginning the discussion of skills and their relation to the curriculum in general education, it may be well to clarify the relation of skills to concepts and logical operations out of which, it has been argued, cognitive and evaluative maps are to be constructed.

A skillful act is more than a reflexive response to a stimulus. The eye-blink or knee-jerk is not a skillful act. As an act acquires the automaticity of a reflex, it calls for less and less thought and judgment. However, skill does require some judgment. A complex act such as mowing the lawn, typing a letter, buying a dress, filling out an income tax form, performing a surgical operation, trying a law case, or teaching a lesson, may contain some components that are reflexive, some learned responses that have become automatic, judgmental acts as to which of several act-sequences shall be used, and judgmental acts that survey alternative routes of purpose and action. Amid this variety of actions, skillful ones are those that exhibit varying degrees of automaticity both in judgment and in performance. To put it in another way, as judgment becomes more and more rapid and sure, and as the smaller act-sequences become more and more automatic, we call the performer skilled. A skillful act is neither wholly automatic nor wholly judgmental.

It is clear that certain skills learned in school conform to this analysis. Handwriting, for example, is made up of movements that in time are performed automatically in a wide variety of situations, but a skillful handwriter adapts quickly to a wide variety of unusual situations, for example, writing in very small spaces or to produce ornamental effects.

When handwriting or reading or composition is used to achieve understanding, communication, and persuasion, judgments involving concepts and logical operations assume the dominant role. Not even the most adept writers and speakers ever reduce to pure automaticity the processes of writing an article or delivering a speech. Yet we recognize the difference between calling a man a good writer, a skillful writer, and a great writer. A skillful writer is one who makes effective judgments about the choice and order of words, concepts, and images, whereas goodness of writing refers to something broader, and greatness refers to something broader still, namely, the ideas of the writer, his imaginative power, his originality. Usually he is also skillful, but he may not be. The good writer is somewhere between the merely skillful and the great.

When we speak of the language *arts* or the computational *arts* in schooling, we combine the notions of skill and goodness, that is, we refer both to what is said and how well it is said, what is calculated and how well it is calculated. We operate on the assumption that if we can make the smaller components of reading, writing, and arithmetic automatic, we can devote attention to making the larger segments of these processes efficient and more or less automatic. It is not that we try to displace judgment by automaticity, but rather that we try to make certain classes of judgment automatic, for example, when to use singular or plural verb forms, when to add or multiply, subtract and divide. However, as the uses to which the skill is put are broadened, automaticity decreases in importance (because taken for granted), thought and judgment increase in importance, and the learning task shades off from a tool or skill subject to a conceptual subject of instruction.

Specialist and nonspecialist alike use certain skills learned in school in about the same way. For all, the use of skills is largely replicative, and for all, certain skills are prerequisites for the special tasks of vocation as well as the common tasks of citizenship and self-cultivation.

The three R's are the most familiar examples of such skills.

All are symbolic in that they utilize words or other signs to stand for ideas, objects, or events. Each is a system of communication, or a system of coding and decoding messages. Each is manmade and each is noniconic, that is to say, the appearance of the symbols, for example, "cat" or the number "687," does not resemble what the symbols stand for. One therefore needs instruction to learn the code and the rules for its proper use.

The three R's are symbol systems and two of them—reading and writing—are called language arts. Mathematics is also a language, but a highly specialized one, and only in its rudimentary form used in general discourse. Hence, when language arts or linguistic skills are referred to, reading and writing will be meant, rather than other symbolic systems (logic or mathematics) that constitute special codes or languages.

The symbolic skills are so obviously *learning tools* that one wonders how their utility could ever be questioned. Yet, no segment of the curriculum is debated so frequently and so acrimoniously as the three R's. A possible explanation lies in the different uses made of these skills. For example, a specialist reads *in his specialty* at a different level of precision than he does in his ordinary nonspecialist reading. A boy who is going to college will have to read in ways that a boy who finishes his formal schooling at the eleventh year will not. The same observations hold for the other two R's. Much of the debate about them would be obviated if these diverse levels of use were specified. Whether Johnny can read, and also *what* Johnny is attempting to read, depends on which of the various uses of reading one has in mind.

Other skills are also important for learning and living: how to use a library and reference books, how to study a lesson, how to carry out school assignments, how to study for and how to take examinations, how to speak effectively, how to organize one's study time, how to play games, how to use tools, how to play a musical instrument and express oneself in paint or through the dance or sculpture.

All "how-to's" are skills. The use of a skill learned in school is replicative, that is, a repeat performance. To be usable, a skill learning must have been established to the point where it can function as needed. Thus, a stenographer who cannot spell correctly does not have a usable spelling skill so far as her job is concerned. A college student who cannot study a textbook does not have a usable reading skill so far as most of his course instructors are concerned. To be efficient, a skill must be developed to the point at which it can be performed semiautomatically, that is, without attention to the component steps of the procedure. Thought and attention should be reserved for making decisions as to how to adapt the skill to the task at hand. These characteristics of skill indicate why the use of a skill learning is neither associative, applicative, nor interpretive, although if we repeat an act of applying or interpreting or associating often enough, it can become automatic and replicative. This is what is meant when thought is said to have become stereotyped.

The secondary school faces the problem of prescribing a level of mastery that will make certain skills usable for tasks which one graduate is as likely to confront as another. This makes the estimates of probable use crucial.

SYMBOLIC SKILLS IN EVERYDAY EXPERIENCE

Presumably, the pupil entering seventh grade has been practicing under tuition the arts of reading, writing, and spelling for six years. What, then, remains to be done in the secondary schools?

If ordinary usage in reading, writing, and speaking is the standard, has not the pupil attained this at the end of the sixth grade? By ordinary usage is meant such activities as reading the ordinary daily newspaper, the weekly large-circulation magazines, signs and maps, directions on packages, notices, and the like. By speaking is meant the common interchange between persons that takes place in the home, in the store, or on the job. As for writing, ordinary usage seems to involve no more than social correspondence, ordering items by mail, and occasionally writing to a business firm for one purpose or another. It is difficult to see what the average seventh grader, proceeding on schedule through the grades, lacks by way of linguistic skill.

At first blush, this seems like an exaggeration, and seems to be contradicted by the bitter complaints about the low quality of linguistic performance by high-school graduates. But whence comes the criticism, and what does it say? It comes from employers, college professors, and some parents. Employers understandably want employees to live up to certain standards of linguistic correctness. Why? It is hard to say, because so far as intelligibility is concerned, written and spoken discourse can tolerate a surprisingly high amount of linguistic laxity. "Yor order shiped tomoro" will be understood as well as the correctly spelled version, but it may create in the mind of the recipient an unfavorable impression of the sender. Hence, the sender discharges a stenographer or secretary who cannot spell and who commits outrageous grammatical improprieties. In other words, the conventions of the business world call for certain standards of linguistic performance that go beyond the requirements of ordinary usage; failure on the part of considerable numbers of high-school graduates to attain them will engender complaints by the businessman.

The college professor, for his part, is unhappy when students do not use the English language at a level commensurate with his professional standards. It goes without saying that the English department is loyal to a linguistic standard well above that required for the outside world, and even for the rest of the university campus. To be sure, the rhetoric divisions of the English departments protest that they will settle for clear and moderately accurate ordinary usage in writing and speech. They have long given up hope for literary elegance in the compositions undergraduates are asked to write. Yet, even this more modest expectation is well above the spoken language tolerated in the factory, the marketplace, and the majority of homes. Colloquial fashion is the only criterion in the nonacademic walks of life. Slang, expressions peculiar to a given factory, parochial forms of profanity and obscenity, ejaculations and intonations, gestures and esoteric allusions create a perfectly viable means of communication for in-group members, however mystifying to the out-group.

Another language style is regarded as appropriate to formal occasions or special situations that demand adherence to certain linguistic conventions. Group members whose modes of speech noticeably depart from the group norm are branded as affected, snobs, or freaks, depending on the nature and direction of the deviation.

Language usage is, however, an important index of class and status. Children who deviate from the linguistic styles of the upper middle class are regarded as culpable in two senses: they have let down the grammarians and also the class, and there is little doubt as to which form of treason is regarded as less unforgivable. But other classes are no more tolerant of linguistic nonconformity.

Much as one would wish it were otherwise, there is little doubt that we do not live in an epoch when literary elegance in writing or speaking has any distinctive value for even the college graduate. Precision is regarded at best as a professional matter, although what is precision for one man is jargon for another. Literary quality is a concern of the professional writer and critic.

One might repeat these observations about mathematics. Despite the increased need for mathematicians in the sciences and in industry, the nonspecialist probably does less computing than his counterpart fifty years ago. Business machines have taken over a great deal of computation once done mentally or by hand. Modern supermarket cash registers, for example, require no more from the operator than the ability to recognize and punch in the amount of money received from the customer and the total amount of the purchase. The amount of change due is then displayed for both customer and operator to see.

The concepts of quantity, of fractions, of percentages, and

of ratios do have a use—an interpretive rather than a calculative or applied use. As for the computational skill itself, it needs to be replicated only in a rather narrow band of life situations, and it is hard to see why the requisite competence cannot be acquired before the end of the sixth grade.

This is not to condone the *status quo*. That the level of language and computational skill required of the nonspecialist in our culture is so low is a commentary on how the technological victory at one and the same time enriches material resources for the group as a whole and reduces the challenge to individual human ingenuity. The adding machine is a victory for the intellect of the few; it benefits the many, but not by making them better arithmetical computers.

The point of this discussion is that to justify the three R's in terms of current adult utility means to justify a relatively low development in them—a level probably reached in the elementary grades. If, however, ordinary life usage of the symbolic skills changes in the emergent culture, then the requirements of general education in the secondary school will also change. If, for example, the citizens of tomorrow cannot get by with reading the headlines of the newspaper, or listening to the five-minute news reports; if post-secondary schooling is to be the rule rather than the exception; if the ordinary citizen cannot read, listen, and talk adequately without a fairly high order of symbolic skill development, then the elementary-school dosages of the language and mathematical skills will not be sufficient.

LANGUAGE SKILLS IN THE HIGH SCHOOL

What, then, are the uses of schooling in the skill area that can reasonably be anticipated? We can begin with reading.

Aside from, or perhaps in addition to, the usual use of reading for ordinary information and diversion, there is reading for citizenship. A large portion of such reading involves the use of concepts taken from economics, psychology, sociology, mathematics, political science, biology, and virtually every other well-developed intellectual discipline. As has been pointed out in Chapters III and IV, the knowledge presupposed is not used applicatively or replicatively; the citizen does not use these disciplines as does the specialist. He uses them for perspective, for interpretation.

For example, reading about the economic state of the nation, even in a newspaper, is not simply the decoding of information by the reader. It is not even like reading the account of a fire or the sinking of a ship at sea. It is more like reading the description of a baseball, football, or hockey game. A foreigner who had studied English in his secondary-school days could make out the account of a fire, but probably not that of a football game. Unless the reader has mastered the special vocabulary proper to the various sports, discourse about such events is virtually unintelligible. Not even all native-born Americans can understand it. In the case of the discourse of economics, what, for example, is one to make of the announcement that the Federal Reserve Board has ordered an increase in interest rates? Can the reader who is ignorant of the workings of the credit system make any more sense out of this than the Russian who reads, "Maris Clouts 60th Round Tripper"?

To verify the point, the reader is urged to examine the Sunday supplements of *The New York Times* or *The New York Herald Tribune*, or the columns of *Newsweek, Harper's, Atlantic,* and similar publications. Can a sixth grader read them? Mechanically, probably. With comprehension, probably not. The case is analogous with mathematics. The citizen of tomorrow may not have to compute any more than he does now; with growth of automatic business machines, even less. But without well-developed concepts of number, statistics, and, above all, a fairly clear notion of how the sciences use mathematical expressions to describe our world, even the columns of his newspaper will be a tower of Babel. And if this should come to pass, then in what sense can he be asked to think for himself and the common good?

This interpretive use of symbolic systems defines their role in the secondary school. Assuming that the purely mechanical aspects could be mastered in the first six grades, what is left for the secondary school to do? It seems obvious that the time in Grades 7–12 should be devoted primarily to the interpretive or categorical use of these symbol systems, their use as cues to decode the meanings and relations of ideas, as vehicles for the logical operations described and discussed in Chapter VI.

This means, first, that much of the "reading" will be done as pupils study subjects other than reading. Every intellectual discipline has a set of symbols whereby it encodes concepts peculiar to itself; ordinary discourse is inadequate to decode it. This gives a more urgent, albeit somewhat different, meaning to the slogan that every school department teaches reading and writing. It means that the symbolic skills peculiar to a logically organized subject are not being taught by the English department as part of general rhetoric and must be taught as a part of the discipline.

It would clarify matters to use a term other than "reading" for the kind of symbolic activity that is called for in economics, chemistry, or history classes. It is a kind of study rather than what we ordinarily call reading. One does not read a textbook as one reads a story or a list of travel directions.

The kind of skimming and scanning that makes for rapid narrative reading will not do for study. Study reading is a kind of rethinking of the thoughts of the author on written or printed cues. Speed is less of a problem than accuracy of insight into the system of relations among ideas; it is not a word-for-word translating process. Nor is it the association of the word with its ordinary or even its dictionary definitions.

Here lies the core of the professors' complaints about poor reading and the reason for the numerous remedial reading clinics that colleges feel called upon to operate for "qualified" high-school graduates. College instruction, for the most part, consists of linguistic presentations to the student, in oral or written form. When a "course" deals with materials that are logically organized, each topic is a set of arguments in favor of one hypothesis rather than another. Within the argument one finds descriptive materials, to be sure, but they consist largely of descriptions of facts, experiments, developments on which the theory of the subject depends. Every such course is or should be a course in the logic of the subject.

The better the college course, the better the instructor, the more the emphasis is on understanding the argument, the interpretation of the facts, and their relation to problems in the domain being studied. Suppose that the entering student "reads" his assignment as he does a newspaper or a novel, that is, merely as a narrative or as a description. Suppose he has formed the habit of answering quiz questions by recalling as much as he can from his reading that seems associated with them. Suppose he mistakes the experiments in the lesson as ends in themselves rather than as illustrations of theory. He fails, or he does far less well than he thought he should, taking into account the amount of "studying" he has done. He and his counselor are likely to agree that something is wrong with his reading, and off he goes for remedial work. But, if he merely learns to read narrative and descriptive materials faster, his basic trouble is not touched. Study reading had better be treated for what it is—a branch of the logic of the subject matter being studied—and this type of "reading" the high school can emphasize with profit. How much of this is a skill can be debated, but since it improves with practice, it has a skill element in it.

Another type of reading also goes beyond the language arts as taught in the elementary grades: the reading of mature literature as an art form. Here, again, is a type of symbolic activity that differs from reading materials for information or for concept reconstruction. Invoking the imagery that is so important an ingredient of literary materials is not a simple decoding of language. The cues are intended to reconstruct or arouse images and subtly shaped feeling complexes. There is a real question whether this kind of decoding is possible without certain kinds of life experience and experience in the *making* of literature (see Chapter XIII).

If ordinary current usage is the standard, the level of literary comprehension can be modest. If, on the other hand, to be genuinely individual in the emergent society entails a high order of literary receptivity, then the sixth grader is poorly equipped to appreciate high-grade poetry or prose either in classic or in contemporary form. Reading literature and poetry is not so much a language art as part of the literary art, just as reading musical notation and the use of paint and clay are parts of their respective arts. If the elementary school develops the rudiments of these skills, the secondary school can be allotted the task of practicing and perfecting them.

To the secondary school one might therefore look for study of the logic and structure of language in general and of the native tongue in particular: of the different types of discourse and propositions; of the uses of language in science, ordinary description, definition, explanation, persuasion, the common fallacies of language.

In brief, a good deal of what is now studied in higher education as linguistics and semantics should become the main fare of the secondary curriculum in the language arts.[1] Whether this should be a separate course, part of every course, whether it should supplement or displace the conventional study of grammar, and kindred questions are topics on which study and experimentation are in progress. There are stirrings in this direction, for example, Project English, but the trends are not yet clear. It may be that the *structure* of language will become the focus of secondary language study rather than syntactical correctness based on grammatical rules.[2]

Another phase of language study involves the psychology and logic of communication. A good description and a good piece of

[1] This deliberate study of linguistics is not the same thing as using the linguistic approach in the teaching of language.
[2] *Why* we have these rules takes us into a study of the development of our language and the family of Indo-European languages of which it is a member. This kind of language study, however, has little to do with correct usage and properly belongs to what are called "developmental studies" in Chapter XII. The development of language is one of the most fascinating episodes of world history.

argumentation do not have the same linguistic structure or the same criteria for "goodness." A lively narrative and an accurate narrative make different demands on the writer. Value statements differ from descriptive ones. Propaganda differs from report. Evocative language designed to arouse emotion differs from language that refers to objects in space and time, and the ritualistic, ceremonial use of language differs subtly from other uses.

Reference has already been made to the artistic or literary use of language. Here words are used to evoke aesthetic responses on the part of the reader; it is the appreciative and aesthetically expressive use of language. We know comparatively little about teaching or learning this use, although we have ample reason to believe that it entails elements not found in the other uses. There are people so literal-minded as to be unable to read poetry or fiction, and some appreciative readers flounder in argumentative discourse.

Accordingly, it might be well to reconsider the traditional combining of composition and literature in the English department. The prerequisites for teaching rhetoric or communication skills are quite different from those required to teach the appreciation of literature or the arts of literary composition. Literary writing and literary reading are both special types of communication, for which the communication experts are as unlikely teachers as people trained in literature as an art are for teaching the language arts in their nonliterary forms. The citizen of the future needs both with equal urgency, but this is not a compelling argument for their amalgamation into one instructional department. This unity made sense so long as the culture was operating in the great rhetorical tradition in which literature provided both the form and much of the content of man's knowledge. This, of course, is no longer the case, so that the lumping of literature and "English" is neither a marriage of necessity nor convenience.

The general transfer value of the study of language as distinguished from the practice of right usage is this: By becoming sophisticated and adept at distinguishing the various uses of language and the diverse rule systems for such uses, the student acquires a conceptual framework for language that serves him well in all types of reading, although it does not teach him the special set of concepts characteristic of a given discipline. This is the justification for the language arts as a major ingredient in secondary education.

This assumes, of course, that the elementary school perfects the mechanics of language sufficiently to enable the student to undertake the new type of language study in the secondary school, and that remedial work in mechanics does not have to be carried beyond the eighth grade. This assumption may, of course, be challenged on the facts; but before one sacrifices the ideal, it would be well to ask whether or not remedial efforts beyond the eighth grade, if the first eight years have been fully exploited, bring sufficient results to justify them.

Some will say that the proposed language-arts curriculum ceases to be the development of a skill and becomes the study of a conceptual system much as any science is. There is a sense, of course, in which the study of the logic and structure of language ceases to be part of language art or skill. Yet there are intellectual skills as well as manual ones. Among the intellectual skills, one can list any symbolic operation that comes to be performed more or less automatically with a certain degree of precision. In this sense, thinking can become a skill, language and concept discrimination can become a skill, study can become a skill, and research can become a skill. As logical operations these are forms of thought; as skills they are the psychological maneuvers we perform again and again in our thinking, studying, and research behaviors.

The same sort of change from skill to concept may come about in the mathematics curriculum, where emphasis is shifting to the study of the nature of number and number relations and away from the memorization of operational rules and the practice of computational techniques. Not that skills are unimportant, but the interpretive use of mathematics demands a conceptual framework that computation as such does not give. On the contrary, it is argued that, given the interpretive competence, the applicative and replicative uses of mathematics are also improved. Given sufficient operational experience with numbers in the earlier years (see Chapter VI), the secondary level of mathematics does become a concept-formation and concept-refinement experience rather than the perfection of a skill.

Just as the interpretive use of mathematics seems to be the proper emphasis in the secondary curriculum, so does the interpretive use of language seem to be the proper emphasis of the language studies. Like mathematics, it does involve skill elements and, also like mathematics, it can be the most general of all studies, because there is no realm of human behavior or study that does not employ a language structure in some form or another. Every discipline can be thought of as a special form of language usage, although this is hardly exhaustive of the activities that make up the discipline. One would expect communication, study, and even ordinary intercourse to benefit from a thorough interpretive training in the language structures employed by man to order and express his experience.

Foreign Languages

Foreign languages present a peculiar problem to a common curriculum of general studies. Does everyone need to study foreign languages? One hears the argument that everyone ought to be adept at some foreign language, but it is difficult to say why, or which one. If there were one international language, the situation would be simpler and better. As matters now stand, one can only say that the national interest makes it advisable, but not strictly necessary for as many citizens as possible to speak another language, and because such adeptness has to be inculcated early in life, some foreign language in elementary and secondary schooling becomes a requirement of the times. Simple, ordinary, conversational usage seems to be all that is envisioned, with some reading knowledge to be acquired in the later years, presumably at the secondary level. In other words, the division of the symbolic skills called foreign languages would constitute in the secondary school about what is taught of the native language in the elementary school. It is tempting to suggest that "speaking and listening" competence in one or two foreign languages be made part of the elementary curriculum, and that during the secondary years opportunities for practice on a noncourse basis be afforded to everyone. This is not a satisfactory solution, and it is not adopted in this book, but neither is the offering of a wide variety of languages feasible, for the variety promises to be endless (see Chapter XV, "A Program of Studies").

Perhaps the difficulty with the question of the foreign languages in the general educational curriculum stems from the fact that people try to justify them on an applicative basis. It would be useful, they say, to know foreign languages if one travels, or it would be helpful to have a reading knowledge of French, German, or Russian if one is to do graduate work in universities that make language competence a prerequisite for the doctor's degree. Or one needs foreign language in order to work in the diplomatic corps or for a foreign branch of one's firm. These observations make sense, but they point to a vocational or a specialist use of foreign language rather than to an interpretive use.

Suppose one were to say that in order to understand the world situation today one ought to be able to read the newspapers of Russia, France, Germany, China, and India. But what about the newspapers of Ghana and Nigeria and Malaya and Indonesia? What about the various regional languages within Russia and China? The absurdity of the requirement of numerous foreign languages for common education does not affect at all what one's special schooling might entail in this regard. So far as citizenship is concerned, we might better put our efforts into developing an enlightened, free, and industrious press to translate into English what is going on in the world, rather than to try to make everyone multilingual.

OTHER ARTS AND SKILLS

In addition to the linguistic symbols and mathematical symbols, the use of which involves a high element of skill, there are other skills that from time to time have had a place in the curriculum. Some of these have to do with symbols, but not of the discursive kind used in ordinary linguistic communication or the kind of symbols used in mathematics.

Artistic Skills

We do from time to time speak of the languages of music, the dance, drama, painting, and the like, and this might lead to grouping these languages with the language arts and mathematics as symbolic skills. But if there are such languages, their structure and use differ considerably from those mentioned. Musical notation is, of course, analogous to mathematics; it is a set of directions for making musical sounds, and the notations correspond point for point to these sounds. Similarly, but in a far less precise fashion, certain dance movements signify emotions or actions. Certain devices, for example, the halo and foreshortening, are conventionalized means of conveying certain effects in painting. Nevertheless, mastery of these symbols or signs tells the beholder very little of what the work of art intends to convey. It would be odd to say that Michelangelo expressed himself through the symbolic means of the cross, halo, angels, and the like, or that Beethoven expressed himself through musical notation and Nijinsky through *entrechats,* or that Shakespeare expressed himself through words and phrases.

The vestibule to works of art is often the knowledge of the techniques used, and appreciation is often facilitated by such awareness. But since these techniques cannot be taught fruitfully apart from the making of art objects, whatever symbolic skills do inhere in them have to be learned in that segment of the secondary curriculum devoted to the fine and applied arts (see Chapter XIII, "Evaluational Maps: Exemplars"). It is understood that this presupposes considerable use of art techniques in the elementary grades. Where this assumption does not hold, it becomes necessary to give the pupil a chance to learn these skills in the earlier part of the secondary grades. The alternative is a kind of aesthetic and artistic illiteracy that effectively closes the door to self-development. How far this skill should be developed is not certain, but the role of technique and "doing" in the appreciative phase of aesthetic experience is important. One would like to think or perhaps dream of everyone being able to express himself in painting, music, and poetry, or in some other set of arts, as freely as he does in language. This degree of competence would take a fairly high order of technical training, perhaps that of a talented amateur. Why such a goal seems fantastic is hard to say; perhaps because so little curricular time in the early years of schooling is given over to it; perhaps because our culture offers no reinforcement for it.

Yet before we dismiss the goal as a dream, we ought to remind ourselves that in the emergent society there are potentialities for self-cultivation in terms of time and money the like of which the world has not yet seen. It may well be that in a leisure-centered culture, self-cultivation will receive the reinforcement that now is reserved for work and its rewards. A school and a curriculum that look to the future should not sell these potentialities short.

The artistic skills of impression or appreciation—the skills of looking and listening and imagining, the skills of making fine discriminations in form and expressiveness—can also be taught from the elementary school onward, but whereas the manipulative skills of expression are best learned early, the skills of impression can be developed fully only in intensive study of works of art, a part of the curriculum that can best be realized in the secondary school.

Bodily Skills

There is a long and respectable educational history favoring the development of bodily skills as part of common education.

The Greeks called it "gymnastic" and included in it not only the exercises conducive to athletic and military prowess, but also the bodily control needed for posture and gesture in the formal dance and the reciting of poetry.

In our time the case for athletic competence is powerfully stated with respect to interscholastic sports and not so enthusiastically for individual physical fitness and bodily grace, although President John F. Kennedy and his Council on Physical Fitness tried to alter this. If it can be argued that such a regimen can be taught with benefit to all, and that it cannot be acquired without formal tuition, then it has a place in common education. In other words, if it is a direct goal of instruction, then it is part of the curriculum on an even footing with all other components of the curriculum. If, on the other hand, physical education is restricted to bodily activities needed for good health, but which do not need tuition, it is on no different footing from eating nutritious lunches, cleaning one's teeth, care of this or that physiological function. It may be carried on at the school for convenience, but it is not necessarily part of the curriculum. Once life outcomes are regarded as formal school objectives, it is difficult to know what to include or exclude. By making social gratification a school objective, the school is forced to justify an expensive system of interscholastic spectacles that has little to do with physical *education* or even with physical fitness as such.

In seeking a rational design for the secondary curriculum as a program of common education, one needs to inquire, as with the symbolic skills, about the use of the bodily skills in life by the nonspecialist.

The average citizen is concerned with his health in two ways: *cognitively*, he needs to understand the workings of his body, the causes of disease, and the principles of hygiene. And in these days of psychosomatic emphasis, this could apply to mental health as well as physical. Somewhere in the curriculum, there should appear the knowledge that enables the citizen to understand these matters.

The other concern might be called *practical*, in the broad sense in which one would say that achieving mental or physical health is a practical as well as a cognitive enterprise. Habits of eating, elimination, exercise, visiting the physician, are included in this area. Although it is easy to see where the cognitive use can be anticipated in the curriculum, it is not so easy to see how the public high school can do very much about anticipating the practical use. Are pupils really to carry on these activities on a practice basis under the eyes of a guide? In a private boarding school this is precisely what is expected, but even there this regimen is regarded as a feature of life at the school rather than as part of the curriculum.

Whether physical training as a means to military fitness or a healthy life should be in the curriculum depends not only on whether or not it requires systematic tuition, but also on whether or not the tuition will produce the desired life outcome. We do not know what the relationships here are. We do not know how many hours a week of physical training and supervised play produce military fitness or habits that endure through adult life. Unless we are ready to extend the school day well beyond its present length, or unless we are ready to utilize summer vacations for this purpose, it is hard to justify curricular time for healthful living as such, although no such strictures need apply to extracurricular opportunities for physical exercise, sports, and tuition in them. One lives in the school as one lives in the home and in the community. The living situation at school should encourage and provide optimal conditions for "good" social and physiological life. Accordingly, games, exercise, clubs, dances are appropriate nonacademic activities to be performed at the school, under school supervision and direction. They are not less important than the academic activities, and for life they may even be more important. Contrary to an often-expressed principle, this does not mean that physical training or social dancing or camera clubs need be part of the program of studies, be awarded academic credit, and so on.

Indeed, the school can stipulate the kind of social and personal life pupils lead while *at* school in order to remain members of the school. Every social institution can in principle do this. Private schools regulate virtually all phases of the pupil's life and charge fees for doing so. Public schools for practical reasons cannot do so, certainly not so completely and systematically.

Health skills and habits as well as social skills can and should be practiced at school; conceivably, if the school gave sufficient attention to itself as a "living environment," it could develop these skills and habits to the point where their replicative use in nonschool life would be assured.

On the same line of reasoning, one can argue that if a school wishes to integrate its living environment with that of the nonschool community, it should be able to do so without setting up a conflict with its instructional program. Interscholastic sports, big school bands, public theatrical performances, impressive proms, and the like are life activities. The school and the community have to choose what kind of life activities the *school as an institution* will represent.

A better case for "general" physical education can be made out if one argues for its need in self-cultivation or self-development. Mastery over one's body, its use as an expressive instrument of the inner life, as an object that gives aesthetic satisfaction, are outcomes that do not accrue automatically and probably do require tuition. Looked at in this way, however, the physical-education program in the secondary school needs radical reorganization and re-emphasis, a task that deserves the attention of physical-education theorists.

In terms of current use, as with the language and computational skills, there is little point in urging either more school time or a different program of physical education. For a different level of use in the new society, the story could be different. With the prospect of more leisure and a decrease in hard physical labor on the job, the maintenance of health and muscle tone may have to become an object of systematic attention and therefore part of the curriculum.

Industrial Arts

Should the industrial arts constitute part of a common secondary-school curriculum? Again, the criteria of vocational, citizenship, and self-cultivation needs in the emerging society should be invoked. In addition, however, one should ask whether such learnings as qualify on the use criterion require formal tuition, and whether the school is the only place in the community where such tuition is obtained.

Under industrial arts one might include: (1) the skills of using certain basic tools and (2) the understandings of the technological processes underlying our culture. The use of a hammer and chisel might be examples of the first, and the understanding of electronics in automation could be an example of the second.

The obvious use of the skills in tool manipulation is clear enough. All householders need these skills, and perhaps it is no longer possible to pick them up informally as one once did on the farm or as chore boy. Today, both men and women paint houses, work in the garden, repair faucets, lay floors, and the like, and do not have much chance to do it until they are adult.

Nevertheless, these skills can be and are picked up at the level of amateur use by trial and error and by following directions on the do-it-yourself kit. Furthermore, with the increasing complexity and delicacy of household appliances and automobiles, even the most daring do-it-yourselfer is balked by lack of special tools and specialized skill. In other words, industrial processes are becoming more specialized, and thus require intensive training, or they are reduced to processes that can be picked up by trial and error and a willingness to follow the directions on the package.

These considerations militate against the inclusion of industrial arts merely as tool skills in general education, even though their nonschool use is obvious.

Knowledge about industrial processes, however, is not in the same case. One can hardly understand our economy without understanding the major types of processing that goods undergo and the technological devices used in the processes. Such understanding, however, is not itself a skill to be practiced, but rather a perspective to be acquired. Since modern technology is rooted in the sciences, part of this perspective should come from the study of science. Part, as is demonstrated in a subsequent chapter, can come from a study of how our culture developed, which includes the evolution of industrial technology. The use of knowledge about technology in common education is interpretive rather than applicative or replicative. The problem, therefore, is not one of whether to include it, but rather where and how to do so.

To anticipate objections that are sure to be raised, it should be noted at this point that the argument that industrial skills and arts are needed to solve or to help solve the dropout problem has not been considered. For one thing, industrial arts and vocational training are not the same thing; for another, the dropout problem is not entirely an educational one. The level of economic activity, automation, and racial discrimination are also factors in the situation. The writers are concerned primarily with a common program of general studies rather than with specialized education for immediate occupational use. They do not deny the need for this, or that the schools should provide it; the question is whether it ought to be done in a secondary school that is to furnish a common education through Grade 12. A later chapter argues that specialized training is so necessary for *everyone* that one layer of our educational system should be devoted exclusively to it, rather than treating it as a substitute for, or as an orphan of, common, general education.

CHAPTER XI

DEVELOPMENT OF CONCEPTS THROUGH THE BASIC SCIENCES

The preceding chapter might be regarded as dealing with schooling for replicative use, because skills are largely so used. However, this book has argued that, so far as the nonspecialist is concerned, the dominant use of schooling is interpretive, although certain logical operations are used applicatively by everyone.

Interpretation of experience has been discussed in terms of two uses of concepts, the cognitive and valuative (Chapters VIII and IX). The next question is: How shall the materials of instruction be organized in order to help the student build the conceptual maps needed to cognize or understand his world? The problem that the school faces was pithily stated by Glenn T. Seaborg, Chairman of the United States Atomic Energy Commission. In his John Wesley Powell Lecture, he remarked: "In the past two decades our democracy has ingested science, but it has not yet digested it—a measure of the infancy of our scientific society."[1]

With regard to the cognitive use of concepts, two types of study are drawn on, basic sciences, discussed in this chapter, and developmental studies, dealt with in Chapter XII. In Chapters XIII and XIV two other types of instruction are examined, value exemplars and molar social problems, which together are designed to provide the materials and experience needed for the development of the valuative maps.

[1] *Science,* CXXV, No. 3503 (February 16, 1962), 505-9.

The basic sciences, according to Tykociner, serve to systematize our knowledge of basic facts and relations.[2] These are the sciences of matter and energy, for example, physics, chemistry, astronomy, and geology; the biological sciences, such as botany, zoology, physiology, and genetics; the psychological sciences; and the sociological ones.

These and kindred disciplines are what we ordinarily mean when speaking about science in the curriculum, but before turning to them, it is necessary to look at language and mathematics as sciences, or as subjects that can be studied as conceptual systems.

LANGUAGE AND MATHEMATICS AS SCIENCES

The previous chapter discussed symbolic skills, including the three R's. But as the discussion probed further into the uses of the language arts and mathematics, it was seen that the skill element in each did not exhaust what one needs to know in these areas. It was seen that the language arts needed as supplements linguistics, semantics, and logic; while mathematics in the secondary curriculum had to go beyond computational skill. The reason for this is that linguistics, logic, and mathematics, among other disciplines, supply "symbols, abstract concepts, and operations for the purpose of ordering and communicating information in a consistent way. . . ."[3]

Because these disciplines are historically related to that part of the curriculum called the language arts, and because the skills of speaking, writing, and computing are not separated in school from the more theoretical aspects of language and mathematics, they were discussed in connection with the teaching of skills. Logically, however, language and mathematics can and should also be thought of as basic theoretical disciplines, and in the higher grades they should be studied as such rather than as skills.

[2] Joseph T. Tykociner, *Research as a Science—Zetetics* (Urbana: Electrical Engineering Research Laboratory, University of Illinois, 1959), p. 37.
[3] *Ibid.,* p. 22. Among the other symbolics of information, Tykociner also lists philosophy of science and general information theory.

With respect to mathematics, the traditional prescription has been a series of courses or subjects beginning with arithmetic and ending with solid geometry and trigonometry for the college-bound. Review algebra or so-called general mathematics has often been prescribed for those in the other curricula. It is, of course, tempting to appropriate this pattern for general education, but if what has been said about the interpretive use of knowledge makes sense, this sequence may not be the solution for general education, however helpful it is for pre-engineering or pretechnical training.

The nature of quantity and quantitative relations, the deductive nature of a mathematical system and its logical properties, the basic mathematical operations and their rationale—these are the constituents of the cognitive frame needed in general education. There is good reason to believe that the newer emphases in mathematics teaching are consonant with this view, but it would be desirable to scrutinize these curricula and to isolate the *key* understandings or guiding ideas they employ. Perhaps there is a minimal set which can be taught over a period of years, either in connection with the development of computational skills or as a separate set of courses. Since the whole problem of key concepts is discussed later in this chapter, it should suffice here simply to reiterate the contention that mathematics for general education is not simply the first one or two courses commonly prescribed for the college major in mathematics. It is rather the set of concepts needed for the mathematical interpretation of experience. How much of what is traditionally found in algebra, plane and solid geometry, and the like, and how many other mathematical concepts should be required for general mathematics, are the targets for many current studies.

With regard to language the situation is different. There is nothing in conventional curricula corresponding to linguistics, semantics, and information theory. Nor are such topics as the history and nature of language, its diverse uses, and logical properties ordinarily studied in the secondary language curriculum.

That general education might well include these topics or some introduction to the post-secondary study of them would seem to follow from the fact that language is one of the most general of all forms of human behavior, lying as it does at the heart of the symbol-making and symbol-using function and cutting across all other intellectual disciplines.

Because of the relative recency with which these studies have found a home in higher education and the fact that the impetus for them has come from persons trained in technical philosophy and structural linguistics, it is unlikely that high schools can recruit staff in sufficient numbers to incorporate these items into their instruction. However, until the need for instruction in these areas is made clear, it is unlikely that teachers will be oriented and adequately trained to meet the demand.

PRINCIPLES OF SELECTION IN THE PHYSICAL SCIENCES

Returning to the physical sciences, the major problem is selection. In principle, at least, every science is needed for a complete cognitive map. If a choice must be made, on what principles should it be made? Consider two possible criteria: the principle of *potential generality* and that of *interpretive use.*

The principle of potential generality was discussed in connection with the cognitive use of concepts in Chapter VIII. There it was argued that concepts can be arranged in a logical hierarchy, with the most general subsuming the less general. Of two sets of ideas that can be used in understanding phenomena, the one that can be used for explaining a wider variety of phenomena is the more general. In this sense, physics is more general than mechanics, the notion of an atom more fundamental and general than that of a molecule, and that of a cell more general than a type of tissue.

In accordance with this principle, the writers propose to limit the study of basic science to general science, physics, chemistry, and biology. The principle of interpretive use should be applied within these disciplines, however, and this means that only the key ideas and relations are taught. This minimal amount should be taught as science, that is, as logically organized subject matter, with the precision required for such study.

INTERPRETIVE USE AS A PRINCIPLE OF SELECTION

Although a full chapter has already been devoted to the interpretive use of schooling, reiteration of this theme is probably advisable. For if study of the sciences continues to be regarded as the first step on the ladder of specialist training, then obviously there will be objections to making the interpretive use primary.

Whether the recently projected National Science Foundation curricula in mathematics, physics, chemistry, and biology are really designed for intepretive use by all citizens, or whether they are primarily intended for the better preparation of the college bound on the way to their prospective vocational careers, is at this juncture not altogether clear. They seem to want to do both. When the materials are first examined, they give the impression that students below the top quartile of the secondary-school population could not master them, and some of the preliminary testing would seem to corroborate this conjecture. On the other hand, the proponents of new curricula in mathematics and science claim that these courses are not restricted either to the gifted or the college-bound student, although it is assumed that they prepare the student for college as well or better than do the more conventional courses. Whether or not any or all of the claims are justified, the intent of the new curricula is to provide high-school students with general rather than special education.

Another way of saying this is that these curricula are intended for interpretive rather than applicative or replicative use. Support for this contention can be found in the following characteristics: (1) the playing down of purely descriptive accounts of physical phenomena and technological application of principles, (2) emphasis on key or guiding ideas, and (3) stress on the methods of inquiry by which the sciences achieved their current status. Even the laboratory work is not intended as a means of developing manipulative skill, or even as a demonstration of the theory it exemplifies, but is designed to help the student appreciate the way in which science and technology interplay, and, above all, to give him the firsthand feeling of what happens when one uses the hypothetico-deductive-experimental method. In other words, the course is intended to provide the student with something very like the experience of the scientist.

One might argue that this kind of science teaching has as its aim the applicative use of science, but unless supplemented by a good deal of the detailed, advanced work in a given field, such study will remain interpretive. It will not be used to advance work in science or even to use science to solve life problems. It may, however, be the very best way for the citizen to learn to grasp almost intuitively the import of science for life and its problems.

The science teacher may not share this conception of science teaching. He may try to re-enact his own specialist training in his high-school teaching, in which case, he wants to teach for application, for the way the specialist uses science. The interpretive use of science may seem to him to smack of superficiality and soft pedagogy, although even a cursory glance at the new curricula should disabuse him of this notion.

There is also the problem of convincing the student himself that the sciences he is studying should be for interpretation rather than for immediate application. Nor is he clear about the kind of learning the interpretive use entails. To get some notion of how the uses of science are perceived by the college student, about three hundred undergraduates at a large state university were asked to rank seven uses of science: cognitive, theoretical, vocational, practical, recreational, methodological, and adjustative.

One-half of the students ranked in first or second place the adjustative use of science, which was defined on the questionnaire as "having sufficient knowledge to feel at home in a world where science is important." However, more than 40 per cent put into first or second place the practical use (putting anti-freeze in your car, washing synthetic fabrics, and so on), what this book calls the applicative use of science.

By rating the adjustative role of science so highly, these students affirmed the importance of interpreting the world scientifically. Yet only 18 per cent assigned the cognitive use of science first or second place. (The cognitive use was defined as "being able to read scientific books and articles with understanding.") How they expected to use science for interpretation without reading scientific materials is not easy to understand. As a matter of fact, twice as many students placed the theoretical use of science (enjoying a knowledge of science for its own sake; obtaining information to satisfy curiosity) in first and second place as ranked the reading of scientific books and articles with understanding in these positions. Again, one wonders how they plan to "do" science or "enjoy" science without reading scientific materials, because to read such materials one needs to have learned the ideas and language of science.

It was apparently not clear to these respondents that to feel at home in a world where science is important means a mastery of the key concepts of the basic sciences, and mastery is not to be confused with mere familiarity. The interpretive use of science involves more than passing familiarity with and diffuse admiration for science. On the contrary, interpretation calls for a highly precise use of concepts, although not in a replicative or applicative way.

Thus, even among many college students the impression persists that the study of science is justified by its usefulness in dealing with such individual, everyday technological problems as coping with the family automobile and household appliances. It cannot be denied that a good course in physics helps make the workings of these appliances more intelligible (knowledge about our technology helps even more), but it does not necessarily help one to fix a broken pump or the transmission system of an automobile. Between the understanding and the doing lies a layer of rules and tools, know-how and skills. When this layer becomes thick and complicated, as it does in our highly developed technology, science as such cannot be used by the layman to fix automobiles and water faucets. For this reason, our society is as dependent on the technician as it is on the scientist: the layman can no more take on the duties of either on a moment's notice than he can quickly take on the duties of a modern soldier. Hence the stress on the importance of differentiating between the applicative and the interpretive uses of science. Science in general education cannot be justified on the grounds that it will help the individual operate and repair machinery, on the one hand, or that he will use it in his vocation, on the other. It is on the grounds of interpretation, on the need we all have to understand our world and society, that the justification must be based.

When science is used interpretively, we ask that it help us think and discourse about such questions as the following: What is it? How is this related to other things? What consequences can I expect from it? How did it come to be what it is? What laws describe the way it behaves? How does its behavior correlate with the behavior of certain other things? We are asking for information that will allow us to place the object of our inquiry into a cognitive or knowledge perspective.

Examining these questions more closely, one sees that some of them ask for classificatory information: To what class of objects does a thing belong? Is this class a subclass of a larger class? For example, is the cancer problem to be classified as a problem of chemistry or as a subtopic of physics? Is it an infection? Is it a type of cell growth? Does it belong to the group of diseases caused by viruses? By tissue injuries? In the early stages of inquiry, definitions are needed to help sort out whatever information one happens to have about infectious diseases, the effects of radiation on cell growth, and so on. Later, as one becomes more familiar with the matter, one realizes that the classification problem has not yet been solved. Indeed, if one could determine clearly to what group of diseases cancer belonged, the next steps would be much clearer. Inquiry is oriented by classification, and by refining classification knowledge is rendered more precise.

In addition to classification questions, there are questions about causal relations and relations of covariation. What causes what and what varies with what are the two most important questions one can ask. The greater the number of items that can be tied together in a logical relational net, the better orientation is, and the more revealing is the perspective. This net of relations is woven by the basic and the developmental sciences, which are discussed in this chapter and the next. One outcome of general education should be the formation of such a categorical or conceptual net.

The specialist, it has been noted, also operates out of interpretive frames: the same in fact as those of the nonspecialist, but the specialist does not stop with understanding. He cannot stop with orienting his problem. The specialist either goes on to augment the knowledge of which his frame is constructed, or he goes on to apply it in practice. For either of these purposes, knowledge has to be more detailed, more self-conscious about the circumstances of its origin and development, and more closely related to technology than is required for interpretation alone.

KEY CONCEPTS AS PRINCIPLES OF SELECTION

The amount of knowledge and the rate of its accumulation and change are so great that the high school cannot solve the problem of selection without making the following decisions:

1. *To limit each basic science or group of sciences to the minimal set of basic ideas and, wherever possible, to concentrate on those notions that are fundamental to the understanding of more than one discipline.* Atomic structure, for example, is as

necessary to chemistry and biology as to physics, while scientific method and temper, which all of the new curricula claim they are fostering, must be so common to all the sciences that the need for stressing them by long and extensive experimentation in each and every course could be avoided.

2. *To regrade certain of these key concepts to lower levels of schooling.* Obviously, not every concept can be taught before there is an occasion to use it. The biologists would like to introduce their subject before large numbers of young people leave high school, but they also believe that biology students need certain concepts of physics and chemistry as prerequisites. The problem would be nearer to a solution if an easier version of the basic physical and chemical concepts could be taught in the lower grades. The experimentation now in progress gives some promise that this regrading can be accomplished.

3. *The notion that a given key concept can be taught at different levels is strategic if Grades 7–12 are to give common education.* Although the new curricula that have been mentioned claim to be suitable for the general high-school population and do not correlate too highly with measures of scholastic ability, it is still doubtful that the materials in their present state are within the range of the lower 50 per cent of the school population.

Granting that the approach through experimentation and induction eases cognitive strain, granting that interesting materials help motivation, it will still be necessary to teach the same concepts at more than one level of difficulty.

An encouraging sign that this is not impossible is furnished by a comparison of the unit on gravitation in the University of Illinois Elementary Science Project in Astronomy[4] with that in the high-school physics text put out by the Physical Science Study Committee.[5] Both treatments have been judged to be scientifically sound; both use the same type of approach in explicating the topic. The astronomy unit on gravitation takes up

[4] *Astronomy: Gravitation*, Book 3 (Rev. ed., 1963), J. Myron Atkin and Stanley P. Wyatt (Co-directors).
[5] Physical Science Study Committee, *Physics* (Boston: D. C. Heath, 1960).

motion and its measurement, matter and mass, acceleration, force, weight, how stars and planets move in the sky, theories of planetary motion, Newton's laws, and ends up with chapters on orbits near the earth, orbits around the sun, orbits out among the stars and far out among the galaxies.

Reading this material even in its trial form gives one the impression that, well taught, it, too, can give a frame of interpretation of which the average citizen would be proud and for which, presumably, the astronomers on the project would not apologize.

Between this treatment and that of the PSSC text, one can think of a continuum made up of treatments varying in levels of abstraction, degrees of complexity, rate of concept-input, amount of experimental data that has to be introduced and kept in mind, length of the chains of reasoning involved—in general, of cognitive strain. Yet, at each level, the key ideas can be taught with precision. The cognitive maps thus formed vary in size and subtlety; they map the same territory with equal accuracy, but with difference in details.

If this judgment is at all correct, there seems to be no theoretical obstacle to devising several or many versions of the gravitational unit and of analogous units. This means that individual differences can be met by different levels of the same course rather than by different courses. If this can be accomplished in a unit in physics, there is no reason why it cannot be accomplished in all the sciences or in all the logically organized disciplines.

KEY CONCEPTS IN THE NEW SCIENCE CURRICULA

That the new curricula in the sciences are committed to key concepts is clear from the statements made in authoritative articles published in the Spring, 1962, issue of *The School Review*.[6] Mention has already been made of the new mathematics

---

[6] Vol. LXX, No. 1. Published by The University of Chicago Press. Copyright (1962) by The University of Chicago. Unless otherwise indicated, numbers in parentheses refer to pages in this issue of the magazine.

programs, so only the reports on biology, chemistry, and physics are discussed here.

Writing about "Renascent Biology," Bentley Glass mentioned the following biological themes that must be treated at all levels of organization: "interdependence of structure and function, regulation and homeostasis, the genetic continuity of life, its evolution, the diversity of type together with unity of pattern, the biological roots of behavior, and the relation of organism to environment" (p. 19). "To insure that adequate attention would be given to the great pervading themes of biology, a special team was established" to see to it that they were introduced and stressed in the text materials (p. 28) prepared by the Biological Sciences Curriculum Study.

On the other hand, Glass was proud to claim, "For the first time, I think, education in the natural sciences, at least at the secondary level, has assigned the acquisition of scientific information and concepts a place of lesser importance than the understanding of the very nature of scientific enquiry . . ." (p. 41). One can agree with the secondary position of information, but the relegating of the concepts to a lower order of importance makes one wonder how seriously one is to take the Committee's devotion to key biological concepts as basic to general education. If scientific inquiry is the primary goal, then perhaps the student could learn it as well in physics. Equally dubious is the emphasis on the tentativeness of "knowledge" in science. From the fact that scientific views change, it is inferred that there is no truth to be found, although science is apparently capable of "accurate and confirmable observations" (p. 18).

The Chemical Bonds Approach Project, described by Laurence E. Strong in "Chemistry as a Science in High School," likewise adopts the pedagogical strategy of using experiments to introduce basic theory. For example, to distinguish compounds from saturated solutions, the effect of temperature on reaction proportions is explored. Structural models for atoms, molecules, and crystals are provided by the assumption that electrons behave as if they were spherical charge clouds, but to deal with the energy relations a conventional electron orbital model is introduced. The orbital and charge-cloud models are brought together by the assumptions that orbitals within the atom can hybridize when molecules are formed, so as to produce the appropriate geometrical relationships (pp. 47–49). Another set of regulative ideas are the three types of bonds: covalent, metallic, and ionic. One is impressed with the number of concepts indigenous to physics that the materials utilize, as well as by the emphasis on the methods by which scientists arrive at their conclusions.

The CHEM (Chemical Education Material Study) grew out of suggestions by a committee headed by A. B. Garrett of The Ohio State University. In 1960, according to J. A. Campbell, in his article "Chemistry—An Experimental Science," the director of CHEM, Glenn T. Seaborg, then Chancellor of the University of California, Berkeley, obtained a grant from the National Science Foundation to "investigate what could be done to produce the most effective high-school chemistry course possible" (p. 52).

In addition to using the experimental approach, the CHEM study gives an introduction to the electrical nature of matter, the mole concept, kinetic theory, dynamic equilibrium, structural properties, energies associated with phase changes, the periodic table, and systematic variations of chemical properties with atomic number (pp. 57–58).

Most explicit with respect to key ideas is the Physical, Science Study Committee, of which Gilbert C. Finlay has said: "The Committee chose to plan a course dealing with physics as an explanatory system, a system that extends from the domain inside the atom to the distant galaxies. . . . Achieving these aims in a one-year course meant that coverage of the field of physics had to be sharply restricted in favor of a deeper development of ideas that are central to a comprehension of the fundamentals of contemporary physical thought. This deeper development meant carrying key concepts to higher levels than have been ordinarily reached in secondary-school courses" (p. 65).

". . . [The] PSSC judged it wise to shift the emphasis away from technology toward a deeper exploration of the basic ideas of physics and the nature of the inquiries that can lead to these ideas" (p. 66). These were the ideas of space, mass, mass conservation, light, the particle and wave theories of light, motion, force, gravitation, the conservation of momentum and energy, electrical forces, electromagnetic radiation, the structure of atoms (pp. 70–71).

Perhaps "key concepts" is not a good term for what these projects have in mind. Key *theories* or key generalizations about the structure and dynamics of the phenomena they are studying probably come closer to the mark. These theories are introduced by having the pupil observe or experiment with a sample phenomenon. This raises questions analogous to those earlier experimenters encountered, and so, in an abbreviated fashion, the pupils re-enact the thinking that went into the development of theory and its testing.

The striking similarity of aims and methods in the curricula discussed leads to speculation about the advisability of uniting them all into one continuous school experience with science. The centrality of physics and logico-experimental method makes it reasonable to suppose that physics should be the basic subject, with biology and chemistry as special exemplifications of physics. The emphasis of all the curricula on the tentativeness of their findings and the rapid changes in the respective disciplines, if taken with the seriousness with which they are proposed, should likewise make the school chary of investing too much time on anything save the most general features of the sciences until the time for special education is reached.

One suspects that the case is overstated. Science is cumulative; developments, not brand-new starts, are the rule. The basic ideas, if reduced to a minimal set, are worth mastering, just as appreciation of the method is worth having. In using science for interpretation, one does not, in confronting a problem, ask, "What experiments can I perform to test an hypothesis?" Rather does one ask (if, indeed, one asks explicit questions), "What concepts in my knowledge are relevant here? What generalizations do I know that will give me the beginning of an explanation? What theories are used to justify these generalizations?" Without such a *categorical net* imprinted by schooling, appreciation of scientific method helps interpretation but little.

Fine as experiments are to motivate the learner and to concretize theory, the functional residue for life use is a set of ideas or concepts so general they accommodate a wide variety of phenomena within a given domain. Interesting as are the theoretical adventures of ideas, and stimulating as they are to learning and understanding, their successful use in interpretation does not necessitate the ability to recount the adventures.

Nevertheless, one should not preclude the possibility of a general science course made up of those concrete operations that lead to an intuitive grasp of the basic notions in physics, chemistry, and biology. Perhaps such experience in the elementary grades can serve as a precursor of systematic study of the separate sciences.

KEY CONCEPTS IN ECONOMICS

A similar trend to theoretical study of basic notions is found in *Economic Education in the Schools*, a report of the National Task Force on Economic Education, Committee for Economic Development.[7]

Some of the most valuable tools for studying the economic system are, according to the report, simple and easily accessible without excessive formal training in economics, and these are the ones that should be emphasized in the high schools. An example of such a concept is the supply-demand-price model that helps us to understand how the three factors generally

[7] New York: The Committee, 1961.

interact under prescribed conditions of competition (pp. 18–19).

In *Economic Literacy for Americans*, the Committee for Economic Development (1962) urged that items used as supplementary materials for a high-school economics course be analytical in nature. The application of this criterion ruled out much of the how-to-do-it type of reading, such as that dealing with how to buy and how to invest (p. 37).

Unfortunately, the number of concepts regarded as basic is large. Under major concepts and institutions are listed such items as scarcity, costs, productive resources, division of labor, economic production, savings, investment, capital formation, labor productivity, principle of diminishing returns, demand, supply, price, market, competition, profit and profit incentive, interdependence—the price and market system, economic efficiency, monopoly, public utility, corporations, government, expenditures, taxes, international specialization, balance of payment and trade, tariffs.

Also, gross national product, national income, per capita production and income, money and real income, price level, equation of exchange, aggregate demand, business cycle, depression, inflation, money—bank deposits and money creation through bank lending, central bank—federal reserve system, economic growth, underdeveloped areas, population problem.

Also, incomes as payment for productive services, personal distribution of income, real and money wages, labor unions—collective bargaining, strikes, picketing, closed-shop, featherbedding, economic security as a goal, social security, farm problem.

Perhaps this list could be condensed, or it may be that the theoretical treatment they require is not extensive. In any event, the intent of the Committee and the kind of course envisioned are both clear.

No doubt other disciplines will undertake to comb their accumulated treasures for key concepts and guiding ideas, and in the degree to which they succeed, an ever increasing proportion of our knowledge can be represented in the secondary-school curriculum. Indeed, the difficulty encountered by the economics group in reducing its "essentials" to a relatively small number is itself an index of the theoretical immaturity of the discipline. Sociology, anthropology, psychology are also in the throes of deciding what are their proper objects, and certainly the debate as to their proper methodology is far from settled. Theories and hypotheses abound, and the list of relevant variables seems endless.

Whether the social sciences can ever grow out of this state no one knows; but so long as they are in it, it is difficult if not impossible to formulate what they ought to contribute to general education, aside from a general respect for the complexity of life.

Hence, although the maturity of a discipline is not listed as a criterion for inclusion in the secondary-school curriculum, the relation of maturity to the possibility of finding minimal sets of key concepts makes it a factor in selection. The diffuse and complex character of the social sciences does not mean that they can be dispensed with in our cognitive maps; it does argue against an attempt to teach them as separate sets of logically organized subject matter in the secondary school.

For these reasons, another way of organizing concepts for instruction, one called "developmental studies," is discussed in the following chapter. Here that discussion can be anticipated by noting that the basic sciences and the developmental studies both furnish cognitive maps, but not of the same kind. The first is, as has been stated, a logical net or, to change the metaphor, a set of conceptual pigeonholes by which the fundamental knowledge about our world is sorted and related. The second views all the events we know anything about as woven into strands stretching back from the present into prehistory. The developmental studies tell how things came to be as they are; the basic sciences tell about the structures, the natures of things as they are.

Taking into account these criteria of selection, especially the criteria that have been called potential generality and interpretive use, so far as the basic sciences are concerned, the following programs could be prescribed:

1. Units on the study of language as a science
2. Units on the study of mathematics as a science
3. Course in general science
4. Course in biology
5. Course in physics
6. Course in chemistry
7. An optional course of college level in one of the basic sciences

The content and organization of this segment of the curriculum are discussed further in Chapter XV. However, a word may be said here about the course in general science. The argument developed in this chapter was for courses in the special sciences based on key concepts, theories, and generalizations. A general-science course, however, means cutting across the special sciences and concentrating on concepts common to all of them. As is indicated in Chapter XV, whether or not there are such common concepts, whether or not a course in such common concepts is worth teaching, and in what grades, if any, it should be taught are all debatable questions.

The writers are fairly well convinced that some such common concepts and logical operations do run through all the sciences, and it may be that children can comprehend these at an earlier age than was previously thought to be possible. Further, it may be that systematic study of the sciences as special disciplines will be helped by a preliminary encounter with the common concepts and operations which a good general-science course could provide.

As to what the central themes of a general course should be, there is a wide variation of opinion. As a sample of candidates for this honor, George Gaylord Simpson has remarked that the unity of science should be sought not in physics but biology, "not through principles that apply to all phenomena, but through phenomena to which all principles apply."[8]

[8] "Biology and the Nature of Science," *Science*, CXXXIX, No. 3550 (January 11, 1963), 81–87.

CHAPTER XII

DEVELOPMENT OF CONCEPTS THROUGH
DEVELOPMENTAL STUDIES

The basic sciences serve to organize and classify human knowledge as it now exists. When so taught and so learned, they can be used as cognitive maps to structure experience with order and some precision. What these sciences do not reveal is how our universe, our institutions, and our culture, that is, our technologies, our ideologies, our arts, and our sciences, came to be what they now are.

Nor do they tell us what we need to know about those disciplines that are devoted to anticipating the needs of our society or to meeting its current problems; yet part of the cultural capital is that great stock of methods which have been developed for accumulating, storing, elaborating, and disseminating the culture. Finally, the basic sciences give only an inkling of man's efforts to make sense of life as a whole and to find a meaningful goal for it. The role of science in the human quest is a tribute to man's highest powers, but it does not justify the quest itself.

Not all sciences are basic in the sense that Tykociner has defined them. That is to say, some of them serve not so much to organize our knowledge as to sustain the life of the social order by projecting its needs and devising ways of meeting them. Agriculture, medicine, technology, and national defense are examples of bodies of knowledge of this kind, and in a somewhat different way, so are political science, jurisprudence, economics, and administration, for they are concerned with the proper functioning of the society as a whole. As examples of disseminative sciences, Tykociner has cited education, educational psychology, vocational guidance, library science, journalism, and mass communication.[1]

Two points stand out when one reflects on this array of non-basic sciences. First is the obvious impossibility of including even a fraction of them in general education. Indeed, these bodies of knowledge characterize what is ordinarily meant by the content of professional rather than general education. How can some of the insights of these fields of study be incorporated into secondary schooling?

We are looking here for a kind of study that will give the student an interpretive map that can organize this vast array of information. The map provided by the basic sciences cannot do this, because much of the knowledge we are trying to map does not have to do primarily with knowledge itself; it does not seek to systematize, refine, and extend knowledge as the basic sciences do. Rather does this map scramble knowledge from the various basic sciences in order to make it useful for solving the problems of the social order. For example, agriculture uses knowledge from chemistry, physics, and biology, but its central concern is with the efficient production of food and fiber. Rarely is an agricultural problem simply a problem in chemistry or biology. Similarly, the problems confronting the citizen are rarely reducible to this or that combination of the basic sciences.

For these reasons, the writers propose that sets of studies called "developmental" be used to supply this sort of cognitive map. Following Tykociner's suggestion, these sets might be called the development of the universe, including life in our cosmos, the development of human institutions, and the development of the culture. Before discussing the contents of these three strands of the developmental studies, it may be profitable to say a word about what is meant by development.

A developmental account of anything, say, the family, can be a historical account of the events that led the family to take one form or another in consecutive periods of time. Strictly speaking,

[1] *Op. cit.*, pp. 30–33.

the historian can record only what happened: there was once this form of the family, and then there was another form, and then another. But such a set of descriptions does not tell why these different forms of the family are related to each other or how. Indeed, it does not tell whether there was any relation at all. Of course, little history is written in this bald descriptive form. The historian does relate events in terms of some theory about what events caused other events and why.

A widely accepted theory of how a given state of affairs developed through time is evolution. We say that the present form of the family evolved from older forms, and we mean by this something analogous to what Charles Darwin meant when he wrote about the origin and evolution of species of living things. Roughly, it means that the pressures of the environment favor the survival of one set of organisms rather than another. Thus, for example, a monogamous family stands a better chance of surviving in an environment where a man can support one wife and their offspring but no more. Some environments might favor polygyny and others polyandry.

Are all developmental accounts evolutionary? Not necessarily. To say that B developed from A is to imply that there is a continuity between B and A such that some elements of A are repeated in B, but that A and B are not identical. In this sense, John at ten weeks of age is developed from John at three weeks of age, or the school of today developed from the Colonial school.

An evolutionary development, especially since the writings of Darwin and Wallace were published, means that a given form of a living thing or an institution is the result of a fitness to survive in a given situation. It implies competition with other forms and victory over them. Thus, Karl Marx's description of the development of capitalism out of mercantilism and feudalism is an evolutionary account of an economic system.

Whether the evolutionary hypothesis can be invoked with equal ease in all types of development is problematic. In the proposed developmental studies, the emphasis is more on showing, if one can, why and how B succeeded A. At some times, the struggle for survival is more illuminating than at others in this story of development. It is more illuminating in the development of living species, for example, than in the development of the solar system.

To paraphrase an ancient doctrine, all development is explained when one can specify the previous state out of which an event emerged, the form or class it exemplified, the immediate cause of its occurrence, and the goal or purpose the change serves. Developmental studies are intended to examine the three major areas where change occurs: the physical environment of man, his socially devised arrangements for living in this environment, and the realms of meaning and aspiration as expressed in his artifacts.

Precisely because development is a temporal process, it can serve as a cognitive map. One can locate an event on this time line and project the trend into the future, a most important type of orientation.

DEVELOPMENTAL STUDIES I

It is generally agreed that the cosmos has undergone change, that it has a history. The planetary system as a whole, and indeed the entire galactic system, are believed to have emerged into their present form as a result of previous events.

Astronomy and geology, for example, are among the sciences which give accounts of these developments. However, these sciences contain much more than theories of development. The theories, after all, are attempts to account for basic data, such as the movements of planets and eclipses and differences in the composition of various layers of the earth. Much of these sciences deals with the results of observation, classification, methods of observation, and tools of observation and measurement.[2]

No one would seriously deny the importance of these sciences

[2] Tykociner has included under this group of sciences the following: cosmogeny (a part of cosmology), geogeny (a part of geology), biogeny (a part of biology), origin and development of species, and development and prehistory of *Homo sapiens*.

for general education and the desirability of studying them systematically if it were possible to do so. Yet, if a choice must be made, and if one asks what aspects of astronomy and geology are most needed for interpretive use, it is to the general theories of how the earth and celestial systems came to have their present characteristics and *how* scientists have developed the means for securing and interpreting their data that one would turn for an answer.

The problem, of course, is how to select the topics and materials with which these outcomes can be achieved. How much astronomy and geology must the pupil *do* in order to construct the cognitive map needed to interpret the import of celestial and terrestrial phenomena? How much does he need even to understand the "story" of the heavens and the earth?

At this stage of curriculum construction, a partnership between the educator and the astronomer or the geologist (unless both roles are happily combined in one person) is imperative. The educator is needed because astronomers, quite properly, want astronomy taught for the purpose of *doing* astronomy. The educator is needed to emphasize the difference between doing astronomy and using astronomy for interpretation. The astronomer is needed because whatever is taught should, first of all, be "good" astronomy, and only the professional astronomer is qualified to make this judgment.

The same sort of considerations can be adduced for constructing the developmental accounts of the development of living things, including man. One must note, however, that a whole group of sciences will have to be drawn upon for this account, so that the extent of collaboration and the number of decisions are enormously increased.

In addition to biology (which is to be studied separately), there are paleontology (the study of fossils), zoology, botany, climatology, various ecologies, and physical anthropology, to mention only a few of the sciences that deal with the development of living things. The same distinction between *doing* these sciences and using them to develop cognitive interpretive maps must be made; there are the same problems of selecting materials and arranging them for instruction as were discussed in relation to astronomy and geology.

Nevertheless, it is a selective rather than originative task. Each of the sciences mentioned does have a developmental aspect. Each, after all, does try to reconstruct the past. Each, in other words, includes a theory about how this reconstruction should be undertaken.

DEVELOPMENTAL STUDIES II

The second segment of the developmental studies reconstructs the development of the family, church, economic systems, governmental systems, laws, and other institutions devised by men to order and nurture their societies.

The materials for this strand of the developmental studies are drawn from anthropology, sociology, economic and political history, as well as the history of jurisprudence. The focus of this segment is on the role of social institutions in social change, and how social institutions develop under the stress of change in other sectors of human life.[3]

Much of this material has a difficult time getting into conventional courses. One student has found that the most widely used textbooks studied in history courses in Illinois high schools throw little light on either the facts or the theories of social change.[4]

[3] Tykociner has included a far wider range of materials in this category: embryological development of the human species, evolution of the family (a part of sociology), evolution of a group (part of sociology and group psychology), evolution of urban, rural, and metropolitan populations, evolution of ethnic groups (part of anthropology), evolution of communities, evolution of states (part of political science), and evolution toward a world community. Corresponding to each of these topics, Tykociner has listed the history of a particular instance of the class, for example, the history of a particular empire and the history of a particular federation of nations (*op. cit.*, p. 29).

[4] John Palmer, "History Textbooks and Social Change," *Social Education*, XXV, No. 3 (March, 1961), 135-36.

Courses in political science, sociology, anthropology, and economics are only infrequently found in the secondary curriculum, and there is little prospect that they all can be introduced as separate subjects. The arguments cited in the case of the sciences having to do with the evolution of the earth and life can be applied here. On the one hand, there is a crying need for the kind of knowledge embodied in these disciplines; on the other, there is no viable way of introducing all of them into the curriculum as separate subjects for systematic study.

In this connection, it may be noted that the Developmental Studies II displace the current courses in history in the curriculum, a point that will hardly elicit applause from the historians. Because historians and the teachers of history have been among the most adamant and vocal foes of the absorption of their subject into an area called "social studies," some further defense of the abolition of the conventional courses in history as a high school subject seems to be required.

One of the most cogent reasons for abolishing the study of history *in its present curricular form* is that it is highly resistant to learning. From time to time, surveys are made to find out how much history American citizens or college students remember. Invariably, everyone, including historians, is shocked by the results, and forthwith pressure is brought to teach more history. The survey conducted by *The New York Times* in the early 1940's and the subsequent debates are an example.

The historians and editorial writers would be less shocked if they reflected a little on how the average citizen uses history. How often does a man recite historical facts? Unless he teaches, writes, or reads a great deal of history, he rarely replicates the learnings of his school days. Nor does he apply them consciously to the current problems of the day. For one thing, the problems of the day are not the foci around which he learned history in the first place. How many of us have studied the history of taxation, international trade, collective bargaining, or the subsidization of agriculture?

But there is a more fundamental reason for the disappointing results that history has on the thought of the citizen. The citizen can "apply" or "interpret" in a situation to the extent that he can subsume it under some generalization. When he does this systematically, comprehensively, and with precision, we call it application; this is what the historical scholar does. When one uses generalizations merely to locate or identify a problem, that is, to gain perspective on it, we call it interpretation. Generalizations are needed for both uses, and it is in generalizations that history and history textbooks are likely to be deficient.

Thus, one writer[5] has said that the generalizations of history are such as the reader already knows, that is, those familiar to common sense. "Changes in mores and folkways are difficult in an established community," and "Political institutions reflect economic realities," are examples.

Furthermore, such generalizations as the historian does use come from disciplines other than his own, for example, psychology, as when Lincoln's death is explained by the assassin's insanity, or Alexander's conquests by a lust for power. Even the concepts used by the historian, such as conservation, social class, national debt, are borrowed from other disciplines.

"Curricula have been formulated and social studies teachers prepared as if what history explains is 'history' itself. Our analysis indicates that it is clearly not the school subject called history that enables us to understand the past but science—economics, anthropology, psychology, and the other sciences."[6]

All of this seems to mean that in order to make the study of history anything more than a bare chronology of names, dates, and places, the pupil should first be grounded in the social sciences. The hope that the basic concepts of the social sciences will be learned as a result of studying history seems poorly founded, especially if one relies on the commonly used textbooks in high school history.

[5] John Passmore, "Explanation in Everyday Life, Science and in History," *History and Theory*, II, No. 2 (1962), 105–23.
[6] John R. Palmer, "The Place of History in the Curriculum," *School Review*, LXXI, No. 2 (Summer, 1963), 214.

Palmer has also noted that few history texts can now justifiably be called "political histories." Geography, sociology, economics, psychology, and the history of science have influenced history texts. This would lead one to hope that history is already on the road to building developmental maps. Unfortunately, as Palmer has said, "It is difficult to acquire much understanding of these subjects by reading history. The flavor is often present but little of the substance. If generalizations from these fields have been used, they are not included in the narrative."[7]

Thus, in an analysis of history textbooks made by the American Economic Association, it was found that ideas fundamental to the understanding of the economy were omitted, although a few exceptions were noted (see bibliographical notes for this chapter).

It may perhaps be unreasonable to expect history to carry the pedagogical burden of giving understandings in the multiplicity of disciplines mentioned above. This is one reason for urging something like developmental studies as a way of organizing materials for secondary-school instruction. This does not dispense with historians, but it does call for greater participation by historians of science, economics, politics, sociology, and technology in the preparation of curricular materials.

Because not all the social sciences can be taught separately and systematically, a course that brings together the key events in the development of social and political institutions seems to be a promising way of evading the dilemma. Many attempts have already been made in structuring materials in this way. Notable examples are provided by the score or so of introductory courses in social science tried out at Chicago, Harvard, Columbia, and other schools concerned with general education programs.

The family, church, government, economic system, and school are among the key social arrangements in our life. Their functions determine much of what we do and are. For the individual to orient himself and the community's problems with respect to these institutions is no small part of general education. Developmental Studies II undertakes to trace the development of

[7] "The History Textbook as a Source of Generalizations," forthcoming.

such institutions in order to show *how* and *why* one form succeeded another, *how* and *why* the functions were modified, *how* and *why* social stress was manifested in these shifts of function.

The "how" and "why" indicate the role of the social sciences as a source of the materials, because the explanatory generalizations necessarily have to come from them. It follows that here again the curriculum-maker is calling for a vast collaborative enterprise. Again, it is a selective rather than an originating task. Much has already been done in these directions, but a clever experiment here and a project there do not make a curriculum. It is for agreement on a unifying set of themes that one can look to the leaders in social-science education.

DEVELOPMENTAL STUDIES III

The development of the cosmos and human institutions go a long way toward filling in our maps for cognitive interpretation. They provide concepts and generalizations and causal sequences into which many life situations can be fitted for interpretation.

There are, however, still other elements needed for our cognitive maps. These are the ideas and the artifacts by which human needs are expressed and fulfilled. The press is a social institution, but the printing press was the artifact that made the press the power it is. Art, literature, philosophy, religion, technology, and the development of the sciences themselves are events that need to be understood.

Once more, the difference between *being* artistic, religious, inventive, literary, or scientific and *knowing about* these activities must be reiterated. While knowledge about art or religion may or may not affect our attitudes and behavior, it is not the same as "doing" these things. As has already been noted, our judgment may or may not coincide with our preferences. It is in the strand of the curriculum called "exemplars" that these two components of value experience are brought together.

Whenever we try to combine knowledge in a subject with knowledge about it, one or the other suffers. Trying to understand the role of chemistry in the development of the culture, for example, is bound to take time from studying chemical phenomena and theory.

Hence, something like cultural history or the history of culture is needed to complete the cognitive map. Just as social institutions affect our thought and action, so do the ideologies and technologies of the culture. Following Tykociner, the general topics to be developed in Developmental Studies III are the developmental accounts of human culture, including its sciences, technologies, art, literature, systems of ideas, and religions.[8]

Naturally, there will be overlapping among the contents of the three types of developmental studies. This is not bad, provided the same materials occur in different contexts. The problem for the curriculum designer is not duplication as such, but rather to strike a viable balance between keeping together in a course of study the elements that go together in existence, on the one hand, and creating a pedagogical hash, on the other. A pedagogical hash results whenever one undertakes to talk about everything at once or in the same course. Integration of topics reaches a point of diminishing returns when details obscure structure. The three strands of developmental study, therefore, "integrate" by distinguishing among the types of phenomena grouped for study. Furthermore, the preparation of materials for any one of these developmental strands is difficult enough without asking for the collaboration of persons competent in all three.

Again, it must be noted that philosophy and the intellectual content of religion, as well as the history of the arts and sciences, can be taught in separate courses, and it should go without further repetition that, given sufficient time, one might choose to study these matters systematically in separate courses. But there is no sufficiency of time, and the interpretive frame provided by de-

[8] *Op. cit.*, p. 29.

velopment of our most human of human accomplishments is the most important of all the interpretive frames.

SOME OBJECTIONS AND ANSWERS

Two sorts of objections to the developmental studies may readily occur to the reader. One has to do with the notorious superficiality of survey courses; the other concerns the displacement of certain conventional courses.

As to superficiality, the charge is more likely to be cogent when the total curriculum is organized on the survey basis. But the curriculum design proposed here has other ways of organizing materials for instruction: the basic sciences as separate subjects, the symbolic skills, value exemplars, and problem-solving, the latter two of which are discussed in the following chapter. The writers quite agree with the critics who say that a developmental course does not by itself teach the structure of a logically organized subject matter or build evaluational models or guarantee facility in problem-solving.

Superficiality is a real danger when too many details are crammed into too little study time, when the course pretends or even honestly tries to give knowledge about individual items rather than about lines of development. For example, if a survey course is used to acquaint the student with the works of Milton, it is pretty sure to fail, because one cannot spend enough time with the works to accomplish this result. Certainly, it will be insufficient to produce an appreciation of Milton. In a developmental course, about all one can do well with Milton is to locate him in the stream of English literature with respect to his contribution to certain ideas and certain literary art forms, just about what conventional survey courses accomplish.

As to the displacement of certain subjects in the secondary-school curriculum, where a displacement does occur, it is in order to achieve the objectives which the course professes, but which in its present form it has rather clearly failed to achieve.

The account of the development of science is itself not a science, and the account of this development does not require the same cognitive strategies as does the study of the several sciences. Although developmental studies have a logic of their own, the logic of causal explanation, it is not couched in the discourse of the topics that are being explained. That is why good scientists are not necessarily good historians of science, and vice versa. The same observation holds with respect to astronomy, literature, mathematics, philosophy, and religion. To understand their development is not the same cognitive task as to understand or to "do" them, although they cannot but affect each other.

It is precisely because so many of the courses in history, civics, sciences, and arts do not achieve the interpretive role we expected of them that the developmental studies must be considered as a necessary ingredient of general education.

It may be asked to what extent the developmental studies resemble the numerous core programs in the social-studies curriculum. The variety of such programs makes it difficult to give a clear answer. Obviously, the three themes around which the developmental studies are organized are cores of a sort, so far as certain disciplines are concerned. On the other hand, the developmental studies are not "core" in the sense of being the only part of the curriculum that is common to all students. Nor do they serve as a core for organizing the total curriculum. However, should certain core programs already in use approximate the developmental studies in scope and style, we would be that much further toward establishing the feasibility of this segment of the curriculum design.

Together with the basic sciences treated in the previous chapter, the developmental studies provide the cognitive maps of interpretation. They provide the student and the citizen with the means of orientation in a complex society and world. Yet it is a cognitive orientation, one that enables one to maneuver problems into position for further inquiry. As the next chapter shows, choice and action require interpretive maps, also.

CHAPTER XIII

DEVELOPMENT OF NORMS THROUGH
EXEMPLARS

Previous chapters have shown that the nonspecialist looks to his
schooling for frameworks in which to fit such questions as:
"What am I to think of this situation?" "What knowledge is relevant to it?" "What terms, what concepts, what categories most
accurately describe it?" Such questions were called cognitive, and
the framework in which the answers were to be sought, a cognitive map or perspective. It was concluded that certain basic
sciences and three strands of developmental study would most
effectively build such perspectives.

However, there are also questions about what is right, good,
beautiful, admirable, and their opposites. Such inquiries are
prompted by the need to answer such questions as: "What ought
I to do?" "What grounds are there for my preferring this to that?"
These questions have something to do with values as well as
with facts. We are not so clear about what validates a value judgment as we are about what supports a judgment of fact, and yet
human action is so solidly based on value commitments that, so
far as life is concerned, value judgments should have the highest
educational priority.

We expect from school some kind of evaluational framework
that will orient us with respect to action, just as the cognitive
framework orients us with respect to interpretation. What elements in the curriculum provide it? What form should these
elements take for the purposes of instruction?

ENLIGHTENED PREFERENCE AND JUSTIFICATION

The most noticeable characteristic of our value experience, as noted in an earlier chapter, is that it contains two components that are only loosely related. One may be called the attitudinal component, the other the theoretical or justifying component. The first tells what one likes; the second tries to give reasons for liking it.

The attitudinal component is being formed from the first day of life, with the result that the origin of many of our likes and dislikes is a mystery to ourselves, our parents, and even to our psychoanalyst. By the time the youngster enters school, he is already equipped with a repertory of preferences, often without knowing how he came by them and whether they are beneficial or harmful. But this much he does know: his likes and dislikes are not turned off and on at will or at mother's or teacher's request. Even when strong arguments are presented to persuade him that his dislike of tomatoes or Fiji Islanders, for example, has no basis in fact, that he would like them if he tried, even when he agrees that he ought to like them, his viscera and emotions continue on their customary course.

This age-old war between heart and head has its pedagogical counterpart in the circumstance that two distinct types of learning are involved in value education. Tastes and dispositions are, in the first instance, products of conditioning that takes place in the home, in the streets, and, to a lesser extent, in the school. It must be remembered that the pupil spends only a few hours a day in school, and that the school does not have the machinery to reinforce systematically anything save scholastic achievement and a respect for the mores of the school community. The school can, at best, modify the tastes already formed. The young pupil's existing preferences and attitudes do not sample the totality of value possibilities very well, either with respect to depth or range. In every value domain —social, recreational, civic, moral, intellectual, aesthetic, and religious—there are levels of preference. In his informal environment, the pupil has probably not encountered the level of preference exhibited by value experts. Just as one expects the school to bring the expert's thought to bear upon the pupil's inexpert knowledge, so it is reasonable for the school to bring the expert's values to bear upon the pupil's rudimentary taste.

This leads to the second phase of value education, namely, justification of taste or attitude. Although it is not the purpose of the common school to turn out specialists in the arts or philosophy, the significant criterion for evaluating the effectiveness of value education is a change of preference in the direction of connoisseurship. Connoisseurship, in turn, means not only liking something, but also liking it because it has certain qualities prescribed by some theory as being essential to admirable objects. The curriculum problem, therefore, is to find works of art or literature or philosophy which can serve as invitations to like and admire, on the one hand, and as exemplifications of the theories in terms of which they have come to be regarded as deserving of esteem, on the other.

One can say that the interpretive frame for valuing and evaluating is constituted by a set of likings and aversions, together with a set of concepts (criteria) of what likings are approved or disapproved by some reference group. The ordinary man's likings and aversions, at any given moment, are shaped by his own experiences of pleasure and pain and by the approval rules of his normal reference group. Adherence to these rules insures that the desire to be approved and esteemed is fulfilled. For this purpose, the ordinary man needs no formal tuition in taste. The milieu in which he lives and works channels his tastes efficiently. His speech, dress, household decorations, as well as his life heroes and heroines, without his even being aware of it, fall into the stereotypes of his reference group. The price of comfortable membership in his family circle and in his work group is acquiescence to the stereotype, but it is a price men are quite happy to pay.

The problem of formal value education arises only when the school wishes the tastes of the public to be shaped by the tastes of a special reference group called experts or connoisseurs. We then say to the ordinary man, "Shape your likings so that they will coincide with the likings of the experts." To follow this advice, the ordinary man not only has to recondition his preferences, he must also change his criteria of what makes an action or an object worthy of his admiration.

The problem of value schooling is to reshape the already formed preferences or likings of the pupils by changing their value reference groups. In a way, this is not very different from what the school tries to do in the cognitive area, for there, too, schooling extends and refines common sense and knowledge by resorting to the thought of the expert. In another sense, the task is more complicated, because (1) changes in attitudes are harder to bring about than changes in belief. (2) There is less consensus on criteria for evaluation than for truth. (3) We know less about teaching for appreciation than teaching for understanding.

In both cognition and evaluation, so far as schooling is concerned, the pupil has to *do* some knowing and liking and judging as the experts do it, and he has to become aware of the operations involved in doing these things properly. The curriculum has to provide means and materials for both types of experience. It also has to decide how to organize these materials for instruction.

Perhaps something further should be said at this point about an apparent gliding over the problem of choosing which standards the school is to encourage or, indeed, if it is to encourage any. To some readers, the decision to use the connoisseur as the standard of value will smack of dogmatic traditionalism. Disagreement among experts in the arts is notorious. Which experts is the school to choose?

Theoretically, it is interesting and important to ask whether there are or can be objective value standards, standards of right and wrong, good and evil, the beautiful and the ugly. Educationally, however, especially at the secondary level, there is only one solution to this problem: to rely on the experts in these fields as the school relies on experts in other fields. The school does not determine what is "good" chemistry, and it does not determine what is "good" literature or art. "Good" means what men who have devoted their professional lives to the study of these domains have agreed is good. Truth here is not simply consensus, but rather the consensus of the body of persons qualified to have expert opinions.

Where these experts do not agree, the school can only proceed on the principle that the major alternatives deserve to be presented as the best guidance available. Expert disagreement does not license the ignorant or change the nature of expertness. On the contrary, this kind of disagreement is the best incitement to inquiry into grounds of disagreement, an important first step to becoming an expert on one's own account. There is enough agreement among the experts as to what the significant examples of the fine arts and the humanities are to supply more than enough material for any secondary-school curriculum. And although, admittedly, the agreement about the more remote past is perhaps greater than about current works, the more recent past has also been studied with sufficient care to permit choices that are not arbitrary and whimsical. Certainly, there is enough agreement not to warrant a fearful withdrawal from the art, literature and philosophical thought of the recent past.

Who are the value experts? Presumably, those men and women who have experienced and reflected upon what gives the highest satisfaction in each value domain. It is to the great artists, writers, philosophers, and saints that we look for wisdom. Because the pupil cannot replicate the expert's life directly, the school has recourse to the reports of value experts, the connoisseurs of life. These reports, in the form of works of art, systems of philosophy, and religions, present the pupil with an array of possibilities far richer and far more subtle than he could ever imagine. But connisseurship is also required to comprehend and appreciate these reports.

These great works represent the aspirations of the race. They are value affirmations that integrated and vividly expressed the character of the successive epochs in our history. Their influence reaches into the present. One may loosely call these value exemplars "classics," not only because they have been admired and preferred by generations of experts, but also because they furnish the experts with the criteria for judging them "excellent." The Parthenon is not artistically superb because it conforms to certain rules; on the contrary, some of the rules for good art were derived from the Parthenon. Classics in any field are not only highly satisfactory objects on their own account, but the source of norms of "proper" satisfaction as well. Therein lies their pedagogical value, for in learning to appreciate them, the pupil not only likes what the connoisseur likes, but he is at the same time exposed to the source of the criteria that the connoisseur has used to justify the liking.

LEARNINGS FOR APPRECIATION AND CHOICE

Value education has two outcomes. One is appreciation—an enlightened taste that combines likings and reasons. The other is a strategy for making choices in situations in which many likings and many reasons jockey for position. A curriculum should make provision for instruction leading to both of these outcomes.

The appreciative act, combining cherishing and appraising, is always directed toward an individual object or action. We appreciate this picture or that poem. We are pleased by this person's character or repelled by that act of cruelty. Appreciation is not identical with choosing or deciding, because we can appreciate without taking the kind of action that forces us to choose. A woman may appreciate more than one man at the same time, but legally she can marry only one; hence, if she marries she has to choose. One does not have to choose between Beethoven and Mozart unless one is forced to make a judgment about their comparative merits or to exclude one rather than another from a concert program. The appreciative act is particular and unidimensional. Choice, however, may mean acting upon alternative and often conflicting strands of appreciation. It can be unidimensional, as when one chooses to buy one painting rather than another, but often it is multidimensional, as when one is asked to make decisions that involve preferences in painting, music, literature, poetry, and morals.

In such complex situations, not only is one referring to and using well-established likings and attitudes, he is also called upon to establish priorities among them and to make cognitive judgments as to causes and probable consequences. Thus, an attitude toward taxation involves attitudes toward the Republican and Democratic parties, toward their respective economic theories, their theories as to the ultimate worth of the person in the social order, notions of social justice, and dozens of other "appreciations" relevant to the situation.

It seems unrealistic to expect training in the appreciation of literature to help one weigh alternatives in problems of taxation, even though some literary judgments might be relative to the decision. Appreciations in the various value areas are related to social problem-solving in the same way that knowledge of each of the basic sciences is related to the developmental studies.

In an important sense, molar (complex) social problem-solving integrates all the other types of learning discussed. For this reason, educational theorists have advocated this type of problem-solving as *the* design for the curriculum. There is no doubt that this integrative experience must be introduced somewhere in school. If the writers reject it as the only way to organize material for instruction, it is because, as is pointed out below, learning to integrate knowledge and feeling does not of itself provide the diverse appreciations and knowledges to be integrated. Educational theorists have always sought the alchemist's stone in the form of a single type of instruction that would achieve learnings in the symbolic skills, basic concepts, appreciations, and judgment. Thus far, no such stone has lived up to its promise, and until one does, we have to regard learnings for appreciation and learnings for choice as two different strands of the curriculum. Learnings for choice are dealt with as a phase of molar problem-solving in the following chapter.

AESTHETIC EXEMPLARS AS MATERIALS
FOR VALUE INSTRUCTION

Appreciations, having to do with likings for individual objects or activities, direct us to the various types of value experience: economic, health, social, civic, recreational, intellectual, moral, aesthetic, and religious. In each field, one can shape preferences and provide justification for them. Each area has its own scholars and experts, its own traditions and disciplines. One way to design the curriculum is to provide instruction in these disciplines: in the fine arts, ethics, aesthetics, literature, and religion.[1]

Can we introduce the formal study of ethics, aesthetics, theology into the high school? Can we add them to literature and the fine arts as fields for systematic study? Is there room in an already crowded program of studies for them?

There is another problem. If literature or the fine arts are to be taught, should they be taught only for *aesthetic* appreciation, that is, for their artistic merit, or should they also be taught as lessons in morality, religion, and social justice? Or are they to be taught *primarily* as means to instruction in the extra-aesthetic values? The argument has been advanced that works of literature (*Grapes of Wrath*) or drama (*Death of a Salesman*) could be used to interest young people in social issues and problems of social conflict.

In summary, should materials be selected for each type of value in which we wish to improve the taste and judgment of the pupil, or is there one type of material that can perform this service for all the value areas?

[1] Theoretically, any value area can be represented in the curriculum, and the writers' reasons for not organizing their curriculum in this way have already been presented in previous chapters.

The disadvantage of the separate-subject approach is that the student can be exposed to the *concepts* for evaluation without necessarily having the direct kind of experience that the experts regard as "good." This could be the case even in courses *about* literature and the fine arts. This is why Aristotle thought ethics an inappropriate study for the young, whose experience with moral predicaments was meager. Vicarious experience can extend and enrich direct experience but cannot be substituted for it. Further, the nonspecialist evaluates "molar" rather than "atomic" situations, that is, complex, holistic problems rather than separate economic, moral, or aesthetic ones. Only the specialist abstracts from the total situation to make judgments in one value dimension.

If, on the other hand, one type of material is used, which shall it be: aesthetic, intellectual, moral, religious? To answer this question, it may help to ask how people shape their value schemata insofar as they are not simply imposed on them. The writers suggest that they do so primarily by introjecting or identifying with a model. This model can be a particular person or a person who represents a style of life, for example, the military leader, the industrial tycoon, the surgeon, or the artist. One forms a self-concept based on such a model and thereafter tries to behave consistently with this concept. To teach values, accordingly, is to shape the pupil's value model.

Where do we get our models? From the family, school, and many other sources, but among the most powerful sources in modern society are the mass media of entertainment. Popular fiction, music, drama, poetry, and painting present value models in the persons of their heroes and heroines, and, unwittingly, their villains as well. Because these life styles are stereotyped, they are easily understood, and because they are repeated so often, they act as conditioning agents. They invite imitation, while the culture is providing strong reinforcement for such imitation. They influence national value commitments by affecting the aesthetic experience of the populace.

Contrary to common impression, the ordinary citizen uses his aesthetic faculties in a wide range of circumstances; he does not restrict them to concerts and visits to museums. For example, the appearance of objects is an important determinant of attention in general. It is an important factor in the price of such objects of ordinary use as refrigerators, automobiles, clothing, and so on. Furthermore, one expects all important activities to be underscored by some sort of aesthetic form. Weddings and funerals have to be carried on amid appropriate sounds, costumes, and gestures. Banquets must have speakers, religions their rituals, special occasions their celebrations. The arts are called upon to render experience more impressive by making it more dramatic and vivid than it otherwise would be.

Not less important is the degree to which common experience relies on appearance for clues to the nature and behavior of objects and people. A certain conformation of landscape betokens serenity or loneliness. A certain type of face warns us against undesirable character traits associated with it, more often than not mistakenly. Science reduces our dependence on appearances as clues to the nature of things, but it will be a long time before we can dispense with them, even in the most sophisticated forms of experience.

Men use models furnished directly or indirectly by the arts to evaluate and even to understand their experience. Oscar Wilde long ago, and many writers in more recent years, noted that we are more likely to test reality by the images the arts have created for us than to test images by reality. Newspapers, magazines, movies, and television, as well as the serious arts, are forever exhibiting models of life, of what we are supposed to find and admire in the world: the way a sunset should blaze, the way a fashionable woman should dress, the way the American man should react to his wife's complaints and to Russian threats. Slogans, trademarks, pictures, and fiction all create shapes and images that trigger certain expectations and emotions.

Ideals, personality traits, life styles, and value schemata

acquire their social power by hypnotizing the public with their charm, a charm that operates through aesthetically grasped images. Popular arts are used in entertainment and advertising to amuse or persuade the customer. The serious artist also portrays his impressions of the world and life, and he, like the advertising man, also wants to charm his public. But whereas the advertiser and propagandist use the work of art as a means to their own and often nonaesthetic ends, the serious artist is committed to expressing what he sees, hears, and feels by creating objects that have high aesthetic and artistic quality—that are aesthetically authentic. The nonaesthetic or extra-aesthetic results are for him incidental, although to the society in which he lives the priorities may be reversed. The school, however, has to insist on both art for art's sake and art for goodness' sake, that is, for social significance.

If this is the social-psychological mechanism for value training, it may be advisable for the school to make use of a similar mechanism. In other words, the school also can present life styles as they appear in the arts, but not in the popular arts. Displayed in literature, drama, painting, and music, life models acquire an attractiveness that engages the emotions as well as the intellect. They are invitations to feel and cherish as well as to understand.

To follow this strategy, one can approach value education through what are called value exemplars, as they are encountered in notable instances of literature and the fine arts. Appreciative learning can be regarded as a type of aesthetic learning, a learning of how to perceive and appraise aesthetic objects, natural and contrived. It means that one looks to the arts, literature, and drama for models rather than to history and philosophy, or, better, one looks to such historical and philosophical ideas as have received high artistic expression.

Let us be clear on this point. To study all value exemplars via their artistic expressions is not a substitute for the study of ethics, aesthetics, and religion. However, given the limitations of time and the fact that attitudinal as well as cognitive components are essential to appreciative learning, the choice of the aesthetic vehicle for value education seems justified.

If works of art are to bear this heavy curricular burden, they have to be *great* works of art as well as *good* ones. A good work of art has met the criteria of artistic quality with respect to form, technique, and aesthetic interest. A great work of art has to have "significant form" and must express an important aspect of life. Usually it covers a wide range of values and portrays them with a clarity and intensity not found in everyday experience. Moreover, each art form has its own distinctive objects and canons of appraisal. To learn to appreciate a painting is not automatically to learn to appreciate poetry. Hence, the samples have to be chosen so that the major arts are represented.

THE TEACHING OF EXEMPLARS

Can we point to some systematic way of teaching exemplars? Or are we reduced to exposing pupils to a wide variety of them and hoping for some mystical alchemy to do the rest? Are we to give pupils a watered-down studio training in one of the arts and hope that this will permeate taste and judgment in other value areas? Or shall we rely upon survey courses? For our purpose, it will be sufficient if a plausible case can be made out for the first alternative, namely, that some systematic way of teaching exemplars is possible.

In appreciation, the use made of schooling is predominantly associative, but one has to be extremely careful about the type of association that occurs. A work of art in any medium is an illusion. Literally speaking, a painting is a pattern of shapes and colors, but it is a work of art if one is led to see the shapes and colors as having lifelike qualities: tension, resolution, opposition, force, cheerfulness, sadness, loneliness, anger—any and every shade of feeling whether there are names for them or not—operating in a space and time of their own. The ability to see and hear life as color or sound patterns requires imagination, or, in other words, it requires a way with images.

However, no work of art can serve as a metaphor to him who does not bring the other half of the metaphor to it. There has to be a store of images that are already analogous to the forms of life and feeling for the work of art to be seen or heard properly. Keeping in mind that the work of art should not make us think *of* this or that but rather that it must look or sound *like* this or that, it is clear that we must learn the images of the culture and perhaps of the race in order to appreciate serious works of art.

The word "snake," for example, elicits somewhat different associations than "serpent," but it is difficult, one would guess, for anyone in our culture to respond to either word without complex imagery and feeling tone. However, it is hard to believe that a man thoroughly steeped in mythology and poetry would respond with an association complex comparable to that of a schoolboy or an adult whose schooling ended in the sixth grade. Part of the task of value education is to provide materials for imaginative construction based on cues and symbols presented by perception in general and art works in particular. In turn, experience with a work of art enriches the store of images.

Appreciative learnings are used replicatively only insofar as the attitudinal component is aroused in the value situation. When judgments about works of art are parroted as learned, they are used replicatively, albeit precisely in the way they ought not to be used. Value learnings are used applicatively only by the expert or the specialist, such as the scholar or connoisseur. As with other learnings, the citizen, for the most part, uses value learnings interpretively, that is, to reflect upon his likings and the criteria for judging them. To construct his evaluational map he uses the exemplars as anchor points for judgment.

LEVELS OF APPRECIATIVE LEARNINGS

There are four levels of aesthetic judgment on which the critical response can be made:

1. The vividness and intensity of the sensuous elements in the work of art: the affective quality of the sounds, colors, gestures, and so on

2. The formal qualities of the object, its design or composition

3. The technical merits of the object, the skill with which the work is carried out

4. The expressive significance of the object, its import or message or meaning as aesthetically expressed

These four levels also mark off the domains of appreciation instruction. The first three are primarily unidimensional, but the fourth need not and perhaps cannot be. The first three are topics in the study of painting, music, poetry, literature, and drama. In each medium, one has to learn how to use the appropriate senses with discrimination, how to discern design and judge its adequacy, and how to relate design to artistic styles and types. Finally, enough training in performance is needed so that one can get the feel of the appropriate techniques. How much of the latter is required by the educated layman for appreciation is still a matter of controversy, but it seems clear that it is not so little as is now required in customary courses on appreciation, and probably far less than is prescribed for professional training of artists.

The case is different with the appreciation of the significance or import of the book or art work being studied. The import always goes beyond the work of art, even though it must be perceptually present in the work of art. What ideal, what conception of this or that aspect of life does a given work of art or exemplar express? Here we are entering upon the field of criticism, and fundamental criticism always is rooted in the total realm of value rather than in one department of it.

The study of exemplars affords the opportunity for all four modes of aesthetic experience, and only when the four are combined is there something which deserves to be called aesthetic education.

It should be obvious that if one is to carry on this sort of education in school, the number of exemplars will be small. Even if the performance skills are fairly well developed by Grade 7, it takes considerable time to learn to cherish and appraise an art work that is rich in significance and high in artistic merit.

We must remember that the worth of any great work of art is not something that can be grasped in a moment. To appreciate and judge an excellent painting, for example, we must do much more than glance at it in a gallery. Ordinarily we must *live* with it until its sensuous qualities, meanings, and forms sink deep into our conscious and subconscious mind. If then, day after day, it works its magic upon us— if its appeal is deep and varied enough to be lasting—we can realize its excellence because our lives are being substantially enriched. The expert critic is one who can sense this amplitude and fineness of value more quickly and surely than the ordinary man.[2]

The choice of a relatively small number of exemplars needs justification, because the current survey type of appreciation course covers a great deal of ground, and performance courses provide a kind of intensive appreciation that is hard to match. The survey course, however, is open to the twin objections of superficiality and irrelevance: superficiality in that it affords only smatterings and flitting exposures to works that are difficult to appreciate under any circumstances, irrelevance in that they tend to give knowledge about the field primarily and appreciation of it secondarily. If aesthetic education is to be a means toward value education in general, appreciation in terms of direct likings is as necessary as knowledge about works of art and the rules for judging them.

As to relying exclusively on performance courses, the fact remains that for people without talent, such training rapidly reaches the point of diminishing returns, except perhaps on a hobby basis. For it is not at all clear that beyond a certain point technical proficiency promotes appreciation in the other three senses enumerated above.

[2] Melvin Rader (Ed.), *A Modern Book of Esthetics* (3rd ed.; New York: Holt, Rinehart & Winston, 1960), p. xxxi.

In short, if the curricular time now given to literature and drawing, art and music can be used for six years of aesthetic education via a study of exemplars, one ought to have a great deal more to show for it than what the secondary school can now produce.

In summary, the area of the curriculum primarily responsible for conveying to the pupil a sense of the style or styles of life found admirable by the connoisseurs of our culture should consist of six years of study devoted to a carefully selected set of paintings, musical compositions, poems, dramas, and novels. In the developmental studies of the culture, knowledge about these exemplars will already have been encountered. The relation of art products and forms to other elements of the culture will have been noted. Perhaps some acquaintance with the names and biographical details of noted artists, writers, and thinkers will have been achieved.

In the exemplar part of the curriculum, the focus of study is a particular work of art. The desired outcome is a change in the quality of the student's perception and feeling about that work. The directions and levels of these desired changes have been indicated. To accomplish this, instruction may have to guide perception by having the student work a while in the medium of the work being studied. Or it may be advisable to discuss styles, periods, and the symbolic conventions illustrated by the work of art. At certain times and on certain levels, a study of the major critical opinions may also be undertaken.

The impact of these diverse modes of instruction is to change the quality of perception, its discernment of details, of form, and, hopefully, of significance. The knowledge *about* the work, while important, is nevertheless a means rather than an end in itself. Until the pupil perceives as the connoisseur perceives, the connoisseur's judgment is not his judgment; his standards are not authentic.

It would be presumptuous of the secondary school to claim that even the most favorable study of exemplars provides the student with a complete interpretive frame. It will be sufficient if a few major guideposts or models in the various arts have been introjected by the student. Indeed, the limitation on the number of exemplars is justified by the opportunities for varied exposure afforded by modern museums, books, and recordings. Much of the power of a work of art comes from the quality and needs of the beholder's experience, and this is not finished and wrapped up by the school. Yet without this frame, we can no more orient ourselves to art than without the basic sciences we can orient ourselves to knowledge.

Whether exemplars of painting, literature, music, and drama should be studied separately or together is an important question that is discussed when the school program is taken up in Chapter XV.

CHAPTER XIV

DEVELOPMENT OF PROBLEM-SOLVING STRATEGIES

The high-school student has been put on the road to acquiring the symbolic, technological, and artistic skills in the elementary school and perfecting them in the secondary school. He has been working with the basic sciences, the developmental studies, and value exemplars. Has the list of school outcomes needed for life in the emergent society been exhausted?

Much of what has been said about the life use of school learnings comes back to problem-solving. Life presents us with a series of predicaments from which we try to extricate ourselves by habit, by luck, by trial and error, and, on occasion, by thinking. Obviously, our culture puts a premium upon the thinking solution of predicaments, and society accordingly expects the school to contribute toward this kind of competence. This holds true even though educators probably overestimate the sheer amount of thinking demanded by ordinary life.

The distinction between the demands of ordinary life and those of life on a higher level applies here as it does in other areas of schooling. By a strange twist, the more developed technologically an appliance becomes, the less thinking does its use entail. Early automobiles, for example, made great demands on the skill and ingenuity of their owners, as well as on their patience and fortitude. The proud boast of modern automobile-makers is that the operator need know nothing about the mechanism under the hood. The increased demand for creative thought by the few (the experts) is accompanied by the decreased need of thought by the many (the consumers).

This phenomenon is not confined to the mechanical appliances that have so radically altered the competences needed for transportation, building, and food preparation. One finds the same paradox in our political, social, moral, and aesthetic life. Prepackaged ideas are as typical of our culture as are prepared foods. Mass-production techniques are applied to the shaping of taste in art and architecture as well as to the formation of our taste in clothes and foods. These developments are products of the ingenuity and even creativeness of experts and professionals, but reduce the cognitive and valuative strain on the individual. He can buy his decisions by the column or by the television program.

If ordinary life is the standard, schooling for thinking or problem-solving is becoming less necessary rather than more. Only if life in the new mass society is to be lived on a level of excellence, does it make sense to ask the school to train the student in the thinking solution to life's predicaments in contrast to a stereotyped and a trial-and-error solution. This assumption, in turn, uncovers another paradox, that life at the thinking, individual level presupposes mass schooling, but of a quality not characteristic of mass production.

Life predicaments present themselves to the individual somewhat after the fashion of a maze. He is stopped in action by a block. As he investigates the situation, he finds many alternative routes. Each one, however, has blocks and alternatives of its own. Like a rat, he can work his way out by trial and error, or he can try a ready-made solution. Each of these is easier than trying to discern the design of the maze as a whole, which is the thinking solution. When each such maze is envisioned as made up of paths lying on different planes drawn in different colors and to different scales, one begins to approximate the complexity and multilateral dimensions of a problem such as taxation or foreign trade. To express the massiveness of such problems, the writers use the term "molar."

Problems are more or less complex, depending on the range and extent of knowledge relevant to them. The problem of finding a gasoline station in any American city is simple; discerning the social structure of the city is less so. Some problems require knowledge mainly from one discipline, as a problem in chemistry may; others call for knowledge from many areas, as does the problem of juvenile delinquency. One learns to deal competently with simple problems by simple means, such as asking for the needed information or utilizing common knowledge. More complicated problems, as noted, require schooling, but only if one insists upon a solution involving thought.

Problems are familiar enough on the school scene. The pupil encounters them within each of the logically organized subjects he studies: mathematics, chemistry, physics. Occasionally, he is involved in group problems, and he has his own stock of personal predicaments with respect to money, friends, choice of a vocation, and so on.

Not all problems are equally useful for pedagogical purposes. Simple problems involving only one dimension of knowledge may not be adequate preparation for dealing with multidimensional problems. This is so because, when a problem is multidimensional, there are steps to be taken before thinking it through or solving it can be begun. One of these steps is making a judgment about what sort of data and what sort of knowledge are relevant to the problem. It is to make this step possible and fruitful that the cognitive and evaluative maps are developed in general education.

CURRICULAR APPROACHES TO MOLAR OR SOCIAL PROBLEMS

What kind of materials, organized in what form, initiate the pupil into molar or social problem-solving or, more accurately, problem-studying? This section examines briefly the claims that (1) the study of certain disciplines and (2) involvement of the pupil in solving his own or his group's predicaments accomplish this. It has long been held, certainly as long ago as the time of Plato, that studying certain subject matters which entail critical and logical thinking makes the learner critical and logical in non-practiced situations. This is the famous but almost universally rejected doctrine of formal discipline. The good mathematician, on this theory, should be able to make good judgments in political science, and the first-rate Latin student should be able to cope rationally with everything from motors to matrimony.

The grounds on which these claims have been made for certain subjects of instruction can be summarized as follows: Some subjects give practice in logical operations that are formally identical in all instances of systematic, critical thinking. The claims for Latin grammar and mathematics were of this sort. Some subjects are thought to be useful in problem-solving more by virtue of their content. For example, the classic literatures were thought to contain information on many topics and wisdom about the major problems of human conduct. Some, like the sciences, were thought to have both highly transferable content and operations.

Leaving aside for the moment the validity of these claims, the fact is that molar problem-solving requires the transfer of both content and operations. The content, however, has its origin, not in one school subject, but in many. No one school subject, for example, furnishes the concepts relevant to a problem such as juvenile delinquency. Furthermore, the problem of delinquency is loaded with value issues and judgments far beyond the scope of any one course in literature, philosophy, or even religion.

As to the logical operations, molar problem-solving employs, of course, the same hypothetico-deductive style of reasoning characteristic of all scientific thought. In addition, it uses the operations characteristic of critical and analytical thinking. As far as sheer logical form is concerned, this could have been learned in any subject that exemplified it, and with some effort it could have been taught for transfer.

What cannot be transferred from any single subject or any set of subjects, however, are the operations called judgments of relevance. A molar problem, being complex and multidimensional, presents a problem within a problem, for one must first decide what data, what facts, what principles, what rules, are relevant to it.

Administrators face this kind of tangle when they have to analyze a wide variety of factors and then synthesize them into a unified action. Where do they acquire this skill, if, indeed, it is a skill? Certainly not in the study of unidimensional problems.

The writers question on somewhat different grounds the claim that practicing problem-solving by the application of intelligence to the predicaments of a child's life in school transfers to dealing with molar problems.

All problem-solving utilizes generalizations. Even so ordinary a predicament as not having enough money to buy both a baseball bat and a movie ticket cannot be treated as a problem without resorting to some such generalizations as: The same money cannot be spent simultaneously in two places. Money is earned in this way or that way. Baseball bats last longer than the pleasures of attendance at a movie. One also uses facts. Bats cost so much; they are on sale at this store. The name of the movie is that and that.

These facts and generalizations can come from common knowledge, but insofar as children's predicaments make use only of common knowledge, they contribute little to dealing with molar problems so far as content is concerned.

The problems of the adult citizen that really matter either in his individual or his social roles are not solvable by the resources of common sense or common knowledge. The requisite cognitive frames cannot be picked up incidentally to the ordinary routines of living. The generalizations or funded knowledge needed for serious problem-solving likewise are not available to the solver without systematic study of the basic intellectual disciplines. When, for example, a generalization from political science is wanted, where is the thinker who has not studied political science to get it? Furthermore, how much of the value schema in terms of which value priorities for choice are established are the result of an individual's getting out of his own predicaments? The role of the expert and the connoisseur in shaping our aesthetic and moral frames of interpretation is no smaller than it is in the shaping of our intellectual (cognitive) frames. In short, the cognitive and evaluational frames needed in the complex problem situation are either learned in school by studying certain subjects and value exemplars or are probably not learned at all.

CONCEPTS AND OPERATIONS IN PROBLEM-SOLVING

The first step in molar problem-solving is to make a judgment about what frames of interpretation are relevant to the problem. For example, with regard to the topic of federal aid to schools, is it relevant to locate the problem in the development of our social institutions, or should one turn to political science or to economics? Are there basic sciences relevant to this problem? Or are there other relevant types of discipline?

As a matter of fact, our culture has developed disciplines for most of the typical social problems that are closer to practical concerns than are the basic sciences. Agriculture, medicine, technology, and military science are disciplines which organize knowledge of diverse kinds to bear upon social needs: food, health, defense, and the like. The problem of urbanization, for example, is more directly related to agriculture and technology than to chemistry, biology, and physics.

The same observations can be made about two other types of knowledge: first, what Tykociner has called the regulative disciplines, for example, political science, economics, jurisprudence, administration and management, and, second, those disciplines concerned with the dissemination of knowledge, the conserving of records and making them available for research. Examples of the latter are education, guidance, library science, journalism, and the like. To put it somewhat differently, each profession organizes materials from the basic sciences so that they are relevant to certain tasks: medicine to the problems of health, law to the problems of justice, education to the problems of schooling, military science to the problems of warfare.

These professional studies are hardly suitable for a secondary school devoted to common education, but even if they were, they would still be only halfway houses to the analysis of molar problems. Taxation, for example, is too big an issue for the intellectual resources of any one profession. Lawyers, economists, accountants, businessmen, financiers, and legislators—all are concerned with taxation. So the individual citizen still has to complete the job of selecting and integrating knowledge.

The concepts needed for the first step in problem-solving are drawn from the segments of the curriculum already discussed. The cognitive and evaluative maps begin to function as maps. They also function in the later stages of the process, when we identify, formulate, and appraise the live issues and options in the problem situation. Much school learning is used associatively as a source of suggestions, reminders, and hunches. Some, but probably not very much, is used replicatively in the form of recollected facts and rehearsed skills.

But by and large, concepts are used interpretively to establish and refine meanings. In this interpretation, the value preferences and judgments learned in the study of exemplars also function. In the problems of federal aid and taxation, not only knowledge but also life styles are operative. The man to whom the frontier individualist is a hero (a life-style model) does not, at first, perceive these problems in the same way as a person to whom a social reformer, say, Jane Addams, is a value model.

The fact has been stressed that concepts are necessary to analyze, interpret, and understand molar problems, and that it is the business of general education to provide them. There is another dimension to molar problem-solving, that of the logical operations by which interpretation is guided and tested. As noted earlier, logical operations are used applicatively for all types of active, systematic thinking. These operations should have been performed over and over again in studying the other segments of the curriculum. Dealing with molar problems is a severe test of how well these logical operations have been learned, as well as of the content of the cognitive and evaluative maps.

It is with respect to the development of the operations that the strongest claim has been made for the activity curriculum. It is held that the scientific method is exemplified in all types of problem-solving, social or personal, and is therefore easily transferred.

Everyone by now must be familiar with Dewey's version of the complete act of thought: predicament; definition and statement of the problem; surveying the situation for relevant data; hazarding intelligent guesses at what would remedy the situation; checking these out one by one for their plausibility; translating these mental predictions into verifying or disconfirming acts; and, finally, carrying out the verifying act.

We are told that in school the process should be re-enacted repeatedly, until the act of thought becomes habitual in the behavior repertoire of the student. A recent book, *Reflective Thinking: The Method of Education*, by H. Gordon Hullfish and Philip G. Smith,[1] is one of the many restatements of the Dewey and Kilpatrick positions that problem-solving in ordinary life re-enacts the main features of scientific thinking. From this, Dewey and others concluded that men, if properly educated, could be as "scientific" about life problems as scientists are about theirs.

It is argued that the method of reflection transfers readily and widely to many types of human predicament; that it embodies the methodology which is at the heart of democracy; that it can be used to arrive at decisions of policy; and that, by sucking into itself a wide variety of data and funded knowledge, it builds for the student conceptual frames adequate to further problem-solving.

It has already been indicated why these claims seem to be

[1] New York: Dodd, Mead, 1961.

excessive. Nevertheless, with respect to the logical operations involved in problem-solving, one is inclined to grant them. If, as has been urged, the logical structure of knowledge is abstracted and given attention in instruction, there is reason to expect a stable disposition to use these operations in problem situations. The chief reason for this faith is the tendency of even the most spontaneous, creative, intellectual act to become a habit with repetition. Hence, the most creative thinkers and artists in time develop "styles" of creating and thinking; if they imitate no one else, they cannot avoid imitating themselves.

The implication of this fact is not that the curriculum must consist entirely of problems to be solved by the choice and action of the pupil. On the contrary, if the logical operations are the constants in all forms of scientific thinking, they can be learned as well in the basic sciences as anywhere else. If the logical operations alone were at stake, a course in molar problem-solving would not be necessary. It is because life problems are so complex with respect to *content* that pupils need a chance to practice the logical operations on sample life problems.

In addition to content and logical operations, there are other operations which, for lack of a better name, can be called "group dynamics." The arts of deliberation involve role-playing, self-examination, and a kind of therapy that enables the group to approach agreement.

In recent years, these psychological dimensions of problem-solving have received a good deal of attention, and the findings are convincing that group thinking is more than thinking about reasonable means to sensible ends. In dealing with social problems, men bring their value commitments with them. Their egos have to be protected at nearly all costs. The reasoning process, accordingly, goes on in an atmosphere highly charged with threats and promises; indeed, the more the problem is a "felt" problem, the more intensely is the atmosphere charged.

There is a kind of social rationality that consists in a system of human relations in which want satisfaction and ego satisfaction are maximized.[2] Achieving this is a matter of wisdom and social engineering as well as correct reasoning. No other portion of the curriculum discussed affords an adequate opportunity to make the pupil familiar with the arts of group deliberation.

This is a point that perhaps needs further justification. Why, it may be objected, is it so necessary to sequester molar problem-solving from other strands of the curriculum? Granted that in no single discipline are the problems sufficiently molar to serve the purpose, and granted that merely "felt" problems of individual students do not furnish the generalizations needed for the intelligent encounter with social issues, why not utilize the social studies core or the course in problems of democracy for this purpose?

Perhaps the writers' reluctance to do so stems from a distrust of the efficacy of any one mode of instruction to accomplish a multiplicity of outcomes. If a course is designed to produce skills, facts, principles, values, and attitudes, it may, like any multipurpose tool, do none of the tasks very well. Long discussions in class, for example, give practice in group deliberation but impede coverage of the materials in the course; if the time is given to coverage, the other outcomes may suffer.

The fact that a whole book could be written on this process of group deliberation[3] indicates that it is not a simple spontaneous process, that it presupposes that certain knowledge has already been acquired, that certain modes of communication have been perfected, that the participants can be made sensitive to blocks in the process, and that there are procedures for removing them.

In short, the writers do not rely upon the problem-solving course to provide systematic knowledge, and they do not rely upon basic science, symbolic skills, value exemplars, and developmental studies to produce as benign by-products the strategies of molar problem-solving.

[2] See Paul Diesing, *Reason in Society* (Urbana: University of Illinois Press, 1962), for a discussion of five types of rationality and decisions encountered in a social order.
[3] R. Bruce Raup, George E. Axtelle, Kenneth D. Benne, and B. Othanel Smith, *The Improvement of Practical Intelligence* (New York: Harper & Brothers, 1950).

MOLAR PROBLEMS AS A FORM OF INSTRUCTION

What shape should molar problem-solving take for instruction? What distinguishes it from the conventional experiences in this area?

The writers envision in the latter years of the secondary school, perhaps in Grades 11 and 12 (if grades are retained), a fairly long transaction each year with two or three social problems of the magnitude of juvenile delinquency, disarmament, the problems of economic democracy, and the like. The latter years of secondary school are to be preferred, because by then the student presumably has reached the age when interest in such problems can be stimulated, if not assumed.

Few problems rather than many are indicated, first, because the objective is not to solve all or even most of our social problems, but rather to become adept in thinking about them systematically. Second, the complexity of these problems makes heavy demands on time. Finally, staff members cannot possibly become masters of a wide range of problems.

This last point is perhaps the most serious drawback to the feasibility of the problems course. Polymaths in these days are rare even at the university level, especially since the current intellectual market favors the specialists. There are two other alternatives. One is to throw any teacher in with the students and have them learn together. This may have its merits. However, the point of the course is not the discovery of problems, but the mastery of strategies of dealing with them. The other alternative is to use the course to train a few teachers in the strategy and the means of teaching and testing it. This alternative is feasible, however, only if the teachers stay with a few problems long enough to be able to lead and guide the class instead of groping along with it.

The practice which is needed and for which plenty of time should be allowed takes the form of (1) clarifying the statement of the problem, (2) exploring its ramifications, (3) making guesses about relevant information and theory, (4) exploring the causes, logical and psychological, for disagreement, (5) formulating alternative solutions and criticizing them.

What outcomes of such practice can the school hope to observe? One would think that a more rapid fitting of an unpracticed problem into its appropriate frames would be one result that could be observed and even measured. Another would be the speed with which the group resolved disagreements about relevance. Still another would be the growth of agreement among the members of the group as to criteria for relevance and evidence; another would be the critical acuity of the group, its semantic fluency. By devoting sufficient time to one problem and concentrating on the strategies of problem-solving rather than on the acquisition of content and attitudes (except attitudes toward the problem itself), it seems not unreasonable to expect results that can be put to immediate use in higher education and in nonschool life.

Let it be reiterated that this kind of "course" or activity is not to be confused with problems studied in chemistry, physics, or mathematics. Nor is it to be identified with the familiar project or core approach, a device that takes the place of studying the several subject matters directly, separately, and systematically. There is a place in the curriculum for both of these problem-solving activities; the study of the basic sciences certainly uses the first, while the developmental studies utilize the second. In the molar problem-solving course, however, the school outcome is not knowledge primarily, or even habituation in the use of the scientific method as such. On the contrary, the school outcomes, which in this instance approximate very closely the life outcomes corresponding to them, are the habits of deliberation, the skills of using diverse interpretive frames, and the practice of the attitudes needed for group thinking and decision.

Such knowledge as accrues would be *about* the way the diverse professions and disciplines operate in our culture, for example, the way research itself operates in it. It should strengthen the interpretive frames (cognitive and evaluative) by testing them on a selected set of problems. More important, however, is the training in the postures—cognitive, evaluative, and personal—needed for the modern tasks of citizenship. One need not accept fully the theory that consensus is the ultimate criterion of truth in policy-making and social decision, but the theory makes sense if it is taken as a way of training citizens to the point where their consensus is a consensus of qualified judges. Such qualifications include the possession of the cognitive and evaluative frames, but also certain ways of behaving in groups, of adeptness in human relations, of using emotional mechanisms that enable them to disengage their egos from the issues under discussion and yet not forget the egos of their codiscussants.

The problems course, therefore, can be regarded as the integrative experience par excellence of the whole schooling process. It should reveal something about how well the other strands of the curriculum have been taught, for it is a small sample of how schooling should be used in life. The sample, to be sure, is so small that inferences and hopes based upon it should be modest, but the school can take comfort in the evidence that this or that student actually did in school the sort of thing that life will expect of him, and that he did it with a certain degree of competence. More than such certification the public has no right to ask of the school, but it has been settling for a good deal less.

It will be objected here, as at other points, that molar problem-solving calls for a high order of intellectual capacity, and that therefore only the brightest students can profit from it. Perhaps this is so, perhaps not. But from this nothing follows about the need for giving every student a chance to try his hand at it and to be a part of a group that is trying its hand at it. One cannot repeat too often that the outcome is not the *solution* of these social problems, but rather the achievement of an intelligent orientation toward them and a disposition to ask the right questions, or at least to recognize the right ones when others ask them. For such learnings all men, if not equally apt, are, at least, legitimate candidates.

CHAPTER XV

A PROGRAM OF STUDIES

The groundwork has now been laid for a common program of general studies from Grade 7 through Grade 12. To do this required an analysis of the educational demands exerted by the emerging culture, the structure of knowledge, the structure of the learning and teaching process, and the uses of schooling in life.

WHY A COMMON CURRICULUM?

It may be advisable, however, to recapitulate the considerations which justify what may seem to be a radical shaking-up of the ideas and practices characteristic of the American high school.

Why, it will be asked, propose a common program of studies devoid of electives? Why this turning of the back, so to speak, on vocational specialization and the diversification of interests in the adolescent years? After all, does not a highly complicated, technologically sophisticated society demand more educational variety rather than less? Why should not diversity of talent and interest find its counterpart in the curriculum? Can a common program meet the needs of the slum and the suburb, the gifted and the dull? These questions are so pivotal as to warrant the repetition of arguments put forward and explicated in previous chapters.

Let us refer once more to the convergent evidence from the analysis of the culture, from recent developments in curriculum, from studies of learning and teaching, and especially from a re-examination of the ways in which schooling is used in a modern society.

From the analysis of the culture, it seems clear that vocational, civic, and personal adequacy *in our time* necessitates a hitherto undreamed-of level of intellectual and moral maturity for most and preferably all citizens.

When one analyzes how schooling is used by the citizen for vocational preparation and for his pursuit of well-being in all its forms, it appears that certain contents and certain psychological operations are not only common to all of these activities, but indispensable to carrying them on properly in our modern culture. Whether a boy is heading for the practice of law or the manipulation of buttons on the instrument panel of an automated refinery, as a citizen he needs highly general cognitive and evaluative maps. On these maps he will maneuver all of his problems for understanding, appraisal, and, hopefully, for solution. This interpretive use of schooling determines the way he perceives his world, the way he thinks and feels about it, and the way he makes choices concerning it. It is also the base on which his specialist training can be built. What sort of secondary schooling builds adequate interpretive maps into the minds and dispositions of our young people?

Because the vast complexity of knowledge makes rigorous selection imperative, one is forced to ask whether or not some content is more important than other content, whether or not some learning operations are more important than others. The writers answer both questions in the affirmative because, as they have argued, some ideas are more general and consequently have a greater explanatory potential than others, and some cognitive operations are more pervasive and more strategic for understanding than others.

In short, looking at the structure of knowledge, and examining the key criteria of value in the moral and aesthetic domains, one cannot escape the conclusion that there are key ideas and criteria and that there are indispensable symbolic and logical operations without which interpretation cannot be adequate. A curriculum which includes these ideas can make a plausible claim to be "needed" by all human beings and therefore to be studied by all of them.

Hence, a curriculum design has been sought that includes as many as possible of the major contents and operations from which the pupil can build cognitive and evaluative maps of great generality and precision. But six or even twelve years is too short a time to include all the desirable ingredients. Therefore, what is included is that which, in the writers' judgment, no individual in a democratic mass society can do without, and from which, therefore, no pupil can be excused. Although many good things could be added to the proposed curriculum, they cannot displace anything already there without meeting the criteria of selection better than what has been chosen.

That there is a need for curricular diversity to match diversity of competence and individual interests is not denied. What is denied is that such diversity must be achieved by an elective curriculum or one that generously affords varied opportunities for vocational training in the secondary school. Diversity of competence can be dealt with in a common program of studies by varying the level at which content is taught. However, a continuation of the already rich extracurricular program in the school should help meet this need. A system of post-secondary institutions should also be created in response to the vocational demands of the emergent society.

If it is argued that this is an unrealistic expectation, one can note that it is more realistic than the expectations of some other proposals for changes in secondary-school curriculum. The hope, for example, that even a large minority of our secondary schools will become comprehensive high schools is certainly not realistic. No more so is the hope that democracy can be maintained by driving a small group of high IQ's through fifteen or more Carnegie units of "hard" subjects, while offering a smattering of vocational skills to the average or less-than-average pupils. Nor, finally, can one any longer believe that the demands of the emergent society can be met by a secondary-school curriculum consisting of exercises associated with the rites of passage incident to adolescence.

It is not that any or all of these proposals are bad as such. If the writers are increasingly dubious about them, it is because they are patched-up versions of schemes that have already demonstrated their inadequacy to the needs of society in our time, however well they may have met the needs of an earlier phase of our national life.

OUTLINE OF A PROGRAM

There are, however, still other questions that a theory of the curriculum cannot ignore. Can the proposed curriculum pattern be translated into a school program? How will such a program provide for variations in the ability of pupils, for diversity of interests, for maximum utilization of time and staff? In order to facilitate a meaningful discussion of these and similar questions, a description follows of a possible program of studies that would exemplify the theory expounded in the previous chapters.

It will be recalled that the curriculum calls for the following main types of instruction:

Symbolics of information: English, foreign language, and mathematics as skills and as sciences

Basic sciences: general science, biology, physics, and chemistry

Developmental studies: (I) evolution of the cosmos, (II) evolution of social institutions, and (III) evolution of man's culture

Exemplars: art, music, drama, literature

Molar problems: typical social problems

The task is to schedule learning sequences in these five areas and to specify the rules governing the passage of pupils through the sequences. The general approach is to divide each area into a number of units constituting a sequence. Each unit is to be taught at more than one level. To achieve maximum flexibility and range, it is recommended that the pupil be allowed to progress through each sequence at his best rate. These notions are discussed in greater detail in the remainder of this chapter, but because the conventional graded high school lends itself uneasily, if at all, to such a program, the discussion begins with a consideration of a nongraded secondary school.

THE UNGRADED SECONDARY SCHOOL

There seems to be no compelling reason for trying to preserve the one-grade-one-year pattern still prevalent in the American school system. The arguments against it are pretty well known. The ungraded or nongraded elementary school has passed beyond the experimental stage, and at least one system seems to be happy with an ungraded high school.[1]

Several factors weigh heavily in favor of the ungraded system in Grades 7–12. First is the fact that once pupils have passed the legal school-leaving age, they drop out at different grade levels. If it is true, as has often been asserted, that many dropouts have the scholastic ability to finish high school, it would be better to have them go as far as they can into an area of study before the law permits them to leave school. On the grade system, they cannot proceed beyond what has been assigned to the last grade attended. And, of course, one must not discount the possibility that being allowed to travel at a pace concordant with ability may inhibit the desire to drop out.

However, dropouts are special instances of the more general need for securing maximum flexibility in adjusting the learn-

[1] Melbourne High School in Florida, as described in *The Saturday Evening Post*, December 15, 1962, by Lewis Lapham, and by B. Frank Brown in "The Non-Graded High School," *Phi Delta Kappan*, XLIV, No. 5 (February, 1963), 216–20. See also Sidney P. Rollins, *The Development of a Non-Graded Secondary School: The Middletown Project* (Providence: Division of Graduate Studies, Rhode Island College, 1962).

ing task to the learning readiness of the pupil. Variability in the adolescent years being no less than in the elementary ones, it would seem that the freedom afforded by the nongraded school should be exploited in the high school.

One aspect of this variability that is especially important at the secondary level is the time needed to prepare for post-secondary schooling. Once the age for legal leaving has been passed, it would be desirable to permit young people to complete their graduation requirements and to enter some chosen institution of post-secondary schooling as soon as possible. If the pupil chooses to remain in the secondary school beyond this point, the work he takes should qualify him for advanced placement in post-secondary schooling. The logical leaving point, in any case, is not the number of years spent at the institution, but rather the level of learning achieved with relation to further learnings the school has to offer.

DIVISION OF SUBJECT MATTER FOR INSTRUCTION

The conventional high school divides the materials of instruction into segments one year long. The student is expected to remain in school four years on the assumption that it takes this long for the average student to complete the work in the required segments of instruction, such as so many years of English, so many of science, and so on.

If one wishes to allow pupils to complete the work at different rates, some provision must be made for other than yearly transfers from one unit of instruction to another. For example, if English I is to be completable in less than a year by Pupil X, he may be out of phase with most of his classmates a good deal of the time. If he completes English I, say, in January, can he forthwith enter English II? Does he go back to the beginning of English II and catch up with the class by June? Or does he start with his new classmates, wherever they happen to be in January, and go on to English III in June?

There are, of course, many ways of avoiding this inflexibility. In the Middletown Project, each subject-matter field except art and music is organized into a sequence of concepts. For example, concept No. 1 in English is called "taking part in conversation," concept No. 2 is "listening for information," concept No. 25 is "listening to evaluate truths, half-truths, and falsehoods," and concept No. 111 is "writing full-length research paper with footnotes, preface, and bibliography." As each semester ends, each pupil is re-scheduled on the basis of progress during that semester. Pupils do not fail, and each pupil spends six years at most in the school but can finish in less. A minimum of specific achievement in each subject-matter field is required for graduation.[2]

Detailed study and appraisal of this and other arrangements lie beyond the province of this book, which is concerned with program designs only insofar as they are needed to illustrate the possibility of a uniform curriculum for the secondary school.

The content of the proposed curriculum is made up of facts, rules, principles, concepts, and skills thought to be essential for all. Hence, to adapt instruction to differences in ability, the variable element cannot be the content. One can, however, vary the way it is taught, the rate at which it is taught, and the level at which it is taught. It is true that these are to some extent interrelated. For example, a lesson dealing with the influence of air currents on climate can be taught with varying amounts of visual aids. The visual aids help to teach concretely and vividly, but this approach takes more time than direct verbal exposition. The lesson can be taught at different levels, bringing out the same principles and salient facts on each. In an advanced class, more technical details, more debatable hypotheses, and more subtle experimentation can be introduced, much of it by direct exposition and discussion; such detail and subtlety would be omitted at the lower levels of instruction. The relation of rate of learning to level is not too clear. Where factual content in a subject

[2] Rollins, *op. cit.*, p. 18.

increases with level, one would expect rate to be slowed down; where the difference in level is merely a difference in generality, rate might remain constant or even be increased.

UNITS AND LEVELS

In accordance with these considerations, one possibility would be to regard the notion of *level* as the key factor in meeting differences in scholastic ability. At any given time, a pupil would be studying a subject at a level corresponding to his scholastic achievement in that subject. To make this possible, the total content (topics or concepts) in a field or area of study would be ordered in a sequence. The total sequence would be divided into segments for teaching assignments. Each segment could be an instructional unit and would be taught for a whole school year. It could thus be used as a unit of credit as well. For example, the English language curriculum for the six-year high school on this proposal would have Units I, II, III, and IV, with a V for advanced placement. The first four units would be taught at *three* levels so that at any given time there would be classes called:

English

(Highest)	IA	IIA	IIIA	IVA	V (Advanced Placement)
	IB	IIB	IIIB	IVB	
	IC	IIC	IIIC	IVC	

Although each unit (IA, IB, and so on) would be taught for a year at a time, a pupil need spend only as much time in any class as his achievement warrants. In other words, the materials studied are attached to fixed time periods, but the pupil is not. The major consideration is that as soon as a pupil is out of step with his class, there will be another class into which he can be placed. Assuming adequate guidance and evaluational procedures, this would give some plausibility to the claim that the student is always at the point of his own maximal achievement.

Something further needs to be said about distinguishing levels and topics. Parts of speech is a *topic* in the study of English grammar; fractions is a topic in arithmetic, the Civil War a topic in American history. A topic is what the instruction is about. A table of contents often lists the topics in a book, and we are familiar with the term "topical outline."

Topics are not literally taught or studied, inasmuch as they are only names designating a cluster of instructional content. Content of instruction, as indicated, always refers to some fact, rule, law, principle, or generalization. Learning to use these elements in thought and speech, one thereby develops the various symbolic skills and logical operations. Thus, in the English curriculum, the *content* of Units IA, IB, and IC is the same. Units IIA, IIB, and IIC embody *content* not found in Unit I, but do not vary in content among themselves.

The important task in arranging a content sequence is to place topics in the right learning order. This is the old question of what is prerequisite to what. The problem can be left to the subject-matter specialist who can specify the logical priorities of content and to the pedagogue who combines logical priority with psychological expediency into a viable teaching strategy.

Given some ordering of content into units, it is suggested that they can be studied at various levels. As has already been noted, "levels" are related to difficulty of learning, but not always in the same way. When we say that course X is at a lower level than course Y, we can mean that (1) in X we take up fewer topics of the same difficulty in a unit of time, or (2) X deals with materials that require a lower order of intellectual operation, for example, in the sense that memorizing spelling or number facts is regarded as intellectually less difficult than reasoning or problem-solving. In general, a course that stresses descriptive materials and the rote learning of rules and facts is at a lower level than one which stresses explanation, generalization, and theoretical considerations. (3) We can also mean that Y is more "advanced" than X. Thus, we can teach fractions for understanding in terms of number theory in both X and Y, but in Y, for advanced students, we may want to work a great deal more on various types of number series and their properties, together with the appropriate proofs, than in X. Y is not distinctive in being theoretical, but it is more detailed, more sophisticated, more technical than X, and consequently exerts greater cognitive demands on the learner.

By "watering courses down," is usually meant that "hard" components, that is, those exerting a high cognitive demand, are either deleted entirely, reduced in number, or taken at a slower pace. The last alternative, one would suppose, is bad only when the pace becomes boring to the student who could proceed faster. As for deletion, everything depends on what is eliminated. When concepts are sacrificed to disconnected statements of fact, and theory to descriptions of congeries of phenomena, this is a watering down, because it dilutes the meaning structure of the subject that makes it worth teaching in the first place. Likewise, when the learning task reduces the cognitive strain on the student by not expecting him to verbalize precisely, to define, explain, classify, and infer accurately, this is also watering down the course.

The proposal to offer the same content at different levels is to be understood as deleting neither any concept nor any logical operation considered essential to the subject of instruction. The difference between one level and another is similar to that described above as obtaining between more and less advanced versions of the same course. The higher the level of the instruction, the more it approaches the complexity, detail, and sophistication of the expert in the field. As indicated in a previous chapter, two instructional sequences on a topic such as gravitation can embody the same basic concepts and be, scientifically speaking, equally correct. Yet one sequence can be comprehended by fifth graders, while the other will tax the intellectual resources of twelfth graders. The difference is largely in the language used and the complexity of data the pupil has to consider in making his inferences. Consider, for example, the following problems in the expansion of binominals:

$$(a + b)^2$$
$$[(a + b) + (x + 4)]^2$$
$$[a + (14\ x + 0)]^2$$

They all exemplify the same principle and rule, yet they differ in complexity. Similarly, the principle of levers is the same whether or not complicated by numerical measurements and special cases.

English language	IA	IIA	IIIA	IVA	V*	
	IB	IIB	IIIB	IVB		
	IC	IIC	IIIC	IVC		
Foreign language	IA	IIA	IIIA	IVA	V*	
	IB	IIB	IIIB	IVB		
	IC	IIC	IIIC	IVC		
Mathematics	IA	IIA	IIIA	IVA	V*	
	IB	IIB	IIIB	IVB		
	IC	IIC	IIIC	IVC		
Science	IA	IIA	IIIA	IVA	VA	VI*
	IB	IIB	IIIB	IVB	VB	
	IC	IIC	IIIC	IVC	VC	
Developmental Studies	IA	IIA	IIIA	IVA	VA	VIA
	IB	IIB	IIIB	IVB	VB	VIB
	IC	IIC	IIIC	IVC	VC	VIC
Exemplars	IA	IIA	IIIA	IVA	VA	VIA
	IB	IIB	IIIB	IVB	VB	VIB
	IC	IIC	IIIC	IVC	VC	VIC
Molar Problems				I	II	

Figure 4.

* Where four or five units constitute the total program within an area, and where the pupil is allowed to finish all four units in fewer than six years, Unit V or Unit VI becomes the equivalent of a lower division college course (or courses) in the areas. Presumably, successful completion of such a unit should enable the student to attain advanced placement in college.

This whole curriculum theory depends on the possibility of teaching an essential set of key concepts, skills, and logical operations to all adolescents in the normal range of intelligence. It relies, therefore, on the assumption that these concepts and operations can be apprehended by pupils of average aptitude if sufficiently cleared of elaborations and details. That is also the theoretical justification of the choice of *levels* as the crucial variable in adjusting to individual differences.

Understanding, then, a "unit" to mean a set of topics and a "unit level" to mean the way this set of topics (content) is to be taught, the total curriculum would look something like Figure 4.

PATTERNS OF PROGRESS

The total curriculum, so far as content is concerned, having been segmented into unit levels, the next question is: How shall pupils pass from one unit level to another?

Before taking up this question, it ought to be pointed out that we are not now discussing such instructional devices as team teaching, multiple classes, and automated instruction. These devices and arrangements, on which there is a rapidly growing literature, may obviate certain objections to the proposed design, for example, those arising from the problems of scheduling, staffing, and plant. Thus, a possible objection to three levels of instruction might be that a small school would have great difficulty in scheduling so many instructional segments, but this problem is lessened if some of the devices being tried by small schools are applicable.[3] Also, two or even one level in all or some areas would be sufficient for schools of less than average size.

It seems reasonable to expect that all students could be carefully tested, upon entry into Grade 7, for placement in one of

[3] For example, see *Designs for Small High Schools*, by Glendon P. Nimnicht and Arthur R. Patridge, and *Small Schools Can Be Good Schools* by the same authors (Greeley: Educational Planning Service, Colorado State College, 1963).

the various levels of the six study areas cited above. (The seventh study area, that of molar problems, is not relevant at that time, as is also indicated by Figure 4.)

Such testing should yield an accurate estimate of the unit level at which the pupil profitably can enter a subject. The patterns of passage from one unit or unit level to another are discussed presently, but something might be said about the rules of exit from the program.

School law being what it is, one possible exit point is the legal school-leaving age. Another is the fulfillment of graduation requirements set by the school, by the state, or by admission policies of post-secondary schools. A third possible exit point might be the inability of the student to profit from further instruction in any unit at any level, and a fourth might be an arbitrarily fixed number of years of attendance, for example, six, seven, or eight. As has been remarked, the entire scheme presupposes the establishment of diverse post-secondary institutions to which every pupil might legitimately turn for specialized vocational education of one kind or another. With these qualifications, one can say, in general, that every pupil proceeds at his achievement rate through the unit and levels of all the subject streams of instruction until he leaves by one of the exits.

Conceivably, therefore, a gifted student could finish the whole program in fewer than six years, but, on the other hand, he might wish to stay on after assembling enough credits for graduation. Or a student might elect to leave the moment he can legally do so and transfer to work or to some post-secondary school; or he might wish to stay until graduation before making this transfer.

What the student cannot elect, on this scheme, is to leave a given stream of instruction at will or to omit it from his program. If the student is not doing well in a unit, he can be shifted into another unit or into a different level of the same unit. But he is doomed, so to speak, to remain in general education until he "leaves."

To make the passage from one instructional segment to another a little clearer, suppose that four students are entering the mathematics stream of instruction. Here are four out of many possible routes:

George (a slow learner): Math IC, Math IB, Math IA, Math IIC, Math IIB, Math IIIC

Jim: Math IB, Math IA, Math IIC, Math IA, Math IIIC, Math IVC, Math IVB

John: Math IA, Math IIA, Math IIIB, Math IVB, Math V

Robert (a rapid learner): Math IIB, Math IIIC, Math IIIA, Math IVB, Math V

Leaving the time spent in each class indeterminate, trusting the testing program and the teachers' discretion to move the individual along, then how long it takes George, Jim, John, and Robert to go through becomes irrelevant to all considerations except that of the school's leaving requirements. Math V is the final measure of Robert's and John's mathematical achievement, Math IVB is Jim's, and Math IIIC is George's.

By keeping the content identical at all levels of instruction within a unit and the teaching-time allotments of the units constant at a year, the motion in the system is confined to the pupil. Courses are not changed to fit the pupil; on the contrary, the matching of pupil and course is achieved by moving the pupil.

The mobility patterns and possibilities become more obvious in Figure 5, where the routes of George, Jim, John, and Robert are plotted. (Certain aspects of the chart are made clear in the discussion which follows.)

In practice, it seems likely that at the A level of any subject, the increase in complexity, abstractness, and sophistication of the material may offset the superior speed with which the brighter student can do the work. If so, the times needed for each unit on the various levels would tend to be equalized.

Assuming also that in an ungraded school the point of entry into a subject is determined by the pupil's readiness, it is possible that some young people entering Grade 7 could begin their mathematics at Unit II rather than I—as does Robert (see Figure 5). As to the point of exit from a given subject, this can be either at the completion of the highest level of the last unit in

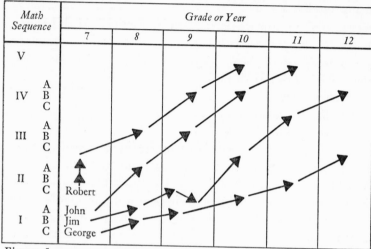

Math Sequence		Grade or Year					
		7	8	9	10	11	12
V							
IV	A B C						
III	A B C						
II	A B C	Robert					
I	A B C	John Jim George					

Figure 5.

the subject, or after six years of study in a subject, or when there is no other segment of instruction in mathematics that the pupil can profitably study.

ENGLISH LANGUAGE

With respect to English, it is anticipated that the earlier units and the lower levels will stress usage and mechanics in reading and speaking, while the later units will gradually shift the emphasis to the structure of language and its more developed uses. If, as is sometimes urged, English is to be regarded as the development of skill in communication, the later units will be concerned with the analysis and construction of more subtle and more complex communication samples.

The A, B, and C levels for each unit will differ more in approach, pace, and cognitive strain than in content. With respect to the mechanics of reading and expression, for example, one can expect some seventh and eighth "graders" to need remedial work on a fairly rudimentary level. There will be some who can improve their skills in these areas, and some who need no further coaching in spelling, punctuation, sentence structure, and word recognition. The first group needs Unit I and perhaps Unit II of English language at the C level. The second group is the average group, whereas the last group can polish up their mechanics in the A level of Unit I or move directly into Unit II or even into Unit III.

Although the slowest pupils will take longer to master the mechanics of language, and although the level of their communicational activity may remain modest, there is no reason for treating them as if they were ten-year-olds. The materials on which they are asked to work can be mature, and what they are asked to express and communicate need not be infantile. Furthermore, there is no clear-cut correlation between the mastery of certain mechanical operations in the use of language and the ability to perform higher intellectual operations in thinking about the language or receiving meaning from verbal materials. There is no reason to make a certain degree of proficiency in mechanics a prerequisite for the study of the structural and logical aspects of language. Hence, when the pupil has reached his limit in the practice of mechanics, he ought to be allowed to try the advanced phases of language study.

The reduction of the program to four units, which enables the pupil to get by with only four years of English in Grades 7–12, can be justified in part by noting that the program does not include the study of English literature, a task that is left to the section of the program called exemplars.

The English teacher or the English department of the school quite rightly will ask for a more detailed account of the contents of the respective units. The principal will want to know in which years the units are to fall, how many classes there would be at each unit level, and the answers to other questions of this sort.

If this book does not satisfy these legitimate demands—and it does not—the reasons are not hard to find. Briefly, they are of two sorts: (1) With regard to the content of the units, that is, with regard to the topics which comprise a given unit, only experts in language instruction are competent to speak with authority. The field is in a state of flux and controversy. While there seems to be agreement that one is dealing here with the art of communication, there is less agreement on the respective pedagogical values of practicing the art, on the one hand, and understanding the structural and formal characteristics of language, on the other.

It has already been noted that in teaching the language of ordinary discourse and in mathematics, the influence of "logical" structure is being felt, and there is a natural and commendable tendency to build this logical component into the curriculum. The writers do not know just where and how this can be done in the secondary school, partly because they do not yet know how the logical dimension and the "usage" dimension affect one another. That is why it is tentatively suggested that, although all units of English language may contain mixtures of usage and logic, the emphasis might shift from the former to the latter in the later units and on the higher levels.

(2) The problems of scheduling and staffing lead to the second kind of reasons for lack of detail. This book is concerned primarily with the type of content and style of the English language curriculum, rather than with the logistics of school administration, important as the logistics are. As noted earlier, there is much trial-and-error activity in these areas, and although a curriculum that cannot be implemented is useless, it still seems unwise to justify the curriculum by the neatness of its fit into administrative designs and instructional devices. The writers hope that language laboratories, multiple-class instruction, and perhaps even team teaching can be used profitably to render the more unusual aspects of the design less disturbing than they otherwise might be. Accordingly, they have fewer qualms about leaving procedural and logistical matters fluid and indeterminate.

The really important matter is the construction of a series of units with a sufficient gradation in levels to meet the variations in ability within a given school, not only in English, but in all areas of instruction.

The reader is offered a hypothetical program. Three levels for each unit of content is simply one of the possible variants, and the same might be said for the number of units. If the idea of the nongraded school is taken seriously, then a unit is not necessarily the equivalent of a year's work for *all* pupils. Accordingly, entry into the study of a unit, movement from one instructional segment to another, and exit from a unit can be adjusted to individual needs and pace.

FOREIGN LANGUAGE

The program calls for study in depth of at least one foreign language. As in English language, the assumption is that one will begin with oral-aural work and gradually shift emphasis to the reading, writing, and understanding of the formal structure of the language.

The amount of foreign-language study a pupil may have had during his elementary school years will affect the level at which he enters the high-school program and which foreign language he chooses to study (if the school gives him a choice). Some schools will be able to afford to offer only one foreign language; others may be rich enough to give the pupil a choice. However, so far as common education is concerned, the case can be made more easily for the study of some foreign language than for the study of any particular foreign language.

There is no conclusive empirical evidence indicating that four units of study will be sufficient to give the pupil a working knowledge of a foreign language. However, the newer methods of teaching foreign language, plus the current practice of beginning foreign-language instruction in the elementary grades, make it plausible to expect that four units at the secondary level will be sufficient for the proficiency commonly envisioned.

Units V in English language and foreign language are designed for the exceptional student who completes the first four units in fewer than four years, or for the student who has a special aptitude and interest in these subjects. Presumably, such an advanced unit could afford an opportunity for independent study and might serve to qualify the student for advanced placement in post-secondary schooling.

MATHEMATICS AND SCIENCE

Many of the considerations and arguments adduced in connection with language study can be repeated for the mathematics portion of the program. The case is somewhat different for the basic sciences, because here one is not dealing with phases of one subject in the various units. Each unit, on the contrary, is concerned with a different science or different science materials.

Units I and II are thought of as devoted to general science, Unit III to be a course in biology, Unit IV a course in physics, and Unit V a course in chemistry. Unit VI would be reserved for those who finish the first five units ahead of schedule. It would be a college-equivalent course in one of the special sciences.

The major problem in this area of the curriculum is the nature of the first unit or units which are to precede the standard courses in biology, physics, and chemistry. It is, of course, the problem of junior-high-school science, namely, whether it should consist of special sciences or of something to be called "general science." Any choice of special sciences for this period is necessarily arbitrary, if one is to be restricted to one or two of them. Out of astronomy, geology, geography, physiology, meteorology, to name a few, which ones shall be chosen or omitted?

Granting the merits of the special science argument, there might nevertheless be conditions which warrant a certain kind of general science in Units I and II.

1. Suppose it becomes the case that, during the elementary-school years, not only a rich store of science "facts" is accumu-

lated by the pupil, but he also apprehends on an intuitive level a good many of the basic concepts and relationships in science. Some of the current studies in the teaching of science give promise that this might happen.

2. Suppose it becomes the case that the standard courses in biology, chemistry, and physics shift their emphasis sharply to the theoretical and investigative aspects and away from the descriptive and applicational phases. Certainly, the work on the science curricula gives promise that this might come to pass.

If these two sets of conditions prevail, there will be a serious split between the relatively unorganized information derived by the pupil from his elementary years and the highly structured courses of the senior high school. A course or courses that would serve as a transition from the descriptive to the analytical approach might have considerable merit. Such a course would provide an even better answer to the problem, if it took as its theme a large domain of natural phenomena to which many principles of science apply rather than a restricted order of natural phenomena.

Some authorities in science education have suggested that material and energy changes in living things might constitute one such theme, and material and energy changes in astronomical, meteorological, and geological events another.

Despite the sweep of such courses, it has been noted that once the "why" questions about these phenomena are raised, the shift to the theoretical, conceptual, analytical level of science is inaugurated. Provided that the discussion and materials are "good" science, such courses might pave the way for the later work in science and provide the kind of integration that study of separate sciences gives only by accident.

What has already been argued with respect to the contents of the basic sciences will not be rehearsed, nor need the contention be repeated that their anticipated use is interpretive rather than the applicative use so characteristic of the specialist. The basic sciences are to be the building blocks of the cognitive map needed by all citizens.

Nevertheless, there will be in each science a wide variation in the cognitive demands made on the pupil. Perhaps the A level might be represented by the PSSC textbook in physics or the materials on the bond approach in chemistry, put out by Strong and his associates. That we can dispense with more modest levels of instruction in these areas seems doubtful.[4]

The C level in the physics course might include the topic of gravitation, just as would the A and B levels, but the examples would be more concrete and familiar. The theoretical implications of phenomena and experiments would be elicited in smaller steps and over a longer period of time. The ratio of descriptive to explanatory materials would go up as the level drops from A to C, although at all levels the comprehension of key concepts would be the primary objective.

DEVELOPMENTAL STUDIES

It should be noted that the developmental studies are scheduled for six units rather than four. The chief reason for this is that they carry a heavy burden of content. It will be remembered that history, geography, some astronomy and geology, economics, sociology, anthropology, not to mention political science, are in a sense "covered" by the developmental studies.

Developmental Studies I, which traces the evolution of our cosmos including man, will have to draw on materials from astronomy, geology, geography, and life sciences, to mention only a few of the relevant disciplines.

The evolution of our social and political institutions (Developmental Studies II) likewise organizes an enormous amount of content into a temporal-causal stream, even after making allowance for great sacrifices of detail.

[4] This may be overcautious in view of the claim that ". . . this course in chemistry is appropriate for the high school . . . and for a student group with a broad spectrum of abilities." Arthur H. Livermore and Frederick L. Ferris, "The Chemical Bond Approach Course in the Classroom," *Science,* CXXXVIII, No. 3545 (December 12, 1962), 1075–77.

Finally, Developmental Studies III, the evolution of our culture with respect to its technology, its fine and applied arts, its economic systems, its ideals and ideologies, also confronts us with a bewildering plenitude of content.

In this connection, it should be noted that although industrial arts as commonly taught have no separate place in the proposed curriculum, a broader version of their function can be incorporated into Developmental Studies III. In other words, industrial arts that emphasize the making of objects or the acquisition of vocational skills are eliminated, but one would not want to omit from general education the understandings of our basic industrial processes and properties of materials and tools. Nor does the course preclude such laboratory experience as would facilitate the industrial understandings, just as laboratory experience is not precluded from any of the other areas of instruction. Much of this material would naturally be included under the evolution of industry and technology.

Similarly, some of the more general concepts in home economics, such as food processing and distribution, textiles, budgeting, and so on, would be encountered both in the developmental studies dealing with technology and those dealing with the evolution of the family as a social institution.

The school materials needed for teaching the developmental studies may present a problem. Although organizing materials of this sort around central themes is not new, grading the materials for three different levels of ability and selecting the content that will bring out the desired developmental concepts is not a simple task.

For one thing, one will have to consult a wide variety of social scientists, some natural scientists, historians, and what, for lack of a better term, might be called students of the culture as a whole. For another, the greater the number of specialists involved in the enterprise, the greater will be the difficulty of securing agreement on matters of selection and emphasis. On the favorable side is the plenitude of writings on these themes and their accessibility to those who may undertake the task of organizing them. As for keeping such materials up to date with new developments, this may become part of the work done in the course itself, especially at the higher levels of the various units.

It is tempting to dismiss the matter at this point. However, sooner or later, the charge will be brought that the developmental studies are nothing other and certainly no more than the old social-studies blocks, those hospitable scholastic seas in which geography, history, economics, and citizenship so often disappear without leaving a trace.

In a sense this charge is valid, and although in Chapter XII the writers tried to indicate their reasons for sacrificing the subject-matter approach in this area of the curriculum, it may be necessary to repeat once more that everything depends on what goes into Developmental Studies I, II, and III. This, in turn, means that everything depends on how qualified are those who organize these materials, especially since it is proposed to absorb not only the numerous disciplines mentioned above, but also something of sociology and anthropology as well. Here, if anywhere, amateurs should not rush in, for it is a place where even experts fear to tread.

The topics in the developmental studies are not nearly so obvious as they seem to be in the skill areas and the sciences, the materials not nearly so well established, and the peaks and valleys of importance not nearly so well acknowledged. However, because in this curriculum the skills, some of the sciences, exemplars, and problems are also to be studied, and studied in a somewhat different way, we can afford to be less definitive in naming topics in the developmental studies than in other areas of the program.

EXEMPLARS

Six units have been assigned to that portion of the curriculum which has been given the name "exemplars."

It will be recalled from Chapter IX that for an individual to fashion an evaluative map, it is necessary for him to introject value models. These models, for reasons set forth in Chapter XIII, had best be sought in the art, literature, and music that have stood the test of critical scrutiny.

There seems to be no simple alternative to organizing these exemplars in some historical order, that is, by periods or styles. Of course, there are alternatives. For example, in some curricula an attempt is made to correlate literature with the history course. In other curricula some major theme, such as freedom, is made the nuclear idea around which the other studies are put into orbit. These alternatives have their virtues, the chief of which is that the diverse materials become related. Much, of course, depends on what sort of relating is desired. Relating large amounts of material around a number of core themes merely raises the problem of how to relate the core themes to each other.

This curriculum has tried to keep clear and relatively distinct both the different types of content and the orders into which content can be arranged. The way materials are related in the learning of the symbolic skills differs from that characterizing the basic sciences and the developmental studies. In the exemplars portion of the curriculum, we are seeking an evaluative order as it manifests itself in works of art rather than in science or in social institutions. It is an order with criteria and rules of its own, and to look for aesthetic order in history and science is to be just as far off the track as to seek scientific truth in painting and literature. The indiscriminate lumping together of materials from diverse orders of experience merely serves to compound the confusion among them and to encourage us to mistake evaluative for cognitive signs on the maps of life.

The suggested organization of exemplars by periods, especially stylistic periods, has the advantage of bringing together works of art that have certain formal, thematic, and technical characteristics in common. Furthermore, the art of a given stylistic period is created by men who work out of a common tradition. They employ the evaluative and cognitive maps of their time, even when they seem to reject them; hence, it is easier to interpret works in various media of a given period with respect to their extra-aesthetic import. Finally, the fact that a period has been marked off and given a name indicates that something reached a high order of intensity and fruition, and that the art of that period exhibits this intensity in a vivid way.

It seems only natural to suggest that each unit of exemplars contain samples of art, literature, music, and architecture. The difficulty with so obvious a suggestion is that it is virtually impossible to find staff who are competent enough in more than one art to handle such a unit by themselves. Accordingly, the next obvious suggestion is team teaching, with specialists in the arts making up the team. Can such a team resist the inevitable tendency to have the unit split into as many subunits as there are specialists?

The integrating factor could be the principles and methods of aesthetic education in general, and one might ask each of the specialists to become familiar with them. What are some of them?

To begin with, there are the common pedagogical problems of teaching and learning appreciation. How much performance does one need in order to appreciate a work of art? At what point in the instruction does one introduce stylistic analysis? What methods seem most promising for guiding the looking or listening of the pupil? How much verbalizing about the work of art should one expect and encourage?

There will, of course, come the time in the unit when the various art samples have to be compared and discussed in relation to each other and to the period of which they are the exemplars. To do this, one might appoint a coordinator or train all the specialists in the aesthetic principles common to all the arts. It is easier, perhaps far easier, for specialists to learn the principles of aesthetics or aesthetic education than for any one teacher to become sufficiently conversant with the various arts to talk about them authoritatively. At several institutions of higher learning, seminars in aesthetic education bring together practicing artists in various media. In at least one of these seminars, the members experience no great difficulty in identifying, studying, and discussing problems that are common to all the arts. There is, therefore, no theoretically insuperable barrier to making such study part of the teacher preparation of those expected to work in the field of appreciative learnings.

To continue with some more of the elements common to the arts, design, harmony, expressiveness, and treatment of thematic material can be discussed in any of the arts. Arts of a period—if the period be well chosen—share a devotion to certain themes, certain outlooks, and certain modes of artistic treatment. For example, the painting, literature, architecture, and music of the Middle Ages are unified by the religious orientation of that epoch. One would want the student to reconstruct imaginatively the outlook that characterized the era, but one would also like him to be able to discern this ethos as it is expressed in the *Divine Comedy*, as well as in the painting, the music, and the architecture of the time.

The symbolism employed by the various arts of a period presupposes familiarity with its myths, beliefs, and conventions. The art of the Greek period, for example, uses a symbolism that makes no sense to anyone ignorant of Greek mythology, and the same mythology is essential to understanding the painting and literature of the Renaissance. For example, in the painting "The Adoration of the Shepherds," by Hugo van der Goes, the scarlet lily and the iris in the foreground are said to be symbols of Christ's blood and the sword of grief that will pierce the Virgin's heart. The seven blossoms of the columbine symbolize the seven sorrows of Mary.[5]

[5] According to Erwin Panofsky's *Early Nederlandish Painting*, cited by John Canaday in *Metropolitan Seminars in Art* (New York: Metropolitan Museum of Art, 1959), Portfolio B, p. 24.

The problem of unit levels in the exemplars is not very different from what it is in the other domains. Although the content is not merely a set of facts and principles, facts, principles, and norms do enter into what is meant by educated taste. Furthermore, although the act of apprehending a work of art may be a unitary and simple intuition, the work of art itself is complex and can be apprehended at varying depths. Hence, the levels at which one teaches the exemplars can vary greatly.

At the C level, one can probably not go much beyond inviting the pupil to view works of art, eliciting some response, pointing out features that he has not discerned, and discussing some of the stories and legends of the period. The goal of each unit is perceptual familiarity with the object, some knowledge about it, and a rudimentary judgment of preference. Perhaps the pupil can begin to seek reasons for this preference and to ask himself whether the features he admires in one work of art he also admires in others. A beginning can also be made in noting the formal elements of a work of art and, to some extent, appreciating them on their own account.

It is not hard to imagine the variations that would be needed to match the pace of the B- and A- level students. Both the art objects and the literature about them are so voluminous and so varied in complexity and sophistication that there should be no lack of variety in either materials or styles of study.

It has been mentioned, perhaps too casually, that in connection with the exemplars, the student must "do" something in the various arts to get the feel of their techniques. This, however, was for the sake of appreciation rather than for improving performance skill on its own account. On the other hand, no explicit provisions have been made for performance training in music, literature, drama, and the visual arts. This can be justified by the fact that artistic "doing" has been practiced in the elementary school. Children have had work in music and the visual arts. The further development of these skills can be regarded as a field for the talented or as a hobby. It has been assumed all along that the secondary school will have a rich array of extracurricular activities among which there will be opportunities to put on plays, play in the band, sing in the chorus, paint, sculpt, or do metal work under professional tuition.

These are legitimate modes of self-development and cultivation, but it is difficult to justify them as essentials of general education in the secondary school. Needless to say, these strictures need not apply in post-secondary schooling, which, to the writers' way of looking at things, has no obligation to general common education.

The exemplar segment of the curriculum is perhaps the most radical departure from the conventional secondary-school program. For one thing, it teaches all the arts for appreciation (evaluated cherishing), rather than for performance, for cognition per se, or for preaching some social gospel, although its end product is value education. For it will be recalled that one important key to value education is the life style or life model. The exemplars present models for edification and introjection directly to the senses and to the imagination.

For another thing, the exemplar segment displaces all survey courses in literature and the arts, as well as separate courses in art and music appreciation. Hence, it carries a great burden of responsibility, and the choosing of exemplars and the approach to them is worth great time and trouble. One would like to enlist the cooperation of our best art scholars and critics in making the selection, lest it merely reshuffle the standard repertory of the high school.

By way of concluding the treatment of exemplars, one can return to the notion of evaluative maps. They determine the way we order our preferences, just as cognitive maps fashion the way we classify and interpret our knowledge. There are, to be sure, cognitive elements in judgments of value, just as there are in judgments of fact. Nevertheless, our operations in the value field are so circumscribed by conditionings that education has a harder task in changing values than in changing beliefs. For this reason, one component of value education is a kind of value reconditioning. Another component is the justification for one preference rather than another. The writers believe that both components are brought into play by the use of value models as they are displayed in exemplars from the arts.

The exemplars portion of the curriculum does not exhaust the requirements of value education. There remains the act of choice itself, especially when it entails the interplay of many values in many dimensions, as it does in what we have referred to as social or molar problem-solving.

MOLAR PROBLEM-SOLVING

The last portion of the curriculum has to do with the social or molar problems discussed in Chapter XIV. There it was argued that the ultimate test of all schooling would be a demonstrated growth in the ability of the pupil to structure problems which spread into many disciplines. The problems of life test our cognitive and evaluative maps. Accordingly, it was proposed that somewhere in the secondary school we deliberately instruct the pupil in the arts of collective deliberation. We ought not to rely on a faith that life will somehow amalgamate the various school learnings so that they automatically display their relevance whenever we assume the problem-solving stance.

In Figure 4, only two units have been allotted to problem-solving, and these have no differentiation of levels. Presumably, these problem-solving courses will come late in the school life of the pupil. This means, of course, that early dropouts may miss them altogether. This is regrettable, but then one regrets all dropouts if they occur before their learning potential is exploited to the full. There seems to be little point in giving problem-solving instruction to those who have not been sufficiently motivated to master the other parts of the curriculum by which intelligent encounters with problems are made possible.

As was indicated in Chapter XIV, perhaps no more than two or three problems need to be tried during the year. The problems need not be the same from year to year, inasmuch as it is not knowledge about the problem, but rather facility in the strategies of problem-solving that is the desired outcome. As examples of suitable problems, one might cite the controversy surrounding racial integration, federal aid to and control of education, the control of mass media, and the emerging nations. We shall need tests especially designed to measure growth in the skills and attitudes that are requisite for good problem-solving behavior, including some of the skills of group dynamics. Of course, the best test would be the tackling of a new problem by the group without help from the instructor and noting whether the group shows any effects of previous instruction. We shall need teachers whose alertness and logical sense are good enough to keep them confident in situations about which they may not, *initially*, know more than their pupils. One would hope, of course, that in time they would become familiar with certain types of problems.

Three levels for the problems sector of the curriculum have not been designated, precisely because part of the skill to be developed is adeptness in operating within a heterogeneous group. Differences in ability and in value commitments are the variables relevant to the problem-solving situation.

By way of summarizing this chapter, the writers can only reiterate their purpose in writing it. Strictly speaking, a theory of the curriculum does not obligate its proponents to supply a program of studies with which to implement it. Any one of a number of programs and many different pedagogical devices could be used for implementation.

However, because this theory does call for a curriculum package that differs considerably from conventional ones, it seemed advisable to indicate how a program of studies could be fashioned from it. The crucial idea of this curriculum, it is to be emphasized, is the notion of a *common* set of *general* studies for the secondary school. These studies are divided into five types of content: symbolics of information, basic sciences, developmental studies, exemplars, and problems. Each of these utilizes a mode of organization of materials designed to fit the outcomes characteristic of them.

The notion of units and levels, the number of units and levels, and even the notion of an ungraded school have been introduced to show that current administrative practices and pedagogical devices give promise that this curricular design can be translated into a program of study. These features, however, are not required by the general theory, and the theory does not depend on them for whatever validity it may claim.

BIBLIOGRAPHY

CHAPTER ONE: EDUCATIONAL IDEALS AND THE SECONDARY CURRICULUM

A very good capsule presentation of the pros and cons of some of the issues in the curriculum controversy is to be found in *The Great Debate—Our Schools in Crisis* (Englewood Cliffs, N.J.: Prentice-Hall, 1959), edited by C. Winfield Scott, Clyde M. Hill, and Hobert W. Burns. For general accounts of curriculum theories, see Joseph Justman's *Theories of Secondary Education in the United States* (New York: Bureau of Publications, Teachers College, Columbia University, 1940), and *Fundamentals of Curriculum Development* (Rev. ed.; New York: World, 1957), by B. Othanel Smith, William O. Stanley, and J. Harlan Shores.

The impact of special-interest groups on American higher education is indicated dramatically in the American Civil Liberties Union's "Statement Concerning the University and Contract Research," reprinted in the *American Association of University Professors' Bulletin*, XLVI, No. 1 (March, 1960), 52–54. The report notes, "In certain fields, such as physics and chemistry, contracts and grants from nonacademic sources account for 90 per cent, or even more, of the research budgets of individual departments" in certain colleges and universities (p. 52). Also see Homer D. Babbidge, Jr., and Robert M. Rosenzweig, *The Federal Interest in Higher Education* (New York: McGraw-Hill, 1962). As pressure is brought on colleges and universities to fill specialized needs, the colleges and universities in turn pass the pressure on to secondary schools by altering collegiate entrance requirements. In the post-Sputnik period, we also find a spontaneous response by public schools in order to meet the need of the dominant interests. One of the most engaging reports is Henry M. Bickell's *Organizing New York State For Educational Change* (Albany: New York State Education Department, 1961). Surveying the changes in formal instructional innovations from 1953 to 1960, Bickell notes that the rate of innovation "in New York State public elementary and secondary schools *more than doubled within 15 months* after the firing of the Soviet Sputnik I, on October 4, 1957. Changes swept not only foreign languages, mathematics and science—which led the field by tripling their rate of change—but all other subjects, *non-academic as well as academic*" (p. 18. Italics in original).

If changes demanded by higher education and mass sentiment are a commonplace in public education, so are the changes demanded by special-interest groups of a non-educational sort. See Mary Ann Raywid's *The Ax-Grinders* (New York: Macmillan, 1962), and Jack Nelson and Gene Roberts, Jr., *The Censors and the Schools* (Boston: Little, Brown, 1963). A classic, but now somewhat out of date, is R. Bruce Raup's *Education and Organized Interests in America* (New York: Putnam, 1936). Also see *Forces Affecting American Education* (Washington, D.C.: Association for Supervision and Curriculum Development, NEA, 1953), Chapters III and IV.

CHAPTER II: CURRICULUM DEMANDS OF A MODERN MASS SOCIETY

The concept of "communal" and "mass" society is based largely upon William Kornhauser's *The Politics of Mass Society* (Glencoe, Ill.: Free Press, 1959). Kornhauser calls attention to the "democratic fallacy," which envisions the masses almost totally under the control of elites, and the "aristocratic fallacy," which sees the elites almost totally under the control of the masses (pp. 23ff.). C. Wright Mills might be an example of one who commits the democratic fallacy, and Ortega y Gasset could be one who commits the aristocratic fallacy (see his classic, *The Revolt of the Masses* [New York: Norton, 1932]).

Mills's popular and influential work, *The Power Elite* (New York: Oxford University Press, 1956), does betray an excessive concern for the abridgment of individual forms of power and control. He is not alone in this. See Fred J. Cook's *The Warfare State* (New York: Macmillan, 1962), which reiterates Mills's contention of at least an informal, very powerful "elite cluster" composed of business, politics, and (especially for Cook) the military. For a more analytic study of the notion of an American elite, see Floyd Hunter's *Top Leadership, U.S.A.* (Chapel Hill: University of North Carolina Press, 1959). Also see Daniel Bell's "Is There a Ruling Class in America?" in *The End of Ideology* (Glencoe, Ill.: Free Press, 1960), Chapter III, for a criticism of *The Power Elite*.

The present writers' contention is that there are sources for individual power and control in our mass society, but these are not to be found in the old locations or means. For an account of how the ground rules for power and control have been shifting, see William A. Williams, *The Contours of American History* (New York: World, 1961), and Edward Hallett Carr, *The New Society* (Boston: Beacon, 1957). The Free Press of Glencoe, Illinois (now a part of Macmillan), has published many fine volumes dealing with the problems and promises of mass society. For examples, see: *Mass Leisure* (1958), edited by Eric Larrabee and Rolf Meyerson; *Mass Culture: The Popular Arts in America* (1957), edited by B. Rosenberg and D. M. White; and *Identity and Anxiety: Survival of the Person in Mass Society* (1960), edited by Maurice R. Stein, Arthur J. Vidich, and David Manning White.

With respect to education, the following works have analyses of the cultural scene which are especially noteworthy: Solon T. Kimball and James E. McClellan, Jr., *Education and the New America* (New York: Random House, 1962), and William O. Stanley, *Education and Social Integration* (New York: Bureau of Publications, Teachers College, Columbia University, 1953). Also see Harry S. Broudy's *Paradox and Promise* (Englewood Cliffs, N.J.: Prentice-Hall, 1961), Part I.

For discussions of the scientific and technical requirements of modern life and education, see the following: George E. Axtelle, "Technology and Social Change," *Educational Forum*, XXV, No. 2 (January, 1961), 133–40; Burton R. Clark, *Educating the Expert Society* (San Francisco: Chandler, 1962), Chapters II, III, and VIII; Fritz Machlup, *The Production and Distribution of Knowledge in the United States* (Princeton, N.J.: Princeton University Press, 1962); Donald N. Michael, *Cybernation: The Silent Conquest* (Santa Barbara, Calif.: Center for the Study of Democratic Institutions, 1962); Leonard S. Silk, *The Research Revolution* (New York: McGraw-Hill, 1960).

CHAPTER III: REASSESSMENT OF THE USES OF SCHOOLING

The literature is replete with lists of school and life objectives. A good sample is found in *Secondary Education for Youth in Modern America*, by Harl R. Douglass (Washington, D.C.: American Council on Education, 1937), which lists citizenship, home membership, effective use of recreation, vocation, health, effective personality and individuality, and preparation for continued study. These are more properly regarded as life objectives than school outcomes.

R. J. Havighurst's *Developmental Tasks and Education* (Chicago: University of Chicago Press, 1949) sets out the needs of the individual which emerge in the course of his development. See also *Toward*

Improved Curriculum Theory, Virgil E. Herrick and Ralph Tyler (Eds.), "Supplementary Educational Monographs" (Chicago: University of Chicago Press, 1950), No. 71, pp. 26–35.

For a classification of educational objectives, see Benjamin S. Bloom *et al.* (Eds.), *Taxonomy of Educational Objectives* (New York: Longmans, Green, 1956), and for a list of objectives as seen in the twenties, consult Franklin Bobbitt, *Curriculum Making in Los Angeles* ("Educational Monographs"; Chicago: University of Chicago Press, 1922), No. 20.

The complexity of the tasks involved in developing critical thinking is exemplified by the research of Robert H. Ennis at Cornell University. See "A Concept of Critical Thinking," *Harvard Educational Review*, XXXII, No. 1 (Winter, 1962), 81–111.

CHAPTER IV: SCHOOLING AS USED BY THE SPECIALIST AND NONSPECIALIST

Because of the way this book classifies the uses of schooling, it is difficult to list bibliographical items that bear directly on the problem. However, almost any volume on general or liberal education contains arguments for differentiating between the vocational and nonvocational uses of schooling. For example, see *General Education in a Free Society*, by the Harvard Committee on the Objectives of General Education in a Free Society (Cambridge, Mass.: Harvard University Press, 1945).

Mark Van Doren's *Liberal Education* (New York: Holt, 1943) and Robert M. Hutchins' *The Higher Learning in America* (New Haven: Yale University Press, 1936) discuss the specialist and nonspecialist distinction, but with a view to justifying one type of study over another. John Dewey, in *Democracy and Education* (New York: Macmillan, 1916), Chapter XX, and some of his followers argue that content is not the distinguishing feature of a vocational or a cultural curriculum. They emphasize, as this book does, the use made of the study, but whereas they tend to stress the need for broadening vocational studies and focusing cultural studies by relating both to the need for reconstructing experience, this book's intent is more modest. It is concerned primarily with the way a given school learning is used under conditions called interpretive and applicative.

For a supportive view of the deficiencies in the teaching of science for nonscientists, see James H. Mathewson, "Science for the Citizen: An Educational Problem," *Science*, CXXXVIII, No. 3548 (December 28, 1962), 1375–78. "Elementary science courses are not taught with a broadening function in mind. They are designed to train the science major in specialized fact. . . . [The non-science major] does not need to become a specialist in a science; he does need to understand the essential nature of science as a whole and his relation to it. . . . Whatever the style or content of a general-education science course may be, the basic objectives are in every case the same: to teach how facts in science are discovered and how they are used in the development of concepts; to describe the effect of scientific ideas in intellectual history; and to train the student to think analytically and critically" (pp. 1376–77). Although Dr. Mathewson's curricular prescriptions do not coincide with those put forward in this book, the writers agree with his general convictions that science for the nonspecialist is not the same as for the prospective specialist in a science.

CHAPTER V: OUTLINES OF A DESIGN FOR SCHOOLING

There are many references that treat the uses of schooling. Perhaps the most comprehensive summary of research investigations as they bear upon the curriculum and the uses of schooling is *Foundations of Curriculum Building*, by John K. Norton and Margaret Norton (Boston: Ginn, 1936). Although this book is somewhat old, it is still one of the best sources of research investigations and curriculum studies that assume the theory of identical elements and the uses of schooling associated with it. The most comprehensive treatment of the curriculum from the standpoint of life situations is *Developing a Curriculum for Modern Living*, by Florence E. Stratemeyer *et al.* (New York: Bureau of Publications, Teachers College, Columbia University, 1957). This reference contains a catalogue of life situations for various levels of development extending from early childhood into adulthood.

The psychological underpinnings of the notion of specific learnings and their direct replicative use are to be found in the works of Edward L. Thorndike. The best single reference for this aspect of Thorndike's work is *Selected Writings from a Connectionist's Psy-*

chology (New York: Appleton-Century-Crofts, 1949). While psychology in general has tended to recognize the deficiencies in the strict stimulus-response theories of learning, mainly there have been only the most absolutely necessary modifications of the theories. One of the most systematic efforts to make fundamental revisions in this theory is the work of O. Hobart Mowrer in *Learning Theory and the Symbolic Processes* (New York: Wiley, 1960).

For a discussion of knowledge and its relationship to the curriculum and instruction, see the essay "Uses of Subject Matter," by Kenneth B. Henderson, and the essay, "On the Reduction of 'Knowing That' to 'Knowing How,'" by Jane Roland, in *Language and Concepts in Education*, edited by B. Othanel Smith and Robert H. Ennis (Chicago: Rand McNally, 1961).

CHAPTER VI: A NEW LOOK AT READINESS

Among Jean Piaget's extensive list of words on the thought operations of children, perhaps the most relevant for our purposes is *The Psychology of Intelligence* (London: Routledge & Kegan Paul, 1950). See especially Chapters V and VI. Also see his brochure entitled *Logic and Psychology* (Manchester, Eng.: Manchester University Press, 1953). Here Piaget gives a condensed version of the operations of thought as they appear at different levels of development. An equally stimulating work on the genetic development of thought and language in the child is that of the Russian psychologist L. S. Vygotsky in his *Thought and Language* (New York: Wiley, 1962). Although there are marked differences between Vygotsky's treatment of stages of development and that of Piaget, the two works are mutually corroborative. Of course, Piaget's work has been extensively criticized by American psychologists, especially because of his theory of stages of child development. One of the best sources of these criticisms, together with views set forth in opposition to Piaget is the monograph of the Society for Research in Child Development (Lafayette, Ind.: Child Development Publications, Purdue University) *Thought in the Young Child*, by William Kessen and Clementina Kuldman (Eds.), Volume XXVII, No. 2, Serial No. 83, 1962.

The notion that the fundamental thought processes can be modified by experience and instruction continues to be one of the chief sources of criticism of the notion of stages of development with respect to thought operations. One of the most extensive studies of this question is that made by J. Smedslund, "The Acquisition of Conservation of Substance and Weight in Children," *Scandinavian Journal of Psychology*, II (1961), 11–20, 71–87, 153–60, 203–10.

Perhaps the best source on the problem of grade placement of materials in accordance with the development of the child, although it is now over two decades old, is the Thirty-Eighth Yearbook of the National Society for the Study of Education, Part I, *Child Development and the Curriculum* (Washington, D.C.: The Society, 1939). See especially the chapter by John E. Anderson entitled "Problems of Method in Maturity and Curricula Studies," pp. 397–422.

CHAPTER VII: STRATEGIC DETERMINANTS OF THE CURRICULUM

"Open" and "closed" or "structured" and "unstructured" situations are terms commonly used in educational discussion. It is difficult to find clear-cut meanings for these particular terms. Perhaps the most extensive discussion of such situations is to be found in Frederic Bartlett's *Thinking* (New York: Basic Books, 1958). This is an experimental and analytic study of thinking, and the reader will find here a rather thorough exploration of the meaning of closed and open systems as they are related to thinking.

Of course, the way knowledge is organized and presented has a bearing upon what is learned and how it is retained. We are only now beginning to find investigations of the effect of the organization of knowledge. The best experimental and theoretical work on this subject is to be found in a set of papers by David P. Ausubel, three of which will serve to introduce the reader to the subject: "The Use of Advanced Organizers in the Learning and Retention of Meaningful Verbal Material," *Journal of Educational Psychology*, LI, No. 5 (Oct., 1961), 267–72; "A Subsumption Theory of Meaningful Verbal Learning and Retention," *The Journal of General Psychology*, LXVI, second half (April, 1962), 213–24; and a general discussion of verbal learning in a paper entitled "In Defense of Verbal Learning," *Educational Theory*, XI, No. 1 (Jan., 1961), 15–25.

There are many general works on the structure of knowledge, some of which are very technical and require thorough acquaintance with philosophy and logic to comprehend. Among those sources which would perhaps be of most help to the curriculum worker and teacher are the following: William Oliver Martin's *The Order and*

Integration of Knowledge (Ann Arbor: University of Michigan Press, 1957); F. S. C. Northrop's *The Logic of the Sciences and the Humanities* (New York: Macmillan, 1948); and Hans Reichenbach's *The Rise of Scientific Philosophy* (Berkeley: University of California Press, 1951).

For a discussion of the role of logic in the handling of subject matter, see "Knowledge About Knowledge for Teachers," by B. Othanel Smith, in a brochure entitled, *The Nature of Knowledge: Implications for the Education of Teachers* (Milwaukee: University Book Stores, University of Wisconsin, 1962). See also *A Study of the Logic of Teaching,* by B. Othanel Smith, Milton Meux, and others (Urbana: Bureau of Educational Research, University of Illinois, 1962).

CHAPTER VIII: CONTENT AS DESCRIPTIVE CONCEPTS AND PRINCIPLES

The literature is replete with sources dealing with concepts and how they are learned. Only one or two psychological references and one or two logical references on this particular subject are given here. Perhaps the most general discussion of the psychology of concept formation is to be found in *The Psychology of Thinking,* by W. Edward Vinacke (New York: McGraw-Hill, 1952). See especially pp. 197–235. A more specific reference, though tied to experimental work, is *A Study of Thinking,* by Jerome S. Bruner *et al.* (New York: Wiley, 1956). See especially Chapters I, II, III, and IV. For concept development from the standpoint of information theory, see *Concept Learning,* by Earl B. Hunt (New York: Wiley, 1962).

The logic of concepts is treated in any introductory book dealing with logic. *An Introduction to Symbolic Logic,* by Susanne K. Langer, is one of the better books (New York: Dover, 1953). See "Concepts" in the general index, and, in addition, read especially Chapters V, VI, VII, and VIII. See also Kenneth B. Henderson's "Abstracting, Generalizing and Explaining—Processes or Relations," in *The Mathematics Teacher,* LIV (1961), 600–605. For a general discussion of definitions, see the monograph entitled *Definition,* by Richard Robinson (Oxford: Clarendon Press, 1950). Some concepts are difficult, if not impossible, to define. This gives rise to special cases of teaching having to do with the question of concepts that are not clear-cut and easily definable. For a discussion of these sorts of concepts and some of the problems connected with them, see the essay, "Language Strata," by F. Waismann, in *Language and Logic*, Second Series, A. G. N. Flew (Ed.) (Oxford: Basil Blackwell, 1959), pp. 11–31.

CHAPTER IX: CONTENT AS VALUATIVE CONCEPTS AND NORMS

There is a very extensive literature on the subject of attitudes, and that on values is quite full. Perhaps the best reference for an overview of attitudes is *The Psychology of Thinking*, by W. Edward Vinacke (New York: McGraw-Hill, 1952). See pp. 311–40. From a logical and analytic standpoint, one of the very best references on the subject is the essay by J. O. Urmson entitled "On Grading," in *Logic and Language*, Second Series, A. G. N. Flew (Ed.) (Oxford: Basil Blackwell, 1959), pp. 159–86. Two general references of special importance on the language and logic of valuation are *The Language of Morals*, by R. M. Hare (London: Oxford University Press, 1952) and *Ethics*, by P. H. Nowell-Smith (Baltimore: Penguin, 1954).

Two of the better books dealing with language in relation to thinking and human behavior are *How To Do Things With Words*, by J. L. Austin (London: Oxford University Press, 1962), and *Language and the Pursuit of Truth*, by John Wilson (London: Cambridge University Press, 1956).

The simplest and most readable introduction to logic, one which teachers will find especially helpful, is *Applied Logic*, by W. W. Little, W. Harold Wilson, and W. Edgar Moore (Boston: Houghton Mifflin, 1955).

For a discussion of rules and norms, see *Models and Metaphors*, by Max Black (Ithaca, N.Y.: Cornell University Press, 1962), Chapters V and VI.

CHAPTER X: USE AND DEVELOPMENT OF SKILLS

For the elaboration of the role of skill in the use of knowledge, see Chapter V on "Mastery," by H. S. Broudy, in *Language and Concepts in Education*, B. Othanel Smith and Robert H. Ennis (Eds.)

(Chicago: Rand McNally, 1961). Also bearing on the problem, but more remotely, is Chapter IV, by Jane Roland, "On the Reduction of 'Knowing That' to 'Knowing How'," in the same volume.

As to the role of the symbolic skills in ordinary experience, it is instructive to read what John Dewey had to say on this topic in *Education Today* (New York: Putnam, 1940), p. 20.

For the directions of new curriculum studies in the language arts and mathematics, see Dorothy M. Fraser, *Current Curriculum Studies in Academic Subjects* (Washington, D.C.: National Education Association, 1962). Further data on the topic should be forthcoming as a result of Project English, now under way at a number of research centers.

For the "official" position of the National Council of Teachers of English, see the curriculum series prepared by its Commission on the English Curriculum. Vol. I (1952) is entitled *The English Language Arts* and Vol. III (1956) is called *The English Arts in the Secondary School* (New York: Appleton-Century-Crofts).

Teaching Language and Literature, by Walter Loban, Margaret Ryan, and James R. Squire (New York: Harcourt, Brace & World, 1961), is an example of the way logic, semantics, and communication theory are infiltrating the teaching of English. These authors devote a section of three chapters to appreciation of literature, the perusal of which may indicate why the present writers doubt that communications, logic, and appreciation can profitably be combined in the same course. The problems of appreciation in music, literature, and art seem to have more in common than do problems of logic, reading comprehension, and expository writing.

The ferment in the discussion of the goals in the English arts curriculum is reflected in "The Basic Issues in the Teaching of English," supplement to *Elementary English* (Oct., 1959), p. 4. The Commission on English of the College Entrance Examination Board was established in 1959 to make recommendations for the secondary-school English curriculum.

The concern of English teachers with the implications of modern language study is evidenced by the establishment in 1960 of its fourth major commission, the Commission on the English Language, and there is reason to believe that the history and structure of the English language will receive careful attention in the coming years.

For a current appraisal of language skills in our society, see "English Language Arts in the Comprehensive Secondary School," *The Bulletin of the National Association of Secondary-School Principals,* XLIV (Oct., 1960), 45–48.

For more detailed reports on the rationale of the new mathematics curricula, see "The New Mathematics Programs," by Edwin Moise, in *The School Review*, LXX, No. 1 (Spring, 1962), 82–101; the *Newsletters* of the School Mathematics Study Group, and the materials put out by the University of Illinois Committee on Mathematics.

CHAPTER XI: DEVELOPMENT OF CONCEPTS THROUGH THE BASIC SCIENCES

For an interesting classification of knowledge and its relation to research, see Joseph T. Tykociner, *Research as a Science—Zetetics* (Urbana: Electrical Engineering Research Laboratory, University of Illinois, 1959). Although this book does not employ his elaborate taxonomy and nomenclature, the division of subject matter for instruction is to a considerable extent influenced by them.

There is no dearth of literature on the nature and philosophy of science. This book follows no one interpreter. For the reader who wishes to explore the topic, one might mention Ernest Nagel's *The Structure of Science* (New York: Harcourt, Brace & World, 1961). An interesting hypothesis about the growth of science is found in Thomas S. Kuhn, *The Structure of Scientific Revolution* (Chicago: University of Chicago Press, 1962). Of special note is Kuhn's observation to the effect that "the study of paradigms is what mainly prepares the student for membership in the particular scientific community in which he will later practice" (p. 11). By paradigms, he means such styles of thinking as are exemplified by Ptolemaic astronomy, Aristotelian dynamics, and statistical mechanics.

In addition to the discussions of the National Science Foundation Curriculum developments in *The School Review*, LXX, No. 1 (Spring, 1962), one might consult *Current Curriculum Studies*, by Dorothy M. Fraser, "A Bulletin Prepared for the Project on the Instructional Program of the Public Schools" (Washington, D.C.: National Education Association, 1962) and *The Revolution in Mathematics* (Washington, D.C.: National Council of Teachers of Mathematics, NEA, 1961).

Special reports and materials on each of these new curricula have been issued by the respective projects. The astronomy project mentioned in this chapter is under the direction of J. Myron Atkin and

Stanley P. Wyatt at the University of Illinois. Books 1 and 2 of their trial materials are entitled *Astronomy: Charting the Universe* (Rev. trial edition, 1962), and *Astronomy: The Universe in Motion* (Rev. trial edition, 1962), respectively.

The American Institute of Biological Sciences issues Biological Sciences Curriculum Study Bulletins. No. 1 was written by Paul De Hart Hurd and is entitled *Biological Education in American Secondary Schools, 1890-1960* (Washington, D.C., 1961).

The question of whether or not the new curricula are suitable for high-school populations is discussed by Frederick L. Ferris, Jr., in "Testing in the New Curriculum: Numerology, 'Tyranny,' or Common Sense?" *The School Review*, LXX, No. 1 (Spring, 1962), 112-31, and in numerous other writings by the same author listed at the end of this article.

Thus far, it is safe to say that the results of the testing are not decisive. "The materials are effectively teachable to high-school students. This conclusion applies to the total student population for which each of these courses was designed," Ferris notes (p. 130). For those who are proposing that all high-school students take science, mathematics, and, indeed, the same set of courses, the evaluation results are reassuring, for example, "It seems clear that the capability of the U.S. high-school student has been vastly underestimated" (*ibid.*). But whether the total spectrum of the secondary-school population can study these materials profitably at the same level of difficulty still seems doubtful.

In connection with the emphasis on key concepts, it is interesting to note that the eminent geologist M. King Hubbert believes that a relatively small number of "master generalizations" are the keys to understanding the physical sciences. He lists the Newtonian laws of motion and gravitation, the thermodynamics of irreversible processes, Maxwell's two laws of electromagnetism, the law of the conservation of matter, the concept of the atomic and molecular nature of the chemical elements and their compounds, the hypothesis that the past history of the earth is in large measure decipherable from the present observation of rocks, the Darwinian theory of evolution, the Mendelian and gene theory of genetics, and the bacterial and virus theory of disease. To bring matters up to date, he adds the equations of Einstein for the equivalence and interconvertability of matter and energy, the Planck equation of the quantum of radiant energy, the Rutherford picture of the atom, and the generalization that by changing the number of protons in the nucleus the transmutation of the elements can be achieved. See "Are We

Retrogressing in Science," *Science,* CXXXIX, No. 3558 (March 8, 1963), 884–90.

Something of how a science study contributes to a cognitive map is expressed in the preface of *Exploring the Universe,* Louise B. Young (Ed.), published for the American Foundation for Continuing Education (New York: McGraw-Hill, 1963). The aim is to provide the layman "with a background of understanding of the principles on which the space age has been built, to give him a glimpse of the mystery and the majesty of the universe, which man has begun to explore with satellites, and, above all, to suggest the methods and nature of the search itself."

For more detailed reports and bibliography in science instruction improvement, see *Science Course Improvement Projects* (Washington, D.C.: National Science Foundation, Oct., 1962).

CHAPTER XII: DEVELOPMENT OF CONCEPTS THROUGH DEVELOPMENTAL STUDIES

The chief source for the architectonic of this chapter is taken from Joseph T. Tykociner, *Research as a Science—Zetetics* (Urbana: Electrical Engineering Research Laboratory, University of Illinois, 1959), pp. 28–30. Professor Tykociner's term for the area of knowledge concerned with evolution and history is "exeligmology" which denotes unfolding. He speaks of "exeligmology of the world at large" (this book's Developmental Studies I), "exeligmology of aggregates of human beings" (Developmental Studies II), and "exeligmology of mankind and its culture" (Developmental Studies III).

For the nature of historical knowledge and history as a source of generalizations see the following: Donald W. Oliver, "The Selection of Content in the Social Studies," *Harvard Educational Review,* XXVII, No. 4 (Fall, 1957), 271–300; Arthur S. Bolster, Jr., "History, Historians, and the Secondary School," *Harvard Educational Review,* XXXI (Winter, 1962), 39–65; A. L. Rowse, *The Use of History* (London: Hodder and Stoughton, 1946); W. H. Walsh, *An Introduction to the Philosophy of History* (London: Hutchinson's University Library, 1951); John Passmore, "Explanation in Everyday Life, in Science, and in History," *History and Theory,* II, No. 2 (1962), 105–23; H. Stuart Hughes, "The Historian and the Social Scientist," *American Historical Review,* LXVI (Oct., 1960), 20–46;

and Patrick Gardiner (Ed.), *Theories of History* (Glencoe, Ill.: Free Press, 1960).

In noting exceptions to the charge that history textbooks are lacking in explicit generalizations, John Palmer mentions Carl L. Becker's *Modern History* (Morristown, N.J.: Silver Burdett, 1958), and he cites the recent world histories prepared by Ethel Ewing (*Our Widening World* [Chicago: Rand McNally, 1958]) and by Leften S. Stavrianos (*A Global History of Man* [Boston: Allyn and Bacon, 1962]) as exceptions to the conclusion that such disciplines as geography, sociology, and psychology are inadequately reflected in history textbooks.

For an account of the core curriculum, see Chapters XIV and XV in B. Othanel Smith, William O. Stanley, and J. Harlan Shores, *Fundamentals of Curriculum Development* (Rev. ed.; Yonkers-on-Hudson: World, 1957). Also see U.S. Office of Education Bulletin No. 5 (1952), *Core Curriculum Development: Problems and Practices.*

CHAPTER XIII: DEVELOPMENT OF NORMS THROUGH EXEMPLARS

The bibliographical notes on Chapter IX are also pertinent to this chapter.

The notions of value areas, levels, and connoisseurship are treated in H. S. Broudy, *Building a Philosophy of Education* (Rev. ed.; Englewood Cliffs, N.J.: Prentice-Hall, 1961), Chapters VI–XI, in considerable detail.

Much of the reasoning in this chapter is based on the analysis of aesthetic experience. A good sampling of the literature in this field is provided by Melvin Rader (Ed.), *A Modern Book of Esthetics* (3rd ed.; New York: Holt, Rinehart and Winston, 1960). The relation of art to social life is well treated in D. W. Gotshalk, *Art and the Social Order* (New York: Dover, 1962).

The notion of art as a means of achieving all educational values is most prominently explicated by Sir Herbert Read in *Education Through Art* (Rev. ed.; London: Faber & Faber, 1958).

One finds in the literature a constant emphasis on values, for example, *The Public Schools and Spiritual Values*, Seventh Yearbook of the John Dewey Society (New York: Harper, 1944), and the Educational Policies Commission, *Education of Free Men in*

American Democracy (Washington, D.C.: National Education Association, 1940).

How such value education is to be incorporated into the curriculum is not always clear. For many of the Progressive school people, character values and social ones were to be achieved through the activity curriculum. For example, see the writings of William H. Kilpatrick. Others have stressed the social studies as the place in the curriculum where the values of the community are overhauled and reconstructed. Still others favor literature as a source of value instruction.

By and large, the values that have been the concern of recent curriculum theories are "the socio-moral rules comprising the core of the culture," and the core curriculum emphasizes these values. See for example, Harold Alberty's *Reorganizing the High School Curriculum* (Rev. ed.; New York: Macmillan, 1953); and Roland Faunce and Nelson Bossing, *Developing the Core Curriculum* (New York: Prentice-Hall, 1951).

An attempt to define the role of aesthetic education in the teaching of values is made in Donald G. Arnstine, "The Aesthetic Dimension of Value Education" (unpublished doctoral dissertation, University of Illinois, 1960).

CHAPTER XIV: DEVELOPMENT OF PROBLEM-SOLVING STRATEGIES

The literature on problem-solving is so voluminous and familiar that extensive references are probably unnecessary. The classic reference is still John Dewey's *How We Think* (New ed.; Boston: D. C. Heath, 1933), because it had so great a pedagogical influence.

The steps and stages of problem-solving by groups are exhaustively discussed in *The Improvement of Practical Judgment*, by R. Bruce Raup, Kenneth D. Benne, George Axtelle, and B. Othanel Smith (New York: Harper, 1950).

Molar problem-solving as distinguished from other types is taken up in H. S. Broudy, *Building a Philosophy of Education* (Rev. ed.; Englewood Cliffs, N.J.: Prentice-Hall, 1961), pp. 304–5, 287–91, 326–29.

There is a growing literature on decision-making, group dynamics, and the language and logic of value judgments. For the first two topics, *The Planning of Change,* Warren G. Bennis, Kenneth D. Benne, and Robert Chin (Eds.) (New York: Holt, Rinehart, and Winston, 1961), is one of the many books that should be helpful. For the third topic, see T. E. Hill, *Contemporary Ethical Theories* (New York: Macmillan, 1952); R. M. Hare, *The Language of Morals* (Oxford: Clarendon Press, 1952); Paul Edwards, *The Logic of Moral Discourse* (Glencoe, Ill.: Free Press, 1955); and A. G. N. Flew (Ed.), *Logic and Language,* Second Series (Oxford: Basil Blackwell, 1953).

For a view that seems to equate all education with group inquiry, see Herbert A. Thelen, *Education and the Human Quest* (New York: Harper, 1960).

CHAPTER XV: A PROGRAM OF STUDIES

The literature on this chapter is scattered among reports on new curricula and new administrative arrangements, such as James B. Conant's *The American High School Today* (New York: McGraw-Hill, 1959) and *Slums and Suburbs* (New York: McGraw-Hill, 1961), and books on secondary-school organization.

Some of these items have been mentioned in the bibliographical notes to previous chapters.

With respect to the language arts, a preliminary English Curriculum Project report (mimeographed) at the laboratory high school of the University of Illinois, for example, notes that "nearly all concepts that are used in the senior year may be discovered and articulated by the 7th grade." Further, early pretesting seems to have shown a wide range of proficiency within a single class, and a surprisingly high level of median performance. What can be done in the communication skills prior to the secondary school has probably been underestimated.

It is also interesting to note that in this project the breaking up of the curriculum into units of grammar, composition, literature, and speech is abandoned. Instead, it is assumed that "the study of English is a continuing analysis of communication" and "the obvious sequence is from easy to difficult analysis." Report by James M. McCrimmon and Daniel A. Lindley, Jr., *The English Curriculum Project at the Laboratory High School of the University of Illinois* (Urbana, Ill.: University High School, 1962), mimeographed.

Typical of the reports on the use of new teaching devices are John A. Brownell, *The Claremont Team Teaching Program* (Claremont, Calif.: Claremont Graduate School, 1961), and *The Norwalk Plan of Team Teaching* (Norwalk, Conn.: Board of Education, 1960–61).

An exhaustive report on curriculum experimentation is to be found in *National Conference on Curriculum Experimentation*, Paul C. Rosenbloom (Ed.) (New York: McGraw-Hill, 1963).

For a report on the nongraded elementary school, see John Goodlad and Robert Anderson, *The Non-Graded Elementary School* (Rev. ed.; New York: Harcourt, Brace & World, 1963).

For some of the arguments on general science, although not their final form or interpretation, the writers are indebted to R. Will Burnett, Professor of Science Education at the University of Illinois.

With respect to the present status of economic education, see Lewis E. Wagner and Lawrence E. Metcalf, "Economic Education in Transition," *Teachers College Record*, LXIV, No. 8 (May, 1963), 706–18.

INDEX OF NAMES

Index of Names

Howe, Irving, 38
Hubbert, M. King, 288–89
Hughes, H. Stuart, 289
Hullfish, H. Gordon, 238
Hunt, Earl B., 284
Hunter, Floyd, 278
Hurd, Paul De Hart, 288

Jackson, Andrew, 146
Jencks, Christopher, 36
Justman, Joseph, 277

Kant, Immanuel, 130
Kennedy, John F., 178
Kessen, William, 282
Kilpatrick, William H., 48, 238, 291
Kimball, Solon T., 279
Köhler, W., 98
Kornhauser, William, 278
Kuhn, Thomas S., 287
Kuldman, Clementina, 282

Langer, Susanne K., 284
Lapham, Lewis, 248
Larrabee, Eric, 279
Lindley, Daniel A., Jr., 292
Little, W. W., 285
Livermore, Arthur H., 264
Loban, Walter, 286

McClellan, James E., Jr., 279
McCrimmon, James M., 292
McGrath, Earl J., 36
Machlup, Fritz, 279
Martin, William Oliver, 283–84
Marx, Karl, 203
Mathewson, James H., 280–81
Metcalf, Lawrence E., 293
Meux, Milton, 284
Meyerson, Rolf, 279
Michael, Donald N., 279
Michelangelo, 176
Mills, C. Wright, 278
Milton, John, 212
Mowrer, O. Hobart, 282
Moise, Edwin, 287
Moore, W. Edgar, 285
Myrdal, Gunnar, 145

Nagel, Ernest, 287
Nelson, Jack, 278
Nijinsky, Vaslav, 176
Nimnicht, Glendon P., 255
Northrop, F. S. C., 284
Norton, John K., 281
Norton, Margaret, 281
Nowell-Smith, P. H., 285

Ogden, C. K., 135
Ohlin, Lloyd E., 40
O'Keeffe, Georgia, 147
Oliver, Donald W., 289
Oppenheimer, J. Robert, 34
Ortega y Gasset, Jose, 278

Palmer, John, 206, 208, 209, 290
Panofsky, Erwin, 269
Passmore, John, 208, 289
Paton, Alan, 110
Patridge, Arthur R., 255
Piaget, Jean, 96, 97, 98, 282
Piercy, M., 96
Plato, 234

Rader, Melvin, 228, 290
Raup, R. Bruce, 240, 278, 291
Raywid, Mary Ann, 277–78
Read, Herbert, 290
Reichenbach, Hans, 284
Richards, I. A., 135
Roberts, Gene, Jr., 278
Robinson, Richard, 284
Roland, Jane, 282, 286
Rollins, Sidney P., 248, 250
Rosenberg, B., 38, 279
Rosenbloom, Paul C., 293
Rosenzweig, Robert M., 277
Rousseau, Jean-Jacques, 91, 92
Rowse, A. L., 289
Russell, Charles H., 36
Ryan, Margaret, 286

Schweitzer, Albert, 56, 57
Scott, C. Winfield, 277
Seaborg, Glenn T., 183, 195
Shakespeare, William, 176
Shore, Maurice J., 5

INDEX OF SUBJECTS